Thrive

Every generation faces challenges, but never before have young people been so aware of theirs. Whether due to school strikes for climate change, civil war or pandemic lockdowns, almost every child in the world has experienced the interruption of their schooling by outside forces. When the world we have taken for granted proves so unstable, it gives rise to the question: what is schooling for? *Thrive* advocates a new purpose for education, in a rapidly changing world, and analyses the reasons *why* change is urgently needed in our education systems. The book identifies four levels of thriving: global – our place in the planet; societal – localities, communities, economies; interpersonal – our relationships; intrapersonal – the self. Chapters provide research-based theoretical evidence for each area, followed by practical international case studies showing how individual schools are addressing these considerable challenges. Humanity's challenges are shifting fast: schools need to be a part of the response.

VALERIE HANNON co-founded the Innovation Unit and the Global Education Leaders' Partnership and is a consultant advisor to OECD and various education ministries worldwide. Recent publications include *Learning a Living* (2013).

AMELIA PETERSON is part of the founding faculty of the London Interdisciplinary School and has taught previously at the London School of Economics and a large secondary school in England. She holds a PhD in Education from Harvard University.

Thrive

The Purpose of Schools in a Changing World

VALERIE HANNON
Independent Scholar

AMELIA PETERSON
London School of Economics and Political Science

CAMBRIDGE
UNIVERSITY PRESS

CAMBRIDGE
UNIVERSITY PRESS

University Printing House, Cambridge CB2 8BS, United Kingdom

One Liberty Plaza, 20th Floor, New York, NY 10006, USA

477 Williamstown Road, Port Melbourne, VIC 3207, Australia

314–321, 3rd Floor, Plot 3, Splendor Forum, Jasola District Centre,
New Delhi – 110025, India

79 Anson Road, #06–04/06, Singapore 079906

Cambridge University Press is part of the University of Cambridge.

It furthers the University's mission by disseminating knowledge in the pursuit of
education, learning, and research at the highest international levels of excellence.

www.cambridge.org
Information on this title: www.cambridge.org/9781108834827
DOI: 10.1017/9781108877152

First published 2021

A catalogue record for this publication is available from the British Library.

Library of Congress Cataloging-in-Publication Data
Names: Hannon, Valerie, author. | Peterson, Amelia, author.
Title: Thrive : the purpose of schools in a changing world / Valerie Hannon, Amelia Peterson.
Description: [Second edition]. | Cambridge ; New York, NY : Cambridge University
    Press, 2021. | Includes bibliographical references and index.
Identifiers: LCCN 2020030112 (print) | LCCN 2020030113 (ebook) |
    ISBN 9781108834827 (hardback) | ISBN 9781108819978 (paperback) |
    ISBN 9781108877152 (epub)
Subjects: LCSH: Education–Aims and objectives. | Education–Social aspects. | Public schools.
Classification: LCC LB14.7 .H367 2021 (print) | LCC LB14.7 (ebook) | DDC 370.1–dc23
LC record available at https://lccn.loc.gov/2020030112
LC ebook record available at https://lccn.loc.gov/2020030113

ISBN 978-1-108-83482-7 Hardback
ISBN 978-1-108-81997-8 Paperback

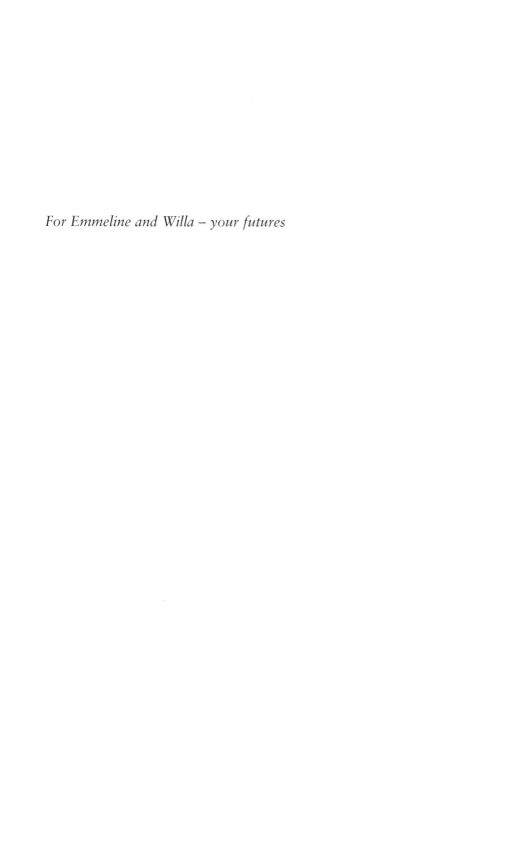

For Emmeline and Willa – your futures

Contents

Figures

Preface

This book arises from discussions with educators, parents, students and employers around the world about new guiding purposes for public education systems. Assumptions about our *purpose* in education are currently under-examined and out of date.

For some, the shock of the 2020 COVID-19 pandemic raised questions about the functions of schooling. If so much could be done online, what were schools for? However, in general there was anxiety to get back to 'normal', albeit supplemented by a greater use of distance learning tools. In the end, within a context of so much disruption, little serious public debate about the fundamental job we need schools to do took place.

Yet, in the context of what some have described as 'the pandemic Great Pause', we are provided with the opportunity to consider this question afresh.

There is no clear narrative or unifying ambition for public education today that both

- connects with the realities people are experiencing, and
- faces up to what can confidently be said to be on our horizon.

The 2020 pandemic illustrated how important a future-focus is. This book sets out the features of the future of our world around which there is strong consensus internationally from scientists and analysts. These features include environmental, technological, demographic, socio-political and economic shifts. Taken together, they show that the scale of disruption our species and planet face is so profound that the risk of *not* changing outweighs that of doing nothing. Changes are needed so future generations are prepared to deal with these shifts – or, better still, to *shape* them. From the evidence, we extrapolate a set of three key shifts or 'pivots' in history that are likely to occur in the lifetime of today's learners.

In short: we have been so preoccupied with asking the *'how?'* of education, we have forgotten to ask the question of *'what for?'* National narratives – around 'economic competitiveness' or 'preparing for the knowledge economy' (or 'digital economy') can now be seen to be woefully inadequate in light of the enormous challenges our species faces – some of them existential. All of these will impact our children's lifetimes, let alone those of our grandchildren. Reflecting on the scale and direction of these shifts, the book proposes the following:

Today, education has to be about learning to thrive in a transforming world.

This formulation has been carefully crafted to challenge some old clichés. Replacing the idea of 'success' is important. It has connotations of qualification acquisition leading to material wealth. Similarly, the idea of 'happiness' is inadequate, because that is an individuated quality. It is possible to be perfectly happy when many of those around you are in abject misery. The idea of 'well-being' too can be perceived to be an individual quality. We need a goal that points to the essential inter-relationships of our world. Thriving – a biological metaphor – perhaps conveys more adequately the notion of healthy flourishing, embedded in one's environment. Today, we need an overarching goal that shows the interconnectivity between things.

When we ask what the job is that we want education to do, elevating the idea of 'thriving' may at least require something of a re-think. It is connected to the idea of *Bildung,* the philosophical concept of fulfilling one's nature or purpose in response to the challenges of a particular historical and societal context.[1] It entails the idea of healthy development across many dimensions. This, in turn, suggests that we must think about the levels of thriving that impact each other.

When we examine what it means to thrive, we see that thriving must happen at four interdependent levels, none of which can be ignored:

- global – our place in the planet
- societal – place, communities, economies
- interpersonal – our relationships
- intrapersonal – the self.

[1] Rowson, 'Bildung in the 21st Century – Why Sustainable Prosperity Depends upon Reimagining Education'.

Reviewing the evidence about the likely trends across these four domains, we suggest that a series of learning goals emerges.

Previous goals for education – where they are enunciated – tend to be at the individual level and are predicated on competition for rationed goods (access to higher education or to high-paying jobs) or a society's success in economic competition. But the evidence suggests that we cannot thrive with these restricted purposes. We need new goals. Designing learning to achieve these new goals will be challenging for educators. But it turns out that this is already being attempted by a number of fabulous educators around the world; if they can do it, so can others – and it would be a lot easier if others joined in.

Moreover, we believe that schools are needed for this task. 'Techno-solutionists' argue that 'schools are dead'; that learning will become 'disintermediated' and individuals, armed with Big Data learning analytics and a plethora of digital offerings, will no longer need institutions.[2] In this book, we argue that they are wrong in principle; and the evidence emerging from the worldwide lockdown, when three in four children lived in countries where all classrooms were shut, shows that schools were wanted – very badly.

However, schools do need to be reinvented as a key part of learning ecosystems – webs of civil society institutions and online connections powerful enough to enable humanity to address the problems that both threaten it – and also offer spectacular opportunities. Schools in diverse settings and conditions are already innovating their foci and their methods to help their learners – not just to pass tests, or even to get a job – but to *thrive*.

This book offers no panacea, recipe or program. Rather it is a catalyst for serious debate about the purpose of our public education systems. To facilitate such a debate, we must update our analysis of the future our young people face, as well as our collective knowledge of the ways that schools are already responding. With this new basis, the work of 'education reform' will take on an authentic energy and depth. However, without seriously re-examining the *purpose* of such reform, the needed scale of change will not materialise.

This new purpose is about how we learn to ***thrive in a transforming world.***

---

[2] Richardson, *Why School?: How Education Must Change When Learning and Information Are Everywhere*; Slayback, *The End of School*.

The transformation of our world becomes apparent when we look at analyses and trends about the future. The book is intended to confront educators, system leaders and political leaders with the contours of a set of profound shifts, about which environmentalists, scientists and entrepreneurs are increasingly clear. Pandemics are but one dimension, but there are other more fundamental shifts underway. Since the first edition of this book, school systems – sometimes led by their students – have just begun to acknowledge these and to respond. Yet these are shifts that challenge foundational assumptions about what education is for. The response needs to be equally profound.

Moreover, since around 2016 there has been a sea-change across Europe and the United States (with global implications) of political culture: the rise of successful populist demagoguery, relying on 'post-truth' campaigns. This shift could be interpreted as a howl of exclusion and impotence that large sections of those populations experience. As much as our environmental and technological challenges, this political challenge requires us to consider the role of schools in the preparation of global citizens.

Amidst these developments, most schools continue with the old prospectus: the promise of 'succeeding' (gaining better competitive access to a limited pool of good jobs) if the right knowledge and skills are acquired. Consequently, most writing about the 'future of educa-tion' ends up with only lists of what students need to learn in order to *succeed* in the future. These get shoe-horned in as new outcomes under old efficiency-oriented models of school improvement.

Thrive shifts the focus to what children and young people need to be allowed to *experience and do now* as part of their time at school – not to develop a set of abstract skills, but to learn to live in new and better ways, taking charge of the future so they can shape it and deal with its challenges. Thinking about the future and how the world has already changed, and will change exponentially faster, should direct us towards new purposes for education. Some of these new purposes will be collective and environmental, rather than just individual or national.

Children and young people *are already facing* some of these chal-lenges in their daily lives, but the pressures are set to increase. What is the role of schools in helping them handle these challenges? What do schools look like when they have re-oriented to address them?

This books aims to:

- set out the evidence about some major disruptions (and opportunities) affecting humanity
- propose a new purpose for education, based on the facts and best predictions about the impact of these disruptions
- illustrate what is already being done to respond to the challenges these disruptions present, and further actions that can be taken.

The examples we profile in the 'pathfinder' chapters are not intended as cookie-cutter recipes. They are deliberately diverse, and we have refrained from over-conceptualising their approaches. We offer them as stimuli for further enquiry, debate and reflection.

Of course, the proposal about fundamental purpose that we suggest, and the goals we consider it gives rise to, are based on our own perspectives and values in the face of these shifts. They are grounded in the contexts of liberal democracies, which we believe to be more fragile and at risk now than in the last 80 years. Not everyone will accept them. Some of those values are up for debate and further improvement. However, we do believe that most of the values in which we ground this book have the potential to be universal, in that they value the future of the planet and its biodiversity, together with human rights to freedom in the context of mutual responsibility.

We welcome debate of these values, but this debate should not lead to rejection of the evidence about the future, nor of what is possible in education. This is because what leaders and the public think education should do is based, whether consciously or not, on what they believe about the world young people will enter. The aim of this book is to update the basis of those beliefs. You have to have a *reason* to change. This book provides it.

Acknowledgements

First and foremost, thanks go to all the interviewees who gave up time to contribute to this book and the school leaders, teachers and students who have shared their insights over the years. The first version of this book would not have been possible without the support of Julie Temperley, who has been a source of much inspiration of the years. A number of colleagues have shared their wisdom with particular generosity, including Rod Allen, Tom Beresford, Mark Blundell, Jo Carrington, Lorna Earl, Sarah Gillinson, Caireen Goddard, Judy Halbert, Matthew Horne, David Jackson, Linda Kaser, Tony Mackay, Jal Mehta, David Price, Tim Sully, Louise Thomas and Sarah Ward.

Becky Taylor, Izzie Collins and the team at Cambridge University Press provided excellent support throughout this process and we are very grateful for their guidance. Likewise we are grateful to Kim Vernon who was a patient and thorough copy editor.

We would like to thank the numerous principals and teachers who have contributed to our thinking through workshops and conferences, following the publication of the first edition, in which we have explored the implications of these ideas for practice; and developed and extended them as a result. To the many friends (they know who they are) who were willing to bear with obsessive behaviour over this book, talk about it, but also require us to think about other things – thank you.

Authors

Valerie Hannon's career spans leadership of education systems, research, teaching and capacity building. She is now an established thought leader in the field of education innovation.

Valerie co-founded Innovation Unit UK and has supported education change programmes in numerous systems, including the UK, Europe, USA, Australia and Africa. She is a founding member and Co-Chair of the Global Education Leaders Partnership (GELP) supporting jurisdictions globally to scale their innovation and transform their systems.

Valerie is an expert adviser on education to the OECD, and a frequent contributor to the World Summit on Innovation in Education (WISE). She is a regular keynote speaker and facilitator at international conferences and workshops. Earlier co-authored books include *Learning A Living: radical innovation in education for work* (Bloomsbury, 2012); and *Redesigning Education: shaping learning systems around the globe* (Booktrope, 2013). Her latest publication was *Local Learning Ecosystems: emerging models* (WISE 2019).

Amelia Peterson teaches Social Policy at the London School of Economics and in 2021 will join the founding faculty of the London Interdisciplinary School, a new university committed to preparing young people to tackle complex global problems. Her academic work focuses on qualification systems and transitions out of secondary school. She received her PhD in Education from Harvard University.

1 | *The Need for Purpose*
Why We Have to Ask 'Why?'

If you ask any audience – of, say, teachers or parents – the question *What is learning for?*, their immediate reaction is likely to be that it is a very silly question; surely the answer is obvious.

On reflection, they soon recognise that it is anything but obvious. We do not have established current answers. To paraphrase Neil Postman, educators were once known for providing reasons for learning; now they become famous for inventing a method.[1] Public debates about education – some of which are hot and polarised – have chiefly revolved around a set of second-order questions:

- *what* should be taught
- *how* it should be taught
- *to whom* (who gets access to what?)
- *how* it should be structured
- *how* it should be paid for

These are all important questions. Perhaps, in times of stability and continuity, they are the ones to focus on. However, those are not our times.

Mass education systems, the first of which emerged in the middle of the nineteenth century in order to serve the needs of the Industrial Revolution, are under intense strain. This is true of most services that the state plays a key role in providing. The disjuncture between the ideal of a public system that provides similarly for all citizens, and the complex and diverse citizenry and goals existent in such systems, creates a perception that public systems are failing the public.

In education, this perception has given rise to what is criticised as the Global Education Reform Movement – or 'GERM'.[2] This reform movement takes the view that the existing model of schooling is essentially sound, but can be enhanced by a mix of better trained

---

[1] Postman, *The End of Education.*   [2] Sahlberg, *Finnish Lessons 2.0.*

teachers and greater use of technology; basically, this view argues that 'school improvement' just needs to be done better.[3] At the other end of the continuum is the view that 'schooling' needs to be disrupted entirely, and that technology in the hands of learners will render schools obsolete. According to this view, 'schooling' is close to being over (and possibly the sooner the better), and learning will be disintermediated, just as many industries already have been.[4] On this view, the de-schoolers of the 1960s were basically right, just ahead of their time. The liberating power of the digital revolution makes their vision a realistic possibility.

Between these two viewpoints is the view that schooling needs to be re-designed, re-imagined. A new paradigm is needed and is overdue; but this book argues that schools as community institutions have a vital role if we are truly to thrive.

The outcomes of the school improvement movement have not done much to persuade critics that it can address the manifest failings of mass schooling systems *even on their own terms*. As Payne so succinctly states: 'So much reform, so little change.'[5]

What are these failings? They include:

- learner disengagement
- the growing costs of the current system with flat-lining gains on existing outcome metrics
- frustrated, unfulfilled education professionals (who are often not treated as professionals)
- little impact on inequality
- profound mismatch with the needs of societies and economies.

These are well documented elsewhere,[6] but the most recent rounds of international surveys provide a contemporary picture. Since 2000, the vast majority of OECD countries have seen no improvement in students' skills as measured by the Programme of International Student

---

[3] Barber and Mourshed, 'How the World's Best-Performing School Systems Come Out on Top'; Tucker, *Leading High-Performance School Systems.*

[4] Khan, *The One World Schoolhouse*; Christensen, Johnson and Horn, *Disrupting Class.*

[5] Payne, *So Much Reform, So Little Change.*

[6] Claxton, *What's the Point of School?*; Mehta and Fine, *In Search of Deeper Learning: The Quest to Remake the American High School*; OECD, *Education Policy Outlook 2015 – Making Reforms Happen.*

Assessment (PISA). Of all the OECD countries, only Portugal has seen sustained improvement in reading, maths and science.[7] In the ten years since PISA last assessed reading (2009–2018), only six countries – Georgia and Montenegro – saw improvement in the performance of low-socio-economic status (SES) students such that they reduced the gap with high-SES students.[8] This was in a period where almost all countries had reducing educational inequalities as a goal.[9] Among teachers, fewer than one third agree that 'the teaching profession is valued in society'.[10] Meanwhile, for students themselves, roughly a third of 15-year-olds across the OECD say that they have no clear sense of meaning in their life, rising to almost half in the UK.[11] That represents a third of 32 million 15-year-olds, who have each spent approximately 10,000 hours in school.[12] That is a lot of time to spend not working out what you care about.

This book argues that one of the reasons for the apparent failure of the school improvement movement is that it is addressing the wrong purposes. To remedy this problem, we need to engage deeply with the questions of what those purposes need to become. The critical questions are:

- What should be the new purpose of mass education systems in the unfolding conditions of the twenty-first century?
- Where are educators addressing the question and what does it look like?

1.1 New Purposes for Our Time

Philosophers of education, from Aristotle to Confucius, Comenius to Freire, proposed purposes for education relevant to their time. The fundamental contention of this book is that our time, the mid-twenty-

---

[7] OECD, *PISA 2018 Results Volume I: What Students Know and Can Do.*
[8] OECD, *PISA 2018 Results Volume II: Where All Students Can Succeed.*, 56–58.
[9] OECD, *TALIS 2018 Results (Volume I) – Teachers and School Leaders as Lifelong Learners*, 98.
[10] OECD, *TALIS 2013 Results, An International Perspective on Teaching and Learning*, 98.
[11] OECD, *PISA 2018 Results Volume III: What School Life Means For Students' Lives*, 165–167.
[12] The average school year across the OECD is 183 days (185 in primary), 5.0 hours per day (4.2 in primary). Students sitting PISA are typically in year ten or eleven of their schooling.

first century, presents unprecedented challenges – some of which are existential – together with stupendous opportunities that demand new purposes of education.

There is increasing consensus about the nature of these challenges, which are discussed in Chapter 3. Taken together they mean that today our species and its home planet stand on the brink of changes that, within the lifetimes of today's young learners, may change them forever. The changes are complex, which makes them all the harder to grasp. Professor Klaus Schwab, Founder and Executive Chairman of the World Economic Forum (WEF), sets out his view of the problem in 2016:

> The changes are so profound that, from the perspective of human history, there has never been a time of greater promise or potential peril. My concern, however, is that decision makers are too often caught in traditional, linear (and non-disruptive) thinking or too absorbed by immediate concerns to think strategically about the forces of disruption and innovation shaping our future.[13]

'Traditional, linear thinking' is exactly what prevails in education today. To take *advantage* of what is now possible, as well as to adapt to the changes that may be inevitable, we need to take this view seriously.

So, it is vital that we address afresh the questions of purpose – and in a way that is grounded in a developed, evidence-based picture of the emerging world, as opposed to being locked in the past. Without doing so, we cannot set a course for the direction of change. And without that, we cannot agree on models, curricula, pedagogies and assessments and all the other structural issues about which we currently obsess. Thomas Jefferson was surely right when he observed that the purpose of public education was not to serve the public but to *create* a public. For his time, that needed to be the focus. However, circumstances are transformed; consequently, this book takes as a starting point the stance adopted by Neil Postman in 1996:

> The question is not, Does or doesn't public schooling create a public? The question is, What kind of public does it create? A conglomerate of self-indulgent consumers? … Indifferent, confused citizens? Or a public imbued with confidence, a sense of purpose, a respect for learning, and tolerance?

---

[13] Schwab, *The Fourth Industrial Revolution*, 2–3.

The answer to this question has nothing whatever to do with computers, with testing, with teacher accountability, with class size, and with the other details of managing schools. The right answer depends on two things and two things alone: the existence of shared narratives and the capacity of such narratives to provide an inspired reason for schooling.[14]

In 1996, Postman's narrative was profoundly humanist, and it continues to be relevant today. He argued for the elevation of a sense of global citizenship and healthy intellectual scepticism. He also argued for an appreciation of diversity. He could not have known that within 20 years, there would be a series of technological, ecological and biological revolutions that would transform the landscape and require a rethink of the 'shared narrative' to address these conditions. The rise in many parts of the West of successful populist demagoguery, with scant regard for truth or evidence, has sent a chilling warning about the fragility of liberal democracy. If faint hopes of 'respect for learning, and tolerance' feel too weakly optimistic today, they must be replaced with something vital and new.

1.2 The Need for New Narratives

This book argues that without refreshed purposes, we will not find the level of collective energy, creativity and focus to create the shifts needed at a *system* level. For the most part, across the world, education renewal is going on in spite of system conditions, not because of them. The work of inspirational educators at the practice level, which is explored in this book, is energised and shaped by their clarity of contemporary purpose. They do not look to systems to guide and support them. Generally, their stories are of finding some space to act, managing the constraints and accountabilities to which they are subject.

It is from the work of these educators that it is possible to see that schools *can* face up to the challenges of this new epoch for the species and the planet; they point the way. Moreover, these schools demonstrate good grounds for arguing that the institution of a 'school' – in the sense of a dedicated community coming together regularly, face-to-face, united in learning – *ought* to survive; and that we should not be seduced by the 'death of school' techno-solutionists. Still, the new

[14] Postman, *The End of Education*.

narrative proposed will entail re-invention of these institutions. The good news is: around the world we see successful examples in action. The bad news is: most public systems still ignore or resist learning from them.

For change to become systemic, we need a new narrative about education's purpose that is authentic, based on evidence of our predicament and in tune with our deepest values. Everything starts with the story we tell about ourselves.

1.3 The Stories So Far …

It's the Economy, Stupid

It is a key task of political leaders to create narratives for their public. These narratives are often what are contested in elections, far more than the technical solutions to whatever specific problems need to be addressed. They are about identity and direction. Arguably, with the renaissance of populism, the dominant narratives have become shorter and less sophisticated: 'Make America Great Again'; 'Take Back Control'; 'Turn Back the Boats'. These are not complicated arguments. Their appeal is partly their simplicity, but also their capturing of notions of identity and social direction.

Education rarely enjoys much of a place in the broad pictures painted by political leaders, other than as an addendum. When we look to identify the dominant narratives around education among politicians today, we see an extraordinary convergence of message and rhetoric.

Predominantly, the message is this: education is what enables individuals to be successful and nations to compete to ensure economic growth. This is only common sense, right?

In 1995 Tony Blair, capturing the zeitgeist, said, 'Education is the best economic policy there is.'[15] Neo-liberalism has become the dominating political framework in the West. So pervasive has it become that it is scarcely even recognised as an ideology. It is seen as neutral, almost as a natural law.

Neo-liberalism sees competition as the defining characteristic of human relations. Citizens are defined primarily as consumers, whose

---

[15] Blair, 'Leader's Speech'.

democratic choices can be best exercised by buying and selling. Efforts to secure more equal societies are inimical to liberty, and futile. The market will see to it.

In addition, economic growth has become the fundamental under-pinning rationale. Occasionally, a dash of 'personal development and citizenship' rhetoric is added to the mix. But the central story has been one of economic growth through competition in the globalised econ-omy, leading to more jobs as well as increased national and personal prosperity – all in a virtuous circle.

Education has become a sort of global arms race, from 'A Nation At Risk' in 1980s America to the contemporary triennial media fair over PISA results. Indeed, in the same speech, Blair went on to couch the issue explicitly in those terms:

The arms race may be over; the knowledge race has begun and we will never compete on the basis of a low-wage, sweat shop economy ... . Education does not stop when you walk out of the school gates for the last time. Education must be for life. This is hard economics.

Twenty years on, even that most thoughtful of politicians, Barack Obama, was drawn into presenting education primarily within the frame of economic competition. Speaking in 2010, he said:

In a single generation, we've fallen from first place to 12th place in college graduation rates for young adults [but ...] we can retake the lead. The single most important thing we can do is to make sure we've got a world-class education system for everybody. That is a prerequisite for prosperity.[16]

Speaking to the same reporter, the then Secretary of Education, Arne Duncan, evoked the spirit of past competitions:

We got a little self-satisfied and other countries have, I think, out-worked us. They have out-invested. They have taken this more seriously, and I think this is a wake-up call.

Where education becomes any kind of focus for political debate, it is generally framed in promises to raise 'standards' by finding more money (and/or greater efficiency) improving buildings, and increasing access to tertiary education.

---

[16] de Nies, 'President Obama Outlines Goal to Improve College Graduation Rate in U.S.'

Another feature of neo-liberalism is that universal competition relies upon universal quantification and comparison.[17] The result is that, in many jurisdictions, education (along with other public services) is subject to a stifling regime of accountability assessment.[18] The philosophy of neo-liberalism promises freedoms, but these do not materialise for educators.

Irrespective of what is to be found in state curriculum documents, the majority of education planning and policy is carried out under the purpose essentially encapsulated by human capital theory.[19] Investment in humans leads to a return on that investment, both to economies (in terms of growth) and to individuals (higher incomes).[20] Clearly, many young people have believed in this narrative: everywhere applications for higher education have increased[21] – in many contexts at the cost of soaring student debt.[22]

It is important to recognise how firm a grip economics – or an out-of-date version of the discipline – has on the public imagination and mindset.[23] As F. S. Michaels remarks in her book *Monoculture: how one story is changing everything*:

In these early decades of the twenty-first century, the master story is economic: economic beliefs, values and assumptions are shaping how we think, feel and act.[24]

How has it come to pass that this discipline, with its poor predictive power and increasingly challenged foundations, has assumed this dominance? It would perhaps be less troublesome were it not for the fact that the pre-eminent model was set out in the textbooks of the 1950s, themselves rooted in the theories of 1850. The infiltration into our very language is clear: it is deemed acceptable to talk of 'natural capital' when we mean forests, fields and oceans; or of 'human capital' when we mean people.

---

[17] Espeland and Sauder, *Engines of Anxiety*; Power, *The Audit Society*.
[18] Lingard et al., *Globalizing Educational Accountabilities*.
[19] Klees, 'A Quarter Century of Neoliberal Thinking in Education'.
[20] Becker, *Human Capital; a Theoretical and Empirical Analysis, with Special Reference to Education*.
[21] Marginson, 'The Worldwide Trend to High Participation Higher Education'.
[22] Chamie, 'Student Debt Rising Worldwide'; finaid.org/loans/studentloandebtclock/
[23] Kwak, *Economism*. [24] Michaels, *Monoculture*.

However, the inadequacies of human capital theory as a basic underpinning for education's purposes are becoming increasingly apparent. Foremost among its critics are those with a humanistic perspective. But it is economists themselves who are now raising questions about human capital theory as an adequate basis for education. In particular, some point out that, for many, the human capital approach has amounted to a kind of con.

Economists Take on the Dominant Economic Narrative

In *The Global Auction* Philip Brown, Hugh Lauder and David Ashton argue that the bargain between individuals and governments has been that both will take on high levels of debt, on the understanding that both society as a whole and the individuals concerned will be well rewarded.[25] But the bargain has not been kept. The rewards traditionally associated with middle-class status have been appropriated by a shrinking subset of society, leaving most at an increasing disadvantage.[26] University-educated workers compete for a diminishing pool of opportunities. This is linked to the global financial crisis of 2008; easy credit and the rising cost of real estate became substitutes for employment-driven prosperity.[27]

Notwithstanding skill gaps in certain sectors, there are not likely to be enough high value-added, knowledge-based jobs created to absorb the supply of university-educated workers.[28] At the time of writing, it seems highly likely that this will be exacerbated by the projected levels of unemployment due to COVID-19. Significant numbers of learners will no longer reap the expected benefits of educational qualifications: employment and the promise of a better future. Disillusion is growing across a number of countries with regard to education being an effective vehicle for social mobility and greater well-being.[29] Around the world, the hope for upward social mobility, spurred by the massive expansion of access to educational opportunities since the 1990s, is now diminishing.[30]

---

[25] Brown, Lauder and Ashton, *The Global Auction*.
[26] Reeves, *Dream Hoarders*.   [27] Streeck, *Buying Time*.
[28] Susskind, *A World without Work*.   [29] Markovits, *The Meritocracy Trap*.
[30] The Sutton Trust, 'Social Mobility and Education: Academic Papers Presented at a High Level Summit Sponsored by the Carnegie Corporation of New York and

Analyses of recent elections in the West highlight the rise of a new educational 'cleavage' – a dividing line in political support – between those with and without university degrees.[31] As education has become for some an identity or mark of success, for others it is an exclusive world, of which they are not seeing the benefit.[32] We have clearly drifted some way from the ideal of education as a public good.

In response to these changes, young people are beginning to question the 'return on investment' of traditionally high status educational routes. On the question of education's contribution to 'growth', there has always been strong scepticism from economists.[33] Even in low-income countries, where systematic reviews of the evidence suggest a clearer economic pay-off to investing in education and skills,[34] there is scepticism about the wisdom of continuing to import the model of other countries. A recent study by the Brookings Institute shows that if the current schooling model is pursued in low-income countries, it will take another 100 years for children to reach the basic education levels present in the high-income world today.[35] In the last analysis, the system of formal education transplanted to low-income countries from the rich is self-defeating as a means of achieving development.

And Anyhow: What Is 'Growth'?

So even economists are unsure of defining education in fundamentally economic terms. However, what is most unsound about the prevalent political response, in the contemporary conditions we face, is what is taken to be the unquestioned good – *growth* – and how that is defined. It has become the primary and overriding objective of the vast majority of global, national and business plans. Growth as a metaphor for prosperity has become deeply embedded through language. We like to see our children grow, or our gardens. Growth seems fundamental

the Sutton Trust'; Volante and Jerrim, 'Why a Good Education Isn't Always the Key to Social Mobility'; Narayan et al., *Fair Progress?*
[31] Hendrickson and Galston, 'The Educational Rift in the 2016 Election'; Surridge, 'What Lies behind the UK's New Political Map?'
[32] Goodhart, *The Road to Somewhere.*
[33] Wolf, *Does Education Matter?*; Blaug, *The Economics of Education and the Education of an Economist.*
[34] Hawkes, Ugur, and EPPI-Centre, *Evidence on the Relationship between Education, Skills and Economic Growth in Low-Income Countries.*
[35] McGivney and Winthrop, 'Why Wait 100 Years?'

to life and progress. But there is another end of the metaphor: that growth can be cancerous.

Despite the widespread adoption of the goal of economic growth for education, the concept of growth has never been more contested. Drawing from a vast range of sources and disciplines, the scientist and policy analyst Vaclav Smil shows how growth has been both an unspoken as well as an explicit aim of our individual and collective striving.[36] But he demonstrates how, now, growth must have limits: only limits on a planetary scale will secure the survival of our civilisation.

If it is to be used as the ultimate arbiter for policy decisions, and in particular for guiding the direction of learning, we had better be clear about what exactly growth means. In terms of national economies, it is conventionally measured as the per cent rate of increase in real gross domestic product (GDP). GDP was created as a metric by the Nobel prize-winning economist, Simon Kuznets, in 1934, and came into use as a measure of nations' economies in 1944. It used to be roughly correlated with the increase in the number of jobs and the size of average personal incomes. Ironically, it was Kuznets himself who cautioned against the profligate use of the measure beyond a limited utility:

The valuable capacity of the human mind to simplify a complex situation in a compact characterization becomes dangerous when not controlled in terms of definitely stated criteria. With quantitative measurements especially, the definiteness of the result suggests, often misleadingly, a precision and simplicity in the outlines of the object measured. Measurements of national income are subject to this type of illusion and resulting abuse, especially since they deal with matters that are the center of conflict of opposing social groups where the effectiveness of an argument is often contingent upon oversimplification.[37]

Such an oversimplification has indeed occurred; perhaps more than Kuznets could have imagined. His own criticisms have gone unheeded.

The definition of GDP matters profoundly for education because it shapes the political world's sense of what is valuable. Kuznets himself

---

[36] Smil, *Growth*.

[37] Division of Economic Research, 'National Income, 1929–1932: Letter from the Acting Secretary of Commerce Transmitting in Response to Senate Resolution No. 220 (72nd Congress) a Report on National Income, 1929–32'.

pointed out a further flaw in the GDP calculation: it does not assign any economic value to the work of care – usually by women in the home. That is *the work which enables the very young and sometimes the helpless to be cared for.* Therefore, housework counts towards GDP when it is paid, but excluded when it is free of charge. As Paul Samuelson, an economist, pointed out, a country's GDP falls when a man marries his maid. Economists are increasingly critiquing the concept of GDP as a proxy for our overall welfare. In *The World After GDP*, Lorenzo Fioramonte points out that a purchase of heroin or an hour of paid sex appears as a plus; 15 hours of volunteer work counts for nothing.[38] Ignoring unpaid work also misrepresents the significance of certain economic activity. Raising well-cared for children is arguably at least as important as building cars. In 2016, for the first time, the UK Office of National Statistics put a value on this unpaid work for the country: £1 trillion.[39] This is excluded from calculations of the national GDP.

It is the environmentalists though who have supplied the most devastating objections to the continuing use of GDP as a measure of real 'growth'. Al Gore points out that growing GDP no longer increases real prosperity nor a sense of well-being: however, it is strongly correlated with the incomes of elites.[40] GDP is based on an absurd set of calculations that exclude any consideration of distribution of income, depletion of essential resources and the reckless spewing of harmful waste into the atmosphere, oceans, rivers, soil and the biosphere. The cost of pollution is not subtracted when calculating GDP; but the cost of the activity of cleaning up pollution is added. Manufactured 'wants' lead to rises in consumption, which in turn is equated with happiness or 'prosperity'. The United States has tripled its economic outcome over the last 50 years with no gains being measured in the general public's sense of well-being.[41] As *The Financial Times* reported in 2016, the average German today owns 10,000 objects, while the average British household owns £4,000 worth of clothes, a third of which will not have been worn over the

[38] Fioramonti, *The World After GDP*.
[39] ONS, 'Changes in the Value and Division of Unpaid Care Work in the UK'.
[40] Gore, *The Future*.
[41] Kahneman and Deaton, 'High Income Improves Evaluation of Life but Not Emotional Well-Being'.

past year.[42] Having only been widely recognised in the early 2000s, 'oniomania', compulsive buying disorder, has been identified in 5–15 per cent of the US and UK population.[43] Many are now responding by trying to 'be more with less'.[44]

The GDP measure takes no account of leisure time, meaning that two countries might have equal GDP but one has workers toiling for 12-hour days and the other only eight. Large amounts of output captured by GDP are also wasteful, such as the hundreds of thousands of tonnes of food wasted in Britain each year, or the Christmas jumpers bought for one day, only to degrade in landfill for centuries.

The context in low-income countries is of course different in that they still have a long way to go to satisfy the basic needs of their citizens. However, emulating the high-income world model is clearly disastrous. Unsustainable patterns of production and consumption point to fundamental contradictions in a dominant model of development that is focused on economic growth. As a consequence of unhindered fossil fuel use and over-exploitation of natural areas, climate heating is producing an increase in natural disasters, already facing poor countries particularly with enormous challenges and even greater risk in the future. As manifested in the Sustainable Development Goals and the United Nations 2030 commitments, sustainability has emerged as the central development concern in the face of the climate emergency, the degradation of vital natural resources such as water, and the loss of biodiversity.[45]

Economic 'Growth' and Ill-Health

The model of consumption exported from the 'developed' world is impacting not only planetary sustainability but human health patterns. Already, the epidemic of diabetes caused by obesity (now affecting 1 in 11 of all adults across the world) has spread from being a 'first-world' problem to a serious problem in the lower-income economies – even

---

[42] Spang, 'Thing Theory'.
[43] Lee and Mysyk, 'The Medicalization of Compulsive Buying'; Maraz, Griffiths and Demetrovics, 'The Prevalence of Compulsive Buying'.
[44] Carver, *Project 333*.
[45] UNESCO, 'UNESCO Moving Forward the 2030 Agenda for Sustainable Development; 2017'.

where there is acute hunger.[46] As Yuval Harari points out, humans today are more at risk of obesity than starvation.[47] If the high-income world is reaching 'peak stuff', the model of growth is still clung to and even exported. When societies lack the basics, it is reasonable for economies to focus on how to produce more stuff, and to measure that form of growth. But we need to shift from old notions of 'growth' to that of value. And what people really hold dear is not being captured by current yardsticks.

The discipline of economics is not the problem here. It is important to clarify this because critics of an economistic worldview are often painted as unpragmatic or untechnical, even anti-science. The goal of economics as a discipline – determining how we can produce and distribute enough resources to survive – is more important than ever. But economists themselves now point out that this work is now too often loaded with unnecessary and inaccurate assumptions, leading to what Kwak calls 'economism' as opposed to economics.[48] In economist Thomas Sedlacek's terms, we need more 'humanomics': an understanding of how to produce and distribute that takes into account humanity's moral principles.[49] This inquiry is related to, but bigger than, the question that Aristotle originally posed: how are humans to live happy lives? Aristotle's response was that happiness resulted from deploying our human intelligence to act creatively. As we shall see in Chapter 3, this dynamic has become, in the twenty-first century, an infinitely more complex one.

---

[46] WHO, *Global Report on Diabetes.*   [47] Harari, *Homo Deus.*
[48] Kwak, *Economism.*   [49] Sedlacek, *Economics of Good and Evil.*

2 | *New Answers to 'Why'*

If economists themselves increasingly acknowledge the inadequacies and distortions that the elevation of 'growth' and its metrics bring with them, it is high time that education was freed from the assumptions of human capital theory and the education arms race. Political leaders need to find a new, more meaningful narrative; one that builds on what really inspires learners (and teachers), and offers a real alternative to being trapped as cogs in an increasingly cranky machine.

But it is unclear where a new vision will come from. When Nobel Prize winners Amartya Sen and Joseph Stiglitz were invited to assess the measures of economic and social progress that currently guide policymaking, they came to a stark conclusion: 'those attempting to guide the economy and our societies are like pilots trying to steer a course without a reliable compass'.[1] The European Union, with its *Beyond GDP* initiative, has begun a search to develop indicators that are more inclusive of environmental and social aspects of progress.[2] It has yet to turn up much. The OECD, more cautiously, has advanced the notion of *'inclusive growth'*; that is, clinging to the concept but trying to focus on distributional fairness.[3] Where direction might have come from the frontiers of the global economy, in Silicon Valley, there are rumbles of discontent. The argument is that the founders of Google, Uber and countless other digital ventures, have sacrificed the world-changing potential of their technologies to the 'growth trap' – the expectation that businesses (and countries, and the world economy) must keep expanding in a way that no healthy organism ever can.[4] Consequently, we are, in effect, doubling down on the industrial

[1] Stiglitz, Sen and Fitoussi Report by the Commission on the Measurement of Economic Performance and Social Progress.
[2] European Commission, 'Beyond GDP: Measuring Progress, True Wealth, and Well-Being'.
[3] www.oecd.org/inclusive-growth/inequality.htm
[4] Rushkoff, *Throwing Rocks at the Google Bus*.

age mandate for growth above all else. Instead, we should accept that the era of extractive growth (in relation both to the resources of the planet, and also the value created by companies) is over.

2.1 If Not 'Growth' – Then What?

Encouragingly, some nations are showing the way. New Zealand declared, in its 2019 budget statement, that it would be the first nation in the world to measure success by its people's well-being. According to the International Monetary Fund (IMF), the New Zealand budget was set to grow (according to GDP) by around 2.5 per cent in 2019 and 2.9 per cent in 2020.So this is already a 'success' in conventional terms. But it was felt that many New Zealanders were not benefitting in their daily lives. While other countries are starting to *measure* well-being, New Zealand is the first western country to design its entire budget around well-being priorities and instruct its ministries to design policies to improve it. The Finance Minister, Grant Robertson declared:

For me, wellbeing means people living lives of purpose, balance and meaning to them, and having the capabilities to do so[5]

This conclusion is highly congruent with the proposition advanced in this book. Moreover, economics, in the hands of a new generation, is shifting to flesh out a basis for policymaking beyond growth. One work in particular illustrates what is taking shape.

Kate Raworth is a former economist for Oxfam, now at the University of Oxford.In place of GDP, she offers the model of 'doughnut economics', in which the objective is to strike a balance.[6] Multiple dimensions of valued resources are arrayed in a circle. The hole in the middle represents a lower bound where people fall short of the essentials of life, where nobody should be. Beyond the outer ring, are the levels at which the collective use of resources pushes beyond earth's life supporting systems. Raworth urges a shift from GDP to the 'doughnut' – a fundamental shift of goals and associated metrics, which is 'growth agnostic'. As she put it in 2019:

---

[5] Roy, 'New Zealand's World-First "Wellbeing" Budget to Focus on Poverty and Mental Health'.

[6] Raworth, *Doughnut Economics*.

The question is: how do you create an economy that thrives whether or not it grows – I don't have the answer to the financial, political and social redesign. But I believe these are the existential economic questions of our time. So we need to start asking them, no matter how jarring they are to mainstream policy debate.[7]

After months of development, the City of Amsterdam has adopted a 'doughnut' model as part of its response to COVID-19.[8] Its aim – to create a *thriving* city.

This question – of how to thrive without endless extractive growth, without necessarily progressing on a specific individual metric – is jarring to the mainstream educational debate, too. It is useful here to delve back into previous ways of thinking about value in education; bases on which we now need to build.

2.2 A More Nourishing Source? The Humanist Alternative

There is among education researchers and writers a long tradition of reflection on the fundamental purposes of learning, schooling and public education. Traditionally, many educators would have met these ideas by studying the philosophy of education as a compulsory part of teacher education. These courses are now increasingly uncommon. While it would be impossible to provide any kind of comprehensive summary here of the many debates that have occurred, reviewing any strand of this tradition is an important reminder that fine thinkers always frame education's purpose in broad and multi-faceted terms. This widening of the frame on what humanity values underpins the shifts that, we argue, need to be made.

Ironically, a bridge to a more powerful, relevant and meaningful encapsulation of the contemporary purpose for education was written by a former economist, Jacques Delors. Delors had been minister of finance in France and later president of the European Commission. From 1993 to 1996, he chaired a commission for UNESCO on Education for the Twenty-First Century, which culminated in the

---

[7] Partington, 'Is It Time to End Our Fixation with GDP and Growth?'
[8] Circle Economy, 'The Amsterdam City Doughnut'; Doughnut Economics Action Lab et al., 'The Amsterdam City Doughnut'; Boffey, 'Amsterdam to Embrace "doughnut" Model to Mend Post-Coronavirus Economy'.

document: *Learning, the Treasure Within.*[9] This report perhaps best expresses the humanist perspective on the purposes of learning as it was perceived at the century's close.

Given his association with UNESCO, it is no surprise that Delors sought to position the purpose of education in a human rights-based development agenda. He tried to re-establish a humanistic tradition, linked to principles of equality, democratic participation and social justice. He was reacting to the rise of neo-liberalism as the dominant paradigm. At that time, he thought there were three crises to be faced: economic, the 'ideology of progress', and 'a certain form of moral crisis'.

From this perspective, the Delors report concluded that 'four pillars' of education were needed. They were defined as follows:

- *Learning to know* – a broad general knowledge with the opportunity to work in depth on a small number of subjects.
- *Learning to do* – to acquire not only occupational skills but also the competence to deal with many situations and to work in teams.
- *Learning to be* – to develop one's personality and to be able to act with growing autonomy, judgement and personal responsibility.
- *Learning to live together* – by developing an understanding of other people and an appreciation of interdependence.[10]

On any assessment (and particularly in their historical context), these are profoundly thoughtful purposes. The reality is that most education systems still concentrate almost exclusively on the first pillar: learning to know. There are ongoing efforts to increase focus on the latter three.[11]

Why did Delors's vision gain so little traction? Clearly it was deeply out of synch with the prevailing ideology of the time (consciously so); and it failed to penetrate the dominant world view of leaders. Nevertheless, it inspired some practitioners, and there is a direct line of intellectual discourse that flows from it.

---

[9] Delors, *Learning: The Treasure within; Report to UNESCO of the International Commission on Education for the Twenty-First Century.*
[10] Delors, 85–98.
[11] Elfert, 'Learning to Live Together: Revisiting the Humanism of the Delors Report – UNESCO Digital Library'; Cappon and Laughlin, 'Canada's Composite Learning Index'.

2.3 Learner Outcomes for Thriving: Beyond 'Knowledge vs Skills'

One line of this thinking runs through into the 'C21st skills' movement. In this movement, the implicit response to the question *What is school for?* was that its purpose is to provide (all) learners with the skills they would need to be 'successful' in the twenty-first century.These skills are sometimes defined in terms of categories (learning and innovations skills; digital literacy skills; and life and career skills); or a discrete 4Cs: communication, creativity, collaboration and critical thinking.[12]

In a sense, contributors to this body of thinking side-stepped the economistic/humanistic dichotomy by proposing that the skills needed to live together are the same as those needed to succeed in a knowledge economy. The notion is appealing and the movement has certainly succeeded to the degree that little discourse around education is conducted now without reference to the need 'to acquire twenty-first-century skills'.

The skills acquisition approach has a great deal to offer, and many educators have embraced it.But there are important critiques that point to the persistent need to ask 'succeed in what?'. Psychologists argue that skills such as creativity or collaboration need to be developed in the context of specific knowledge domains, bringing back in a question of what kinds of activities, experiences and disciplines schools should focus on.[13] In addition, recognition that skills are in themselves only instrumental has led to a focus on character, including not only 'grit' but ethics.[14] But then we have to engage with the question of what kind of values and principles to reify. From where do the ethical foundations arise? What – if in our contemporary secular societies religion does not provide it – is the basis for what we prioritise in developing knowledge, skills and character?

It is the concept of 'success', therefore, that needs to be better understood and defined, in the light of a clearer conception of humanity's predicament. Without grounding our goals in this unfolding

---

[12] Trilling and Fadel, *21st Century Skills*; Bellanca and Brandt, *21st Century Skills*.
[13] Willingham, *Why Don't Students Like School?*
[14] Fadel, Trilling and Bialik, *Four-Dimensional Education*.

reality, we risk being banal and abstract. We can no longer afford that; leaders and educators need to confront that reality squarely.

Some contemporary writers have sought to update and develop the humanist perspective and skills-based approach.[15] The OECD's *Framework for Education and Skills 2030* proposes that the outcomes for learners should be *competencies*: defined as knowledge + skills + attitudes + values.[16] The great strength of this approach is that it avoids the sterile debate about whether education should be 'about' the acquisition of knowledge (the conventional view) or 'about' the acquisition of skills (the 'progressive' view). Of course this is a false dichotomy. And what the OECD 2030 *Framework* does is to show that even the right combination and blend of knowledge and skills is insufficient: values and attitudes are also critical in all forms of learning, including disciplinary learning. Each discipline, or way of knowing, has itself an associated set of values and attitudes. In science, for example, these include a respect for evidence; an openness to new ideas; sustained intellectual curiosity.

The OECD *2030 Framework* introduces (and hopefully will help to legitimate) one further concept that is absolutely critical, not only to the acquisition of competencies, as described above, but also to the broader, deeper objectives that learning should be devoted to. This is the idea of *learner agency*. Discussed in greater depth in Chapter 12, the concept is introduced here for two reasons.

First, it lies at the heart of new conceptions of active learning.The Framework observes: -

Knowledge and skills, attitudes and values form a complex, interrelated system resulting in a person taking action ... Defending and asserting one's rights, interest, limits and needs ... lies at the very heart of responsible, autonomous action. It means that individuals capably put themselves forward as a subject, of whom account has to be taken, and adeptly assume their responsibilities and choices as a citizen, family member, consumer and worker in a world of different cultures, interests, values and beliefs.

Accordingly, the Framework proposes that learners should be enabled to become reflective responsible agents, investing themselves actively to

---

[15] Biesta, *Beyond Learning*; Egan, *Learning in Depth*; Facer, *Learning Futures: Education, Technology and Social Change*; Biesta, *Beautiful Risk of Education: Interventions Education, Philosophy, and Culture*.
[16] OECD, 'The Future We Want'.

achieve goals that they have understood and endorsed. This is the case both for their own learner journey (the process) but also for the application of their agency in the world (the outcome). Interestingly, the Framework uses the same metaphor adopted by Sen and Stiglitz: we are all in need of a *compass*. The learning compass is what education needs to confer on young people for their life journey.

Second, without newly released levels of learner and citizen agency, it is impossible to see how the goals of thriving in a transforming world can be achieved. Agency is a challenging concept for schools to take on, and is often referred to in a very diluted and superficial sense. However, the multiple examples set out in the pathfinder chapters to follow, as well as the specific initiatives being taken which are discussed in Chapter 12 give grounds for real optimism and hope that schools can be re-imagined with this outcome in mind, so that learners can become shapers of the future not just victims or objects of it. We turn now to why that purpose is more urgent than ever.

2.4 Beyond Humanism as a Basis: We Are Part of Something Bigger

Contemporary visions of education move beyond the Delors report by taking up the challenge inherent in the notion of 'interdependence' and 'learning to live together'. The *2030 Framework* is one initiative that appears to hold much promise. Launched in 2018, this learning framework starts from where we believe it should: with the issue of *purpose*. The proposal it makes is that the overall purpose of learning should be the creation of 'the future we want'. This is a massive advance: it is future-focused and purpose-driven. However, who is 'we'? And are we again trapped in an anthropocentric world view in which all that counts is the human species, and its wants and desires? The Framework proposes that it is for societies in context to determine the nature of 'the future we want' – and lists a set of key indicators as a starting point for debate. These are based on the OECD's 11 *Better Life* indices: housing, income, jobs, community, education, environment, governance, health, life satisfaction, safety, work-life balance.[17] It remains within a wholly anthropocentric world view. We want to

---

[17] 'OECD Better Life Index'.

argue that human 'well-being' is no longer a sufficiently comprehensive purpose.

Once, it might have seemed whimsical to suggest that nature has rights. But we are now witnessing a set of legal moves in jurisdictions around the world that are seeking to recognise interdependence and animacy in the living world, and these have come to be known as the 'nature rights' or 'rights-of-nature' movement.[18] One example is the Lake Erie Bill of Rights, drafted by the City Council of Toledo in Ohio.[19] Now hotly contested by some business groups, including frackers, the Bill confers upon the lake legal personhood, and accords the consequent rights in law – including the right 'to exist, flourish, and naturally evolve.'[20] The move had been driven by Toledo residents appalled at the degradation and pollution to which the lake was being subjected. Before being dismissed as an absurdity – because the lake itself could not defend its rights by taking a case – we should note that neither can a baby or an adult in a vegetative state. The Bill states that, 'we … extend legal rights to our natural environment to ensure that the natural world [is] no longer subordinated to the accumulation of surplus wealth and unaccountable political power'.

This Bill is an example of what might be called a 'new animism': that is, a bold ontological claim that lakes, trees, forests are not just resources for humans but have independent validity – and rights. These claims have been advanced through the activism of indigenous groups.[21] This included change to the constitutions of Ecuador and Bolivia in 2008 and 2009 to recognise Rights of Nature and more recently similar claims as that for Lake Erie have been made for Whanganui River in New Zealand and the Columbian Amazon.[22] These rights have been proved hard to enforce and their desirability is a contested and complex legal and philosophical question.[23] It in part highlights the limitations of the rights-based approach that has come to dominate international law. Suffice it to say here that the

---

[18] Chapron, Epstein and López-Bao, 'A Rights Revolution for Nature'.

[19] 'Toledo, Ohio, Question 2, 'Lake Erie Bill of Rights' Initiative (February 2019)'.

[20] Margil and Dickinson, 'Toledo Passed a "Lake Erie Bill of Rights" To Protect Its Water. The State Is Trying to Stop It.'

[21] Bunten, 'What Do the Rights of Nature Have to Do with Indigeneity?'

[22] Torres and Macpherson, 'The Tour to Save the World: Colombia Wins the Yellow Jersey for the Rights of Nature'.

[23] Pietari, 'Ecuador's Constitutional Rights of Nature: Implementation, Impacts, and Lessons Learned'.

search is on for a new framework for manifesting and legally enforcing values in which the human is entangled in the midst of a vast set of life ecosystems – and is not the masterful, knowing centre. As the consciousness of that reality emerges (hopefully in time to avert some imminent losses and crises), we will discern a new set of purposes and roles for education in its enactment.

Amitav Ghosh in *The Great Derangement* sees the epoch as one in which Earth is revealing itself as both acutely vulnerable and restlessly lively:

The uncanny and improbable events that are beating at our doors seem to have stirred a sense of recognition... that humans were never alone, that we have always been surrounded by beings who share elements of that which we thought most distinctively our own: the capacities of will, thought and consciousness.[24]

If it is no longer viable to take an exclusively human-centred approach to wider institutions such as law and politics, so too we argue that this is the case with education. We need to recognise that we are indissolubly a part of a bigger ecology of which we are not the centre, nor the ultimate or pre-eminent adjudicator and beneficiary. A systematic look at the evidence in Chapters 3 and 4 suggests that this understanding is about to be forced upon us. We go on to show how this requires a re-assessment of the idea of *thriving*.

---

[24] Ghosh, *The Great Derangement*.

3 | *The Context for a New Purpose*

An Age of Disruption

3.1 Our Present: Learners' Futures

The current dominant narratives about the purpose of education have failed on every count: they do not inspire teachers and they fail to promote the changes needed for education to work for everyone. But most damningly, they do not connect with the lived realities of many young people; rather, they rely on selling learners a false promise that cannot be delivered. Even in low-income countries with desperate youthful populations, for whom education is seen as the panacea, there is a powerfully growing need to think about these issues differently. As the Director General of UNESCO, Irina Bokova, wrote in July 2015:

I am convinced we need to think big again today about education ... The world is getting younger, and aspirations for human rights and dignity are rising. Societies are more connected than ever, but intolerance and conflict remain rife... inequalities are deepening and the planet is under pressure. Opportunities for sustainable and inclusive development are vast, but challenges are steep and complex. The world is changing – education must also change.[1]

The implication is clear. Our starting point for thinking big about education is to understand how the world is changing.

The disconnect between schooling and today's world is obvious. But if that disconnect is a fissure, the relationship between today's education and the needs of the future is a canyon. Therefore, serious consideration about the nature of the future awaiting our species and its home planet may – just possibly – drive home the need for a new set of purposes and a different paradigm to serve them. There are some grounds for optimism around this approach. Arguably the biggest shifts in objectives and practice (in terms of their reach, if not their depth) have occurred in the movement towards taking '21st century

---

[1] UNESCO, *Rethinking Education*, 3.

skills' seriously. This is perhaps because the pressure came from a broader alliance than usual. Not only educators and theorists, but civil society and in particular business and technologists, united in advocating for an enhancement – although not a rethink – of the outcomes of schooling. While the resulting curricular reforms are still contested and assessment remains a major challenge, this is a foundation that might be built upon.[2] It has created a crack in the solid edifice of a model of education predicated on the transmission of knowledge and its recall.

Where we need to go further is to recognise the *magnitude and speed* of the shifts and disruptions that are impending, and that we can say, with considerable confidence, will impact the lives of learners entering schools today. If the evidence for these shifts is strong, what moral basis is there for education systems to adopt the ostrich position?

3.2 Using 'the Future' Wisely

There is of course a number of problems around the use of 'the future' to guide action. But let's be clear that to use ideas and evidence about the future simply means being explicit about what is currently implicit. The dominant human capital theory itself uses assumptions about the future (specifically, the future of job markets and economic growth) to justify particular educational ends and means. Making no changes is in itself making a bet about the nature of the future. The evidence suggests it is a very bad bet.

This book profiles schools and other organisations that are seriously considering the need to design education with a view to the wider, transforming world in which young people live. Each example looks different because it is responding to a particular society, community and group of students. It is an interesting reflection that the human capital theory, and the 'school improvement' movement led to a convergence around the nature of schools. What we are witnessing now, as schools begin to focus on their learners' thriving, is increasing *divergence*.

The acknowledgment that the human capital model has within it an implicit theory about the future should alert us to some very clear problems. One is around the phenomenon of 'selective attention'.

---

[2] Reimers and Chung, *Teaching and Learning for the Twenty-First Century*; Griffin and Care, *Assessment and Teaching of 21st Century Skills*.

This concept, developed by psychologists, refers to a tendency on the part of people who are so determined to focus intensely on a particular image they are oblivious to other images present.[3] We select things to which we pay attention principally through habit or preference. The selection of metrics is also critical: as we have observed, the metric of GDP includes some values and arbitrarily excludes others. Thus too with the outcomes of schooling: we pay selective attention to a set of metrics – which are limited and habitual, and which obscure others. Therefore, in the account that follows of the best outlines of the future, we can do no more than be aware that further selective attention may be at work, and ask critical questions. 'Futures' are always constructions. They reflect the vision, values and tools of the analysts. They will be as complex and multi-faceted as history has been.[4]

The difficulties of adopting the future as a guide to action have been much debated by futurists.[5] Al Gore in his magisterial book, *The Future*, discusses the human history of thinking about the future, from oracles and entrails to algorithms.[6] The fragility of prediction is apparent. Amusing memories of past predictions include: 'What can be more palpably absurd than the prospect held out of locomotives travelling twice as fast as stagecoaches?' (*The Quarterly Review*, England, March 1825); 'There's no chance that the iPhone is going to get any significant market' *(USA Today*, 30 April 2007).

It has been predicted that oil would run out (predicted in 1923, 1960 and 2000) and its price would rise indefinitely (the price of oil dropped to c. $30 a barrel in 2016 from c. $100 in 2014; to negative value in 2020; and volatility continues).

There have also been predictions of catastrophe/utopia that do not come to pass. When the moon landing took place, there were predictions of moon-colonies. Time-scales are important: the latter suggestion may yet occur. Predictions around the impact of the SARS epidemic proved to be wildly inaccurate. (Though some countries learned from the experience to plan for the future that unfolded with

---

[3] Beautifully illustrated in *Gorilla on a Basketball Court*: www.theinvisiblegorilla .com/gorilla_experiment.html
[4] Facer, 'The Problem of the Future and the Possibilities of the Present in Education Research'.
[5] Miller, 'Futures Literacy – Embracing Complexity and Using the Future'.
[6] Gore, *The Future*.

COVID-19). Trends may be accurate, yet wild cards in human history – asteroids, discoveries – can never be discounted.

While prediction about human behaviour and its consequences can never be made with the same degree of confidence as those in the physical sciences, advances have nevertheless been made, not least through the availability of immense computing power to assist the process. New methodologies have been developed, for example *Foresight*, a social technology developed 30 years ago and now used extensively in the spheres of business and government.[7] Naturally, time-scales are critical: the longer the time-scale, the lower the degree of confidence. Trends may actually accelerate in entirely unanticipated ways when we are dealing with *emergence* in complex systems. There may be sudden shifts in a clear pattern, when the potential for change builds up without that being apparent until it reaches critical mass. Then we have the phenomenon of disruption. If any word were to capture the nature of the most serious evidence-based assessments of our futures, that word would be *disruption*.[8] Whether one cheers or sighs at this word, it helps to break from the linear thinking that controls education debate today. Whether at the level of policy or practice, current recommendations for the future are based on what has worked in the past. This will not work if trends are subject to disruptive change.

3.3 Trying to Grasp the Magnitude of Change

It could be argued that change is always with us. What is different about the current epoch? Perhaps humans have always perceived themselves to be in an era of extraordinary and unprecedented change. The evidence presented below suggests otherwise: no era in humanity's history has stood at the cusp of a set of changes such as these, with implications for our very nature and existence.

In *The Future*, Gore concludes:

There is clear consensus that the future now emerging will be different from anything known in the past – not of degree, but of kind. There is no period of change that remotely resembles what humanity is about to experience[9]

---

[7] Conway, 'An Overview of Foresight Methodologies'; Giaoutzi and Sapio, *Recent Developments in Foresight Methodologies*.
[8] Dobbs, Manyika and Woetzel, *No Ordinary Disruption*.
[9] Gore, *The Future*, xv.

We do have very good evidence of this. The work relied on here is not that of speculation, fantasy or science fiction, but is based in empirical research, from a wide variety of sources. The level of consensus is striking, and cannot easily be attributed to group-think.

However, the problem is not just one of evidence and data. If it were, we would be in a very different position. The issue is really one of what the human mind can bring itself to believe or confront. In his book *We Are the Weather*, Jonathan Safran Foer recounts the story of an eminent US Supreme Court justice, Felix Frankfurter, who in 1943 was given compelling incontrovertible evidence of the systematic exterminations in the concentration camps. Himself a Jew, he concluded that he would do nothing about it because he could not believe it. He observed: 'I didn't say that this young man [his informant] is lying. I said I am unable to believe him, My mind, my heart, they are made in such a way that I cannot accept it.[10]

Similarly, while we may not think that the scientists are lying and other data sources on the range of issues reviewed below are false, we appear unable to incorporate them into our the world view that determines our actions. Thus, despite the clarity of the science, in the United States about a third to almost half of the public believes that the seriousness of the global emergency is generally exaggerated.[11] We need to grasp these issues viscerally, not just intellectually.

The tsunami of studies published recently on the subject of futures cannot and should not be ignored by educators nor by those charged with guiding public education systems. This work has been accelerated and made more sophisticated by one of the very phenomena it charts – what Gore calls the development of 'the global mind'. Interconnected data-sets and Big Data analysis through massive computing power, multi-disciplinary global research teams, distributed 'citizen scientists' and instantaneous communication have changed our relationship to the world of information; we can use this to better comprehend the trends and scenarios that are unfolding.

It is possible to splice and dice the concepts and arenas in a variety of ways. However, for the purposes of this book, an overview of this field of futures analysis will be discussed through three lenses:

- *our planetary environment*
- *technology*
- *and human evolution.*

[10] Foer, *We Are the Weather*, 18.
[11] Kamarck, 'The Challenging Politics of Climate Change'.

Of course, one cannot be understood without reference to the rest: they are inter-relating complex systems. But each one can now be seen to be at a *pivot point*, or inflexion in history. These pivots, or great disruptions, are likely to occur in the lifetimes of today's young learners. Each will be explored in more depth in subsequent chapters, but here is a preview of the key evidence. This synthesis is offered to educators as a key backcloth for the task of telling a different story about education's purpose.

Pivot 1 Earth's Predicament, Therefore Ours

Preoccupation with the colossal impact of COVID-19 has in some quarters diverted attention away from an unrelenting trend that is of far greater consequence than transient pandemics. If greenhouse gas emissions continue to rise, we will pass the threshold (two degrees above pre-industrial levels) beyond which global warming becomes catastrophic and irreversible. This pivot-point will result in rising sea levels, polar melting, droughts, floods and increasingly extreme weather. No nation will be unaffected; in fact, some have already begun to feel the effects.[12] Since 2016, each year has become the hottest in recorded history. The long-term development is most telling: the decade that ended in 2019 was the hottest ever recorded.[13]

On current emissions trajectories, earth is headed for a rise of around five degrees. The relationship between human activity and the earth's ecological system has become radically unstable.[14]

The world's readiness for the inevitable effects of the climate crisis is 'gravely insufficient'.[15] This lack of preparedness will result in poverty, water shortages and levels of migration soaring, with an 'irrefutable' 'toll on human life'.[16] However, the consequences are not just in the future. Louisiana in the United States is already losing an area of land the size of a football pitch every 45 minutes to sea level rise.

[12] Chow, '5 Places Already Feeling the Effects of Climate Change'.
[13] Hodgson, 'Hottest Decade Ever Recorded "Driven by Man-Made Climate Change"'.
[14] Klein, *This Changes Everything*.
[15] Global Commission on Adaptation, 'Adapt Now: A Global Call for Resilience on Climate Resilience', 1.
[16] Global Commission on Adaptation, 3.

All of this can be seen as a pivot point, as we have entered what scientists have named the Anthropocene Age, a term that entered the Oxford English Dictionary in 2014. This is the epoch of geological time in which human activity is considered such a powerful influence on the environment, climate and ecology of the planet that it will leave a long-term signature on the strata record. The nature of that record will be oceans full of plastic (which is inert), mountains removed to access coal, and dispersed artificial radionuclides as a result of weapons testing.[17] The Anthropocene Age commenced around the onset of the nuclear age and coincided with the 'Great Acceleration' – massive increases in population, carbon emissions, species extinctions and the boom in the production (and discarding) of plastics, metals and concrete. Many of these changes will persist for millennia or longer, and are altering the trajectory of the earth system, some with permanent effect. They are being reflected in a distinctive body of geological strata now accumulating, with potential to be preserved into the far future.[18]

The mass loss of biodiversity witnessed in this age has been called the 'Sixth Extinction'.[19] The key difference with this phase is that while previous periods of accelerated species loss were driven by natural planetary transformations (or catastrophic asteroid strikes) the current one arises from human activity.[20] In this 'Anthropocene defaunation', 50 per cent of all species could be extinct by the end of the century.[21]

It is important not to be apocalyptic about these trends; most writers in the field are determinedly optimistic that things can be done to arrest them.[22] (Though in current political climates, that same optimism is being tested).[23] One significant factor will be the astounding pace of developments in convergent technologies, touched on in the next section, with their potential to ameliorate or reverse some of the trends in motion. Still, this phase of history can reasonably be termed as pivotal because the following question is being asked: are we closer

---

[17] Harari, *Sapiens*.
[18] Anthropocene Working Group (AWG), 'Results of Binding Vote by AWG'.
[19] Leakey and Lewin, *The Sixth Extinction*; Kolbert, *The Sixth Extinction*.
[20] Ceballos and Ehrlich, 'The Misunderstood Sixth Mass Extinction'.
[21] Dirzo et al., 'Defaunation in the Anthropocene'.
[22] Klein, *This Changes Everything*; Abraham, 'An Inconvenient Sequel – The Science, History, and Politics of Climate Change'.
[23] Klein, *On Fire*; Wilkinson, 'Al Gore's New Inconvenient Truth Sequel Is a Strange Artifact of a Post-Truth Year'.

Our planet at a tipping point?

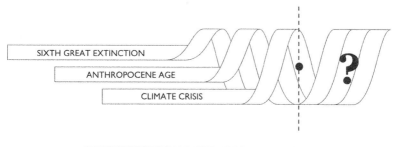

Figure 3.1 Our planet at tipping point?

to the point where the ecological balance of our planetary home can no longer support civilisation? The justifiable fear is that a sudden point of no return may be reached because of our slowness in apprehending the level of danger. Hope resides in the establishment of this issue into the centre of our collective consciousness, and through that the development of all means to restore the balance. This then needs to be one of the key purposes for education. How can we thrive if our planet does not? (See Figure 3.1.)

Pivot 2 The Apotheosis of Technology

For some writers, the speed and scale of advances in technology is the starting point for analyses of the future; this is possibly because while there are challenges inherent in the magnitude of the developments, there are also extraordinary opportunities. The power and penetration of technology to reshape the world have attained unprecedented levels. Technocratic solutions are sometimes assumed to be capable of resolving any and all problems.

In the blink of an eye (in historical terms), we have seen:

- the construction of a planet-wide electronic communications grid, connecting the thoughts of billions of people at ever faster speeds, and linking them to exponentially expanding volumes of information and data

- webs of sensors being embedded ubiquitously across the word, such that the Internet of Things and 'the age of surveillance' is here[24]
- the development of increasingly intelligent devices and robots.

The communications grid – the global network – is set to grow at an extraordinary pace. In the next decade, the unprecedented convergence of 5G and satellite networks will bring four billion new minds onto the web. The cause for optimism, as journalist Steven Kotler and entrepreneur Peter Diamandis argue, is that if network size, density and fluidity have turned cities into the best transformation engines humanity has managed to create, then the fact the entire globe is about to be linked into a single network means that the whole planet is the largest innovation lab in history.[25]

The implications of this development for the future of work and employment are discussed in Chapter 5. Technology underpins the industries of the future. Fields with great potential for expansion include:

- robotics
- genomics and life sciences
- 'code-ification of money'
- cybersecurity
- Big Data.[26]

One obvious consequence is that any individual without knowledge and skills in science, engineering, maths and technology (the so-called 'STEM subjects') will be at a considerable disadvantage in labour markets, limited to the less profitable health and care sectors, which are also likely to continue expanding.[27] But equally, we will argue that in this new reality, the humanist and creative arts perspectives – which are equally essential for all to create and share meaning – are at risk.

There is a consensus that in technological development, a point of disruptive change is arriving. To conceptualise it, writers describe it in relation to what has gone before: Karl Schwab has called it *The Fourth Industrial Revolution*; Andrew McAfee and Erik Brynjolfsson of MIT call it the *Second Machine Age*.[28] Previous industrial revolutions

---

[24] Zuboff, *The Age of Surveillance Capitalism*.
[25] Diamandis and Kotler, *The Future Is Faster Than You Think*.
[26] Ross, *The Industries of the Future*.   [27] Bakhshi et al., *The Future of Skills*.
[28] Schwab, *The Fourth Industrial Revolution*; Brynjolfsson and McAfee, *The Second Machine Age*.

changed our relationship to agriculture, made mass production possible and brought digital capabilities to billions of people. Schwab argues that this 'revolution' is fundamentally different. It is characterised by a range of new technologies that are fusing the physical, digital and biological worlds; and impacting all disciplines, economies and industries. It is even challenging ideas about what it means to be human. The evidence of profound change is already around us: ubiquitous, mobile supercomputing, sophisticated robots, self-driving cars, neuro-technological brain enhancements and genetic editing. However, new developments are happening at dramatic speed, many of them grounds for optimism for the potential of technology when harnessed to meaningful goals. Alphabet, the parent company of Google, has established a range of projects known as 'X-projects' or 'other bets'.[29] They include serious extension of assistive technology into medicine, building on existing trends such as connected implanted blood-sugar monitors.

All of this amounts to spectacular progress in improving the quality of life and mitigating suffering. Some of it touches on our own personal destiny – death. However, the most profound 'pivot point' regarding technology is the breakthrough in artificial intelligence (AI) which points to a new generation of computers/robots with the capacity to learn, and therefore self-program.

The capacity of robots to assume jobs and tasks currently performed by humans is now evident. The nature of this, and the implications, are reviewed in Chapter 6. However, this is not the key pivotal shift. The prospect of computers that can acquire the capacity to learn will mark a unique juncture in the relationship between our species and its technologies. The Frankenstein (or the Sorcerer's Apprentice) syndrome has been resurrected many times in fiction. This is the fear lying behind what is otherwise a supreme engineering and neuro-scientific endeavour. The idea that human beings are the source of meaning as well as power is about to be challenged.

Technology is now extending our cognitive capacity. And there are countless things that only a human can do at this present time, and that no computer as yet seems close to. But how can we ensure thriving, as this relationship unfolds and the balance shifts? (See Figure 3.2.)

---

[29] 'X – The Moonshot Factory' https://x.company.

Technology in control?

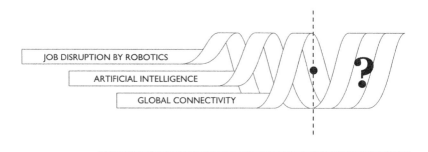

Figure 3.2 Technology in control?

Pivot 3 Home Sapiens – Now Subject to Our Own Design?

This disruptive change in the relationship between technology and humans brings us to the third great shift: the pivotal point that our own species has reached in its capacity to intervene in its own evolution.

Yuval Noah Harari, in *Sapiens: A Brief History of Humankind*, masterfully plots the progress of humans through key turning points over time: he sees these shifts occurring over four revolutions:

- *Cognitive*: we developed language, conceptualization, co-operation.
- *Agricultural*: we domesticated nature, and made permanent settlements.
- *Scientific*: we 'admitted ignorance' and developed the scientific method.
- *Industrial*: we created new ways to convert energy and produce things.[30]

The space between each of the previous revolutions has grown shorter. Now, we are being carried forward at unimaginable speed towards another new reality. The most profound revolution, or pivot

---

[30] Harari, *Sapiens*.

point, is related to that final set of adaptations in our health and our life expectancy.

The convergence of the life sciences with the digital explosion has created the capacity to reshape the very fabric of life: it is changing not just what we can do, but who we are. The cost of gene mapping has plummeted. Individual gene sequencing will shortly be able to identify the exact nature of a particular cancer and its pathways. Genetic engineering of pigs is taking place to harvest lungs for transplant (and soon hearts and kidneys). Genomic screening and trait selection are advancing. In 2016, British scientists were given permission to genetically modify human embryos.[31] Surplus embryos from IVF procedures are being used in trials (and must then be discarded and not implanted) in order to better understand the process of miscarriage and improve IVF procedures. We are within mere decades of genetic and other forms of bio-engineering enabling far-reaching changes to our physiology, immune systems, cognitive and indeed emotional capacities. (Genomics has entered the mental health field: it is known that 100 genes play a role in schizophrenia). The potential is enormous and the consequence very hard to grasp.

This capacity to alter the direction of our own evolution is further entwined with the technological revolution discussed in the previous section.

We have long been physically enhanced by technology (the majority of adults now have something – glasses, a new hip, pacemaker, dental implants or lens replacements). A range of artefacts (from wheelchairs to bicycle gears) can now be controlled through thoughts transmitted by headsets. The convergence, through implants or by other means, of human bodies with artificial intelligence is currently being researched – sometimes referred to as 'transhumanism' or 'superintelligence'.[32] Nick Bostrom, the leading thinker in this field, argues persuasively that the future impact of artificial intelligence is perhaps the most important issue the human race has ever faced: the *potential for designing our own evolution*. It is entirely possible that human beings are not an evolutionary end point, but that we are destined to evolve further, playing a major role in the design and direction of the process. (See Figure 3.3.)

---

[31] Siddique, 'British Researchers Get Green Light to Genetically Modify Human Embryos'.
[32] Bostrom, *Superintelligence*.

New humans?

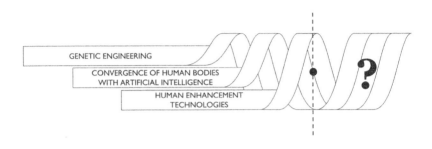

Figure 3.3 New humans?

Four Levels of Thriving

If the evidence and arguments presented above are accepted, then a number of things follow:

- Never in human history has such a set of profound shifts or pivots been faced. They are literally without precedent.
- Not all trends are inevitable. Opportunities sit side by side with great threats. The actions we (and particularly the young) take in the coming decades will be critical. It is as fallacious to resign to an apocalyptic nightmare as it is to pretend that the future will be like the past.

In light of this, it is morally indefensible to continue with a process of mass schooling that is indifferent to and ignorant of, the scope of these disruptions, and which promotes a value system (competition, growth, efficiency, homogeneity) that steers us towards the darker of the potential paths ahead. Acknowledgement of the possibilities emerging is the first step to equipping young people with the ability to shape the future.

We need a new animating purpose for learning, which relates to our new reality. We need to learn how to *thrive in the transforming world* in the fullest most authentic sense. If that is our purpose (and what is the alternative?), then we can discern learning goals at *four levels* (see Figure 3.4):

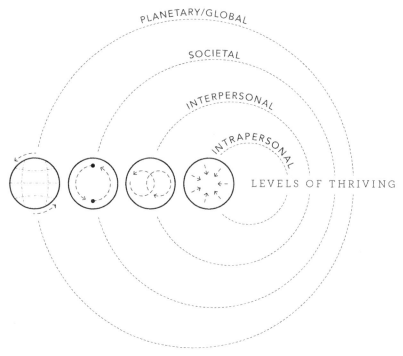

Figure 3.4 Four levels of thriving

- *Planetary/global*: how can we contribute to the thriving of our home planet and within the global community of which we are now all a part? Thriving will mean to live sustainably and with global competence.
- *Society*: how can we learn to build thriving communities and nations? It will mean navigating new landscapes of work and reinventing democracy.
- *Interpersonal*: how do we learn to build thriving relationships? In a technologised environment, how can we learn empathy and love?
- *Intrapersonal*: how can we learn to grow the thriving self? This will mean finding personal meaning and inner growth; calm conscious-ness and awareness.

The next chapters take each of these connected aspects of thriving in turn, and explore the work of schools that are reinventing themselves to address these – the real challenges we face.

4 | *What Does It Mean to 'Thrive' – Globally?*

If one theme emerges from recent scholarship about our contemporary condition, it is the idea of the single interconnected entity of earth. The human correlate is the *Global Mind*.[1] Others see the world as now 'united in a single ecological and historical sphere'.[2] We now share the same information field. The penetration of globalisation into all fields (including the cultural and educational), combined with the connectivity of research, thinking and knowledge creation, drives home the extent to which we have become One World. Spatially we are shrinking too, as travel has become faster and easier. Furthermore, the presence of extreme global inequality and the impacts of poverty and conflict now cannot be contained to discrete locations, as migration drives them not just into the consciousness, but also into the communities of many who would have previously remained untouched. Addressing these issues is no longer (only) a moral imperative, but also a practical one.

Therefore, the ultimate objective of *thriving* requires us to 'think big' about education, moving beyond local and national boundaries, to the condition of our planet and our species as a whole. As discussed in Chapter 3, all the evidence suggests that the predicament is historically unique.

We therefore propose that the explicit challenge for education in this global context should be that young people learn:

- To *live sustainably within the earth's resources, protecting its ecosystem and biodiversity, and*
- To *acquire global competence*

These goals are directly related to the pivot points identified in Chapter 3. The nature of the changes underway explain why these goals should be a part of education's task.

[1] Gore, *The Future*.   [2] Harari, *Homo Deus*.

4.1 The World in Our Hands

Ultimately, we cannot thrive if our planet does not. Three phenomena imminently threaten the capacity of the earth to remain a congenial home for our species. These are: climate crisis, resource depletion and destruction of biodiversity. These three threats are distinct but, of course, inter-related. They must be in sharp focus when we set our purposes for learning both because of the weight of evidence concerning the imminence of irreversible disaster, but also the huge potential for young people to take different approaches to these challenges than previous generations. Only by placing these three crises at the heart of education can we translate fear and urgency into action.

Thriving – On an Unliveable Planet?

In one sense the issue of global warming has moved into the mainstream of public consciousness. But climate-heating deniers (whether of the phenomenon itself or of the causal contribution of human activity) are still to be found; some of them have achieved election to high office. This, despite the science becoming ever more irrefutable, and the impact more directly experienced. Climate warming demands to be a central focus and theme for the purpose of education.

The effects are already apparent. We saw in Chapter 2 that temperatures records are being broken on a regular basis. Extreme weather events are increasingly common. Of 260 such events studied since the early 2000s, 68 per cent can be attributed to human-made climate change.[3] From Australia to California, the now-familiar pattern of increased bush-fires and droughts is spreading. The relationship with human activity is conclusive.[4] At the other end of the spectrum, the types of catastrophic floods, which used to occur every 100 years or so, are now happening every 10–15 years.

It may be that, experientially, it will be this phenomenon that drives home the reality of the climate emergency in societies formerly used to temperate conditions; regular flood threats and extreme storms, with all their human and economic costs are possibly starting to act as a wake-up call. For some communities, this will be too late: island states in the Pacific are already starting to disappear as rising temperatures

[3] Carbon Brief, 'Mapped'.   [4] The Weather Club, 'Wildfires across the Globe'.

melt polar ice-caps and cause the sea itself to expand.[5] New assessments of the topography of coastlines around the world now estimate that more than 300 million people are at risk from rising sea levels.[6] This is more than three times above the previous estimate of 80 million. Land that is currently their home will flood at least once a year by 2050 unless carbon emissions are cut significantly and coastal defences strengthened.

If this is the present reality, what does trend analysis and computer modelling tell us about the years to come – in the lifetimes of today's learners? In 2012–2014, the World Bank commissioned a series of three reports studying projected warming and associated risks. Carried out by the Potsdam Institute for Climate Impact Research and Climate Analytics, the first report warned that without concerted action, temperatures are on pace to rise to 4°C above pre-industrial times by the end of this century. They concluded:

A 4°C world is likely to be one in which communities, cities and countries would experience severe disruptions, damage, and dislocation, with many of these risks spread unequally. It is likely that the poor will suffer most and the global community could become more fractured, and unequal than today. The projected 4°C warming simply must not be allowed to occur.[7]

Putting it another way, Kevin Anderson, the Director of the Tyndall Centre for Climate Change Research said in a speech to DfID in 2011:

4°C of warming is incompatible with any reasonable characterization of an organized, equitable and civilized global community.[8]

As the reports trace, 4°C of warming could raise global sea levels by 1 or even 2 metres by 2100, drowning islands such as the Maldives and inundating coastal areas such as those in Ecuador, the Netherlands, California, parts of the North-East United States and large swathes of South-East Asia. A number of world cities would also face serious consequences. Ironically, disappearing sea-ice allows more and more ships to access once unreachable regions in high latitudes. As a result,

---

[5] Nosowitz, 'How Alarming Is It That Islands Are Just Disappearing?'; Klein, 'Eight Low-Lying Pacific Islands Swallowed Whole by Rising Seas'; Braunschweiger and Rytz, 'Interview'.

[6] Kulp and Strauss, 'New Elevation Data Triple Estimates of Global Vulnerability to Sea-Level Rise and Coastal Flooding'.

[7] World Bank, 'Turn Down the Heat', xviii.

[8] Anderson, 'Climate Change Going beyond Dangerous'.

plans are underway to drill for oil and gas in the Arctic, thus enabling further release of carbon emissions.

Estimates in 2014 were that around 1.5°C warming is already locked in.[9] As we consider rising temperatures, one last point to note is the ever-present possibility of a critical point of emergence (or 'non-linear tipping points') – a point when interaction between various dimensions of the complex system are such that remediation is not actually capable of human control.[10] Pushing global temperatures past certain thresholds could trigger abrupt and potentially irreversible changes, with massively disruptive impacts. In 2019 an unprecedented joint statement by 11,000 scientists from across 153 countries concluded that, taken together, most of their 'vital signs indicators' of such tipping points are going in the wrong direction and add up to a climate emergency.[11]

Political consciousness of this clear and present danger has been growing, but the rise of populist deniers is a new challenge. We have already remarked upon the dismal level of action to achieve the pledges that were made at the Paris Agreement (CoP2015). However, 'green' parties appear to be making political progress and many mainstream parties are looking to craft a 'Green New Deal' as part of their agendas. Citizens' protest and lobbying groups such as Extinction Rebellion in the United Kingdom have seized media attention, and there are signs that the issue is starting to figure in the public consciousness. Unsurprisingly, this is especially the case among the young. In the United Kingdom, the number of British adults who regarded climate as a priority in 2019 was small: only 27 per cent saw it as one of the top three issues. But this is the highest it has been on record, and that figure doubles among 18- to 24-year-olds.[12] Most significantly for the purposes of reflecting on education, the resonance of this issue with school-age students is dramatic. The Greta Thunberg phenomenon has become global, and school strikes on the climate crisis galvanised an estimated 6 million school students across the world. So widespread and powerful were these events that, based on 'intensity of use', the Collins Dictionary names 'climate strike' as its 'word of the year'.[13]

[9] World Bank, 'Series'.   [10] World Bank, 'Turn down the Heat', xvii.
[11] Ripple et al., 'World Scientists' Warning of a Climate Emergency'.
[12] Damian Carrington Environment, 'Public Concern over Environment Reaches Record High in UK'.
[13] Collins, 'The Collins Word of the Year 2019 Is …'

What other issue creates such a level of engagement, anger, energy, concern, curiosity and focus among school students? There is a powerful message here for educators when we think about what young people need and want for their futures; but it also has its dark side, which we discuss below.

We can no longer conceive of the quality of human life without seeing ourselves as *a part* of nature. By any measure, the impact of the climate crisis is and will remain the major determinant of whether both we and the environment together can thrive. If we do not prepare to adapt to it, it will subsume and overwhelm anything else we might prepare for.

The many aspects to the climate crisis cannot of course be done full justice here. The objective has been to shift the focus – to overcome the selective attention that has blinkered us – and reframe any discussion about what education's purpose is, towards the most pressing, existentially threatening issue of our time. New, more authentic political commitments may be created and may hold; we must hope, most earnestly, that they will. But we cannot entirely outsource the issue to distant political negotiators, technologists or environmentalists. The young cannot be consigned to be observers of the process that defines their future. There has to be a change in the way in which we help them to see themselves in relation to the planet – the stories we tell about our place on earth. It requires a fundamental shift in mindset, and in how we live. Nor is this to relegate the problem (and the opportunity) to a lifestyle issue. It is a fundamental *education* issue: what learners know, can do and value. It impacts what people will choose to prioritise in their democracies and the leaders they elect, the companies they are prepared to buy from or work with, the skills they seek to acquire, as well as the personal choices they make.

Thriving – As We Run Out?

It is estimated that humanities' eco-footprint (a measure of consumption) is one and a half times the earth's ability to sustainably provide the resources to meet that level of consumption. That shortfall is being met through the depletion (or degradation) of what has been called 'natural capital' – resources such as fresh water, soil, forest land, wetlands. Natural resources, both renewable and non-renewable (such as minerals) are being hit by a double-whammy: increasing human population plus increasing per capita consumption. But it is not just our consumption that has created the problem. As New Zealand sustainability writer Michael Lockhart summarises:

More people on the planet leads to more:

- Sewerage and stock effluent
- Fertilisers, herbicides and pesticides
- Fossil fuels extracted and burned
- Oil leaked and spilled
- Land deforested and developed
- Soil eroded and degraded
- Minerals mined
- Waste and toxic by-products of manufacturing[14]

All of these lead to depletion or degradation of natural resources. Of course, some of these processes are intimately bound up with the extractive economies that have driven climate change: it is the same mind-set and attitude towards the earth that underpin both. As with climate change, the current, existing impact is manifest. Already, water scarcity affects one in three people on every continent of the globe. But it is the trajectories into the future that are concerning.

Global demand for water is projected be 55 per cent higher in 2050 than it was in 2000, at a time when the groundwater table in many regions of the world is falling and large areas are suffering from shortages due to drought, large-scale irrigation, pollution and dams.[15] The differential impact of resource depletion is no protection for currently temperate, high-income nations: resource depletion drives migration, and there is an argument that water may be the source of future conflict just as oil once was.

Energy efficiencies, renewable energy and a massive increase in more efficient recycling will be needed. Some are calling for a 'circular economy', a comprehensive rethink of our current model of production and consumption, which is regenerative and restorative; where one company's waste is another's raw material.[16]

---

[14] www.econation.co.nz/resource-depletion/
[15] Global Water Forum, 'Water Outlook to 2050'; Smedley, 'Is the World Running out of Fresh Water?'
[16] Circular Economy, 'Circular Economy – RSA'; 'What Is a Circular Economy?'

Alongside this rethinking are the possibilities being created by the development of new materials. The new technologies of molecular manipulation have led to revolutionary advances in the materials sciences and hybrid materials possessing a combination of physical attributes, far exceeding those of any materials developed through older techs of metallurgy and ceramics.[17] Equally, nanotechnology offers great promise in the development of materials that can address global challenges. In the quest for enough water, for example, the hope lies in single-cell mebranes that could make affordable desalination at scale – currently well beyond reach.[18]

Thriving – When It's Just Us?

It is hard to argue that our thriving as a species is not indissolubly bound up with the thriving of our planet. (Unless you posit exodus to another handy candidate in the solar system. No serious futures thinkers anticipate this anytime soon). So far, so anthropocentric. However, the third aspect of the earth's current dramatic shift, introduced in Chapter 3 is the destruction of biodiversity. Does this matter to us or impact our thriving? There are four separate questions here:

- What has already happened?
- What is likely to happen?
- Does it matter to our species?
- Can the younger generation address this matter?

What has been called 'the Sixth Great Extinction' is already well under way, precipitated by humans.[19] To put the rate of extinction into some perspective: some 875 documented extinctions occurred between 1500 and 2009, with degradation of highly biodiverse habitats such as coral reefs and rainforest. In 1995, when the sixth extinction was first widely discussed, the rate of extinction was estimated as being up to 140,000 species *per year*.[20] In the most comprehensive report yet produced, the UN Report on Biodiversity and Ecosystems, *one in eight*

---

[17] Gore, *The Future*.
[18] Yang et al., 'Large-Area Graphene-Nanomesh/Carbon-Nanotube Hybrid Membranes for Ionic and Molecular Nanofiltration'; Ramirez, 'Inching Towards Abundant Water'.
[19] Kolbert, *The Sixth Extinction*; Leakey and Lewin, *The Sixth Extinction*.
[20] Pimm et al., 'The Future of Biodiversity'.

species were found to be at threat of extinction.[21] As the summary message communicated:

Ecosystems, species, wild populations, local varieties and breeds of domesticated plants and animals are shrinking, deteriorating or vanishing. The essential, interconnected web of life on Earth is getting smaller and increasingly frayed. This loss is a direct result of human activity and constitutes a direct threat to human well-being in all regions of the world.[22]

As for future trends, surprise, it is anticipated that the biodiversity destruction rate will increase as we, the 'global superpredator', continue to over-fish, destroy habitats, and acidify the ocean. In a nutshell, the projections show a range of extinction of between 20 per cent and 50 per cent of all living species on earth within this century.[23]

So what? Can humans thrive, albeit a bit lonelier (despite there being 7 billion of us)? Leave aside the moral, value-laden question here, and focus entirely on the practical. Based only on those grounds, there are consequences for our well-being. Since the sixth extinction began to draw global attention, scientists have spent over two decades studying its potential consequences for humans. Contemporary scholarship concludes that the projected extinctions could reduce the resilience of the human species, through reduced efficiency and 'carrying capacity' of the earth's 'ecosystem services' and, potentially, reduced protection from infectious disease.[24]

Of course, it is most fervently hoped that those are not the only grounds on which this matters. The morality of what we have done – and what we might still do if we do not change strategies – is surely indefensible. It is not only homo sapiens that has a right to life and to thrive; an entirely selfish anthropocentric world is not the one we want, or that our children deserve.

As Harari puts it:

The future may see sapiens gaining control of a cornucopia of new materials and energy source, whilst simultaneously destroying what remains of the natural habitat and driving most other species to extinction.[25]

What would we be then?

---

[21] IPBES, 'Global Assessment Report on Biodiversity and Ecosystem Services'.
[22] Martin, 'UN Report'.   [23] Gore, *The Future*, 339–341.
[24] Cardinale et al., 'Biodiversity Loss and Its Impact on Humanity'; Yule, Fournier and Hindmarsh, 'Biodiversity, Extinction, and Humanity's Future'.
[25] Harari, *Sapiens*, 392.

4.2 Implications for Education's Purpose

Understood in their totality, these features of our predicament are not susceptible to partial fixes. Leave it to the politicians. Hope for a techno-fix. Recycle more. Education can just carry on teaching subjects with an additional dash of environmental issues ('teaching about climate change') to geography and biology classes. As Klein points out, all we must do to bring about the most dysfunctional (possibly apocalyptic) of outcomes is just . . . to carry on what we are doing.[26] Nothing else required.

A central argument of this book is that we need a holistic response to addressing environmental issues. That includes a new frame of reference and narrative for education, which legitimates educators prioritising the creation of a different relationship between humans and the environment. This will lead to curating the conditions whereby learners re-imagine the relationship between people, place and other species. If so, then a *fundamental learning goal* will become learning how to live within the earth's renewable resources, protecting its ecosystems and biodiversity.

To deny young people the opportunity to learn this will be seen, in future times, as another form of abuse: as basic as learning how not to soil your space. However, it can and should become a positive endeavour. Instead of just protecting the planet from human impact, the educational question can be: Why not redesign our activities to improve the environment? We can *learn* how to undertake interventions for a beneficial, sustainable footprint. Young people need the chance to share in the design and development of a new economy that is sustainable, built on innovative technologies and deeply embedded in an emerging ecological literacy.[27] A good start has been made in many higher education institutions.[28] But the truth is that without an intentional re-orientation, the default goal of most schools for their kids is to position them for the acquisition of individual material wealth and increased consumption. This may well not be educators'

---

[26] Klein, *This Changes Everything*.
[27] Clarke, 'The Grave Disconnect: Aligning School Reform with Ecological Change'.
[28] For an example, see Facer, 'Learning to Live with a Lively Planet: The Renewal of the University's Mission in the Era of Climate Change'.

deliberate intention: but it is an outcome of tacitly held old assumptions about the job we want education to do.

Moreover, as observed above, increasingly this issue is at the front and centre of many young people's minds: they are demanding that it be brought properly into focus in their daily learning. But educators will have a delicate path to tread. There is already some evidence of 'climate anxiety' in children: a sense of fear and imminent loss.[29] Researchers suggest that this is a rational fear based on events and stories from around the world, underpinned by the weight of evidence of the change. Moreover, this is among children who have not yet directly experienced the effects. Among those who have, unprecedented levels of stress and anxiety are produced, for example, in Greenland where people are struggling to reconcile the traumatic impact of global heating with their traditional way of life.[30] It is being referred to as 'ecological grief'. The challenge for educators, therefore, is to centre these issues in a way that empowers and not disables; that gives hope rather than a sense of impotence and doom.

It is a ghastly commentary on the state we are in that the people who have perhaps the best understanding into the necessary relationship between humans and the planet are indigenous communities – who are themselves, in so many contexts, at risk of cultural extinction. Diverse indigenous communities have much to contribute through their evolved insight and experience over millennia. In western knowledge systems, we are just starting to understand the notion of 'trusteeship', by which humans' role is conceived as trustees of living creatures and future generations. As we shall explore further in Chapter 5, the role of indigenous leaders in a number of cultures as distinctive and assertive educators is a beacon of hope. The challenge is to build on the insights of indigenous knowledge a perspective that fully addresses the conditions of modernity, in a 'post-natural' world.

As we show in Chapter 5, educators have an increasing variety of models and approaches upon which to reframe their goals and practices. Part of this might entail the recognition of something like another form of intelligence, to develop in young people and guide decision making. Howard Gardner, in revising his initial propositions around

---

[29] University of Bath, 'Rise of "Eco-Anxiety" Affecting More and More Children Says Bath Climate Psychologist'.
[30] McDougall, 'Ecological Grief'.

the theory of multiple intelligences, recognised that another distinct form of thinking had been omitted, and in 1995 added the notion of *naturalistic intelligence*.[31] This he saw as a 'sensitive, ethical and holistic understanding' of the world and its complexities – including the role of humanity within the greater ecosphere. Some educators now define this as becoming 'naturally smart':

Intelligence is not ours alone, but a property of the earth.
We are in it, of it, immersed in its depths.
Each terrain has its own intelligence, with its own sky and its own blue.
How do we become naturally smart
and share what we learn to enhance well-being ?[32]

This perspective drives home that what we need is not just increased scientific knowledge and understanding; rather we also require an imaginative multi-dimensional sensibility.

4.3 Humanism Revisited

Over the last 30 years, the principal alternative rationale to the economistic narrative for education has been humanist. That philosophical approach is problematic in the light of everything that has been said about homo sapiens' evolution – and aspects of enhancement. What, after all will 'human nature' or 'human values' become? No forms of neo- or post-humanism have yet been fully or satisfactorily articulated. However, given that humanism elevated anthropocentric values and goals above all else, that view is now in need of reconsideration. It is a big stretch for humans to reconceive of our place within the totality of the universe with humility: to accept the idea that other species and living beings are not our playthings. But *it's not all about us*.

Leaders in all domains need now to understand and develop this narrative. Interestingly, Pope Francis began that process with his 2015 Encyclical *On Care for our Common Home*.[33] This is a work of several hundred sections, providing a religiously framed but scientifically informed account of the risks to the natural world. Entreating a different relationship with nature, he writes that,

---

[31] Morris, 'The Eighth One: Naturalistic Intelligence'.
[32] Paul Clarke, unpublished writing. See Clarke, 'Naturally Smart'.
[33] Pope Francis, 'Encyclical Letter Laudato Si' of the Holy Father Francis on Care for Our Common Home', 24 May 2015.

Nature cannot be regarded as something separate from ourselves or as a mere setting in which we live. We are part of nature, included in it and thus in constant interaction with it.

If more leaders can develop these kinds of informed and inspiring accounts for their communities, we would see a powerful dynamic force for change. Such a new narrative would give a clear base for the redesign of learning. As our examples in Chapter 5 demonstrate, some schools are already starting to rethink their practice around forging children's relationships with the natural world, and in some cases working more concertedly on ways to protect, sustain and regrow it. Solutions are within reach, and some people are already energetically engaged in the work:

The work ahead is to design and develop sustainable systemic responses where teachers and children are able to work on site-specific models of intervention and actions, and as they undertake this work they need to be assisted in the process of sharing their learning within a networked platform ... thus accelerating the opportunity for ... transferable regenerative learning.[34]

4.4 Enriching Our Ideas of Global Competence

We said in Chapter 3 that thriving at the planetary level would mean learning to live sustainably and with *global competence*. 'Global competence' could be crudely conceived as whatever it takes to win the great global economic competition. Part of the problem of incorporating more sophisticated ideas of global competence into a new narrative around education springs from the deeply ingrained sense of the supremacy of the nation-state. Some people still derive their sense of personal identity from that idea. But to be globally competent need not entail surrender of a secure cultural identity – albeit that some fluidity in that domain may perhaps be no bad thing.

The Asia Society[35] sees the movement for global competence as:

An urgent call for schools to produce students that actually know something about the world – its cultures, languages and how its economic, environmental and social systems work.

[34] Clarke, 'The Grave Disconnect: Aligning School Reform with Ecological Change'.
[35] http://asiasociety.org/education/global-competence

This knowledge base is foundational. With it would come not just greater tolerance, but respect. And as the examples in Chapter 5 show, the more profound approaches teach students not just to know, or to respect, but also to take action. Thriving in this century rests on the degree to which interdependence and cooperation are recognised and achieved.

Two issues illustrate the need:

- the future of economic globalisation
- migration.

Intensification of Globalisation?

Globalisation in the last century had winners and losers. We have already suggested how the planet was a clear loser. However, among people, big capital, entrepreneurs and those with mobile, high skill-levels benefitted from the opening up of world markets. Millions in low-income countries, such as China and India, moved out of poverty into a new middle class. Meanwhile, just as many remained firmly in poverty, and people living in high-wage societies, such as Europe and the United States, were exposed to competition, not just from lower-cost labour, but also from countries hungry to develop new skills and adopt new technologies.[36] In looking at the future, most commentators see the intensification of global competition as grounds for doubling down on education as the best hope to 'succeed'. So some forms of 'global competence' are seen as part of that *competitive* solution. This is not the perspective we adopt here.

Distance-shrinking technologies and transport cannot be un-invented. So while the movement of information, money and people across borders continues to increase, there are other factors that might reduce this flow and cross-border trade in goods has been slowing.[37] New forms of nationalism (especially in the United States and Europe), geopolitical rivalry allied with economic protectionism could

---

[36] The pattern of winners and losers is represented in Christoph Lakner and Branko Milanovic's 'Elephant Curve', showing growing incomes for most of the middle of the global income distribution, very low gains for those in the upper percentiles (the middle classes of the high-income countries) and vast increases in income for the top percentile: the global 1 per cent.

[37] Lund et al., 'Globalization in Transition'.

conceivably slacken it further, if not altogether terminate it. The COVID-19 pandemic further strengthened critics of globalisation, who advocated for the localisation of trade. Advocates of the continued integration of markets doubt that a reversal of globalisation will take place.[38] In either eventuality, the challenge for education is to give young learners experience of the complexities and diversity of a globalised world: in one scenario – globalisation redux – better to take an active place in globalised, multi-ethnic and multi-cultural economies. In the other scenario – globalisation in retreat – better to counteract resurgences of xenophobia and racism. Intercultural fluency will be more imperative than it has ever been.

Global Migration

Yearly levels of migration now exceed anything previously witnessed, even in the aftermath of World War II. Global displacement reached a new high by the end of 2017 with 68.5 million individuals forcibly displaced worldwide due to persecution, conflict, generalised violence and human rights violations.[39] Of these, 25.4 million are registered refugees. Migration is seen by some as a defining feature of the age, alongside the climate crisis and population growth. Migration creates huge changes in ways of living through movement across countries, but also within them: continued urbanisation means that it is estimated that by 2050, 68 per cent of the world's population will live in cities, up from 55 per cent today.[40]

In this interconnected world, international migration has become a reality that touches nearly all corners of the globe, often making distinctions between countries of origin, transit and destination obsolete. Modern transportation has made it easier and cheaper for people to move – and it is this that suggests that, rather than being a fleeting phenomenon, it is likely that this global population churn will continue – unless a marked reduction in conflict and economic inequality is achieved. The climate crisis also impacts on migration.[41] While

---

[38] LeGrain, 'The Future of Globalisation Is in Doubt'.
[39] IOM, 'Global Migration Trends'.
[40] UN DESA, '2018 Revision of World Urbanization Prospects'.
[41] Podesta, 'The Climate Crisis, Migration, and Refugees'; 'The Climate & Migration Coalition'.

people have always had to move due to weather, the numbers are predicted to rise; already tens of millions each year are having to leave their homes due to natural disasters.[42]

While migration is almost always represented as a problem, there are many positive aspects and opportunities offered by migration, both internal and international. In countries of destination, refugees and migrants often fill critical labour shortages, become entrepreneurs and overall add to the economy in terms of taxes and social security contributions.[43] Still, migrants remain vulnerable to exploitation, are often the first to lose their jobs in the event of an economic downturn, often working for less pay, for longer hours and in worse conditions than the local population. In schools, provision for supporting young recent migrants varies widely. These issues are acute as the number of unaccompanied child migrants has risen. In 2015/2016, related to the overall rise in asylum seekers, UNICEF estimated that there were five times as many children migrating alone than in 2010/2011.[44]

International migration is now a multi-dimensional reality of major relevance for the development of countries of origin, transit and destination. For schools, questions of support and integration are societal ones that can become acute at any moment with the arrival of new students. These situations for societies and for schools require coherent and comprehensive responses. An understanding of the connections between the world's countries, cultures and systems must be the basis for this response. This means making *global competence* an explicit goal of education systems.

4.5 Building on International Foundations

Here we may be pushing at an open door. The link with 'successfully competing in a globalised economy' has perhaps been the lever to insert global competence into the discipline-dominated curriculum.

---

[42] UN News, 'Migration and the Climate Crisis'.
[43] Newland and Capps, 'Why Hide the Facts about Refugee Costs and Benefits?'; Banulescu-Bogdan, 'When Facts Don't Matter: How to Communicate More Effectively about Immigration's Costs and Benefits'.
[44] UNICEF, *A Child Is a Child*.

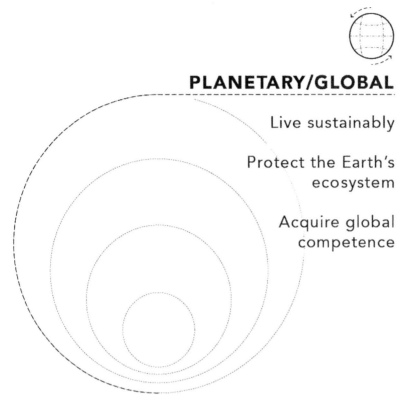

PLANETARY/GLOBAL

Live sustainably

Protect the Earth's ecosystem

Acquire global competence

Figure 4.1 The planetary/global level

The OECD's Programme for International Student Assessment (PISA) has not only produced a thoughtful and comprehensive Framework for teaching global competence but it also, for the first time in 2018, included global competence in its suite of international benchmarking assessments.[45] That may be enough to make education policy makers pay attention. In the United States and Australia enough agencies are now endorsing the idea, and providing resources and frameworks to

---

[45] OECD, 'Preparing Our Youth for an Inclusive and Sustainable World: The OECD PISA Global Competence Framework'; www.oecd.org/pisa/pisa-2018-global-competence.htm

promote it, to suggest that – if other systemic conditions are attended to – there may be real progress in making global competence available to more learners.[46] Hopefully, it will be done in a spirit that is directed towards thriving in the fullest sense. Chapter 5 shows what this spirit looks like.

---

[46] Asia Society and OECD, *Teaching for Global Competence in a Rapidly Changing World*; Boix Mansilla and Jackson, 'Educating for Global Competence: Preparing Our Youth to Engage the World'.

5 | Pathfinders for a Thriving Planet

Mainstream school systems have been incredibly slow to respond to the crisis we are looking at, or join in the effort to address it. Maybe we are starting now to see how that can happen.

Paul Clarke[1]

Paul Clarke is a patient man. For 20 years, he has been teaching students in Australia and in the United Kingdom about permaculture: the practice of developing sustainable agricultural systems. Yet only recently has he found more schools cropping up interested in ways to introduce their students to this knowledge. In response, he co-founded the Pop-up Foundation, a UK-based organisation that works with schools and communities to create 'pop-up' sustainability projects. It is now developing into a network of 'Naturally Smart' schools.

One of these is Nazareth Catholic Community School[2] in Adelaide, where the primary school students work to create a kitchen garden. Students in every year of the school are involved in maintenance of the garden; it is a central part of the science curriculum. Each year, students learn about another type of life or entire cycle that is sustained by the garden.

These projects aim to develop students' 'ecological reasoning': their ability to reflect on and make decisions about a situation in terms of interdependence and sustainability. The projects also aim to develop in students 'an ethic of care': care for the sustainability of the environment as part of caring for one's own and others' futures. At Nazareth Catholic Community School, this latter aspect aligns well with their values.

Nearby, Holy Family Catholic School[3] has taken this focus even further. 'Ecology' is one of the three parts of the school's mission and

---

[1] Interview with Paul Clarke, May 2016   [2] www.nazareth.org.au/
[3] www.holyfamily.catholic.edu.au/

feeds through into a wide variety of actions. Each class in the school is responsible for a part of the school garden, and the school now grows its own fruit. They have secured a grant to install solar panels and create a wetland next to the school.

Recalling Pope Francis's words from Chapter 4, it is perhaps not surprising that both of these are Catholic schools. There is no tension for these schools in placing ecology and sustainability at the heart of what they do. Catholic Schools South Australia, the body responsible for the governance of all Catholic schools in the state, put out back in 2010 'an ecological vision for schools in South Australia' entitled, 'On Holy Ground'. It describes how 'caring for fragile ecosystems' as 'a core element of Christian responsibility'.

For those of us who are not Catholic, and likely not religious at all, there still seems something to learn from this approach of care. One of the big shifts in this approach to environmental education is away from the notion of standardised curriculum – 'all students must learn about climate change' – and towards teaching knowledge and practices that are specific to and directly relevant for the regeneration of a particular local environment. The students at Nazareth and Holy Family are motivated not by an abstract desire to care for the natural world, but by the possibility of creating a more sustainable and hospitable environment for themselves and the people they care about. They learn that the position of beds, the choices of what to plant when, are all related to the specifics of their location, and that caring for that location has tangible consequences. Students learn that the better they sustain the garden through its yearly cycles, and the more they reduce waste, the better they can provide food not just for their own kitchens but also their community. This is celebrated at Market days where the children sell excess food from the gardens, alongside parents who can bring their own excess produce.

As discussed in Chapter 4, it is possible for humans to learn how to improve rather than degrade their natural environment. Schools are ideally placed to teach young people how to do this for their own communities. In the process, we must hope that this generation develop a different attitude to humans' relationship with their planet. It is our species' last and best hope.

Clarke believes that when young people are fully engaged in working with their natural environment, it 'throws up something profound about intelligence: it's not just us who are intelligent, nature is. We are part of a much bigger form of intelligence'.[4] One of the big challenges, however, is helping schools and individuals open up to this kind of realisation. 'The trouble is, it's hard to talk about this stuff – in spite of the emerging scientific evidence – without sounding as though you are coming over all hippy.' When cynics have the advantage of representing the easy road, it is all too easy for us to close our mind to the 'intelligence' of the natural environment. So maybe we need to find more human channels for it to reach us.

5.1 Listening to Different Voices

As Clarke's comment reflects, in western, post-Enlightenment societies, it has become difficult to talk about any way of relating to nature other than as an object of scientific study. But in our work in different countries, we have been fortunate to have conversations with people who approach the question of environmental sustainability in a very different way from our home culture – and from the multilateral agencies promoting sustainable development. We have noted that many of these people come from societies where indigenous peoples – groups that were the primary population before western colonisation – have an increasingly strong presence in public dialogues.

Writing about 'indigenous peoples' is inherently reductive given the considerable diversity that exists between cultures of First Nations people even within one land mass, let alone between countries such as New Zealand, Canada and South Africa. Nevertheless, we want to suggest that there are some important commonalities in ways of knowing and perceiving the world, in what some researchers now describe as 'indigenous knowledge systems'.

Arihia Stirling is the Principal of Te Kura Maori o Nga Tapuwae, a Maori-medium School in Auckland, New Zealand. She is an inspiring leader of the resurgence of Maori identity through education as a means of restoring Maori culture, identity and dignity. For her, the connection with place is central:

It is vital for us as Maori people – in order to restore our culture and our language – that we strengthen our connectedness with our environment. In the words of the people of Whanganui: Ko au te awa, ko te awa ko au – translating – I am the river and the river is me. We aren't separate, we are

---

[4] Interview with Paul Clarke, May 2016

forever entwined, with the environment. And we intertwine this in our pedagogy. Tribal schools fundamentally locate both our pedagogy and our curriculum with genealogical links to the tribal lands.[5]

As we come to learn more about the limitations of western science when it comes to understanding and predicting our complex natural ecosystems, how might non-indigenous communities learn from alternative ways of knowing and responding to our natural world?

On the other side of the world from Clarke, a group of educators are grappling this exact question.

Vancouver Island is the land mass that stretches from Victoria, the capital of the province of British Columbia, up and away into the Pacific Ocean. Right at its tip lies School District 85,[6] covering over 8,500 square miles, and encompassing 11 communities, including the 3 towns of Port McNeill, Port Alice and Port Hardy. The district is home to several fishing communities, but since time immemorial it has been the home of the Kwakwaka'wakw Nations, speakers of the Kwak'wala language.

All students in the district now have the opportunity to learn about and experience authentic Aboriginal content, and study First Nations languages and history as part of courses such as the integrated English First Peoples course at the high school level; however, school leaders are also working to ensure that First Nations knowledge is a greater part of all subjects, including science. This reflects a commitment of the new provincial curriculum in British Columbia, which includes First Nations knowledge as part of all subjects.

In 2016, under the leadership of former Principal D'Arcy Deacon, district 85 held its first STEM (Science, Technology, Engineering and Maths) Challenge, for sixth and seventh graders to apply methods of design and engineering they have been learning. The challenge was initiated by a presentation on aboriginal methods of Food Harvesting, and the children then had to design ways to harvest local foods such as salmon and clams without destroying natural life cycles. These projects are part of a two-sided effort in schools to spread valuable eco-literacy while also engendering increased knowledge about and respect for the First Nations that make up their community.

It might seem difficult to promote these kinds of authentic learning experiences without the relationships, support and guidance from First

[5] Interview with Arihia Stirling, April 2016   [6] www.sd85.bc.ca/

Nations communities, along with collective district leadership, to ensure that knowledge is transmitted accurately and respectfully. But opening ourselves to the accurate and profound value of indigenous knowledge is as much about an attitude as specific activities.

Across the other side of the province, School District 10 covers the lake-dotted terrain of the Kootenays, a vast region stretching to the Rocky Mountain range where British Columbia meets Alberta. The district is small and geographically spread with six tiny schools in diverse communities, and locals get by through a mixture of self-sufficient living and a fledgling tourist industry. The Kootenays are home to the Sinixt, Ktunaxa, Secwepmec, and Okanagan First Nations and people here show a similar respect for their land and relationship with their ecosystem. Over the past decades, the schools in the district have been developing methods of 'place-conscious learning', using their incredible mountain surroundings to inspire and motivate learners in rich learning experiences such as writers' workshops with visiting Canadian authors, using place and art to help further the journey of reconciliation with indigenous peoples, and intentionally teaching children the necessary skills to preserve and sustain their specific natural environments. At Lucerne, the only all-through elementary and secondary school in the district, students and teachers have created a kitchen garden, greenhouse and sustainable food program similar to that at Nazareth.

As Clarke suggested, it can be difficult to be focusing on the natural world when human concerns are always pressing. Some school and district leaders demonstrate how it is possible to create a moral urgency around changing our relationship to our place without constantly talking about it. Terry Taylor, superintendent of the district, had chosen to call place-conscious learning the 'signature pedagogy' of their district, and actively supports teachers and school leaders to find innovative ways to educate their students outside, or take one more step in their quest for fully self-sustaining schools.

There are some days when no children are present inside their classroom walls, something that Taylor and the parents and community celebrate. Instead in School District 10, teachers regularly take their primary students outside for learning each day using GIS devices to map their community, finding natural materials to create visual art or engaging in inquiries about protecting the habitat of local animals. Teachers journey with their middle school or secondary learners up to the tops of local mountains studying geographical formations, study the impact of climate change on local glaciers and snowpack, and paddle with parents and community volunteers for four or five days on Slocan Lake as they learn about local indigenous culture and the water cycle in science. Intermediate students practice physical and mental well-being, walk and hike trails, ski in the mountains and swim in mountain lakes. They study botany and geometry through learning about local plants and trees, and examine fish habitats with local fisheries experts and wildlife conservation with local bear biologists. Solar panels on the roofs of local schools in the district were installed by students alongside solar engineers, electricians and carpenters as the students learned hands on skills in renewable energies.

The possibilities for place-conscious learning are endless, with teachers encouraged and supported to collaborate designing innovative place-conscious learning environments that deeply engage their students. The students' learning also has a positive impact on the well-being and stewardship of their local communities.

Taylor's regular collaborator, Professor Leyton Schnellert, describes it as 'balancing things'. 'Without saying "this is our moral purpose", everything [Taylor] does is saying "what are we doing, how are we going there?"'[7]

Taylor herself describes it as all about having an inquiring attitude:

We 'possibilize' together in community. We don't know what's possible, but we can take charge of the future by coming up with possibilities.[8]

Here, perhaps, is an attitude that one can embrace without fearing being side-lined a lefty green. If we keep our eyes and minds focused on real places, real possibilities, the next generation and their teachers might really have the power to create a better world. Nor need educators any longer feel defensive about this stance. For many, among the lessons learned during months of COVID-19 closures, the most profound has been a new relationship with nature.

5.2 Educating Global Citizens

Clarke and Taylor emphasise the importance of local place, connecting students with the land they live on and the local ecosystems that sustain

---

[7] Interview with Leyton Schnellert, March 2016
[8] Interview with Terry Taylor, March 2016; personal communication, December 2019

them. Meanwhile, other schools have set their sights on the problem of global interdependence. For these schools, the global learning challenge that is most pressing is a *social* and human one: preparing students to engage in dialogue and collaboration across cultural and political boundaries. As we saw in Chapter 4, educationalists have called this new skillset 'global competence'.

Avenues School[9] stands on the lower west side of New York, looking down on the skyscrapers of Manhattan's financial district. Established in 2012, Avenues is a private school subtitled 'The World School' and with 'global readiness' at the heart of its mission. It was created by a group of educators convened by entrepreneur, Chris Whittle, one of the founders of online provider EdisonLearning. The group, which included former principals of some of the United States' most prestigious private schools, gathered around a mission that to be fully educated citizens today, students needed an education that would give them a global perspective.

Tyler Tingley, part of the initial design group who then came out of retirement to become Avenues' Director of Curriculum, says he was drawn to the school as an opportunity to really prioritise the study of other cultures and languages. All students at Avenues learn a second language, not just for a few hours a week but in a partial immersion method where 50 per cent of their lessons take place in that language. The ultimate aspiration of the founders is to have 20 Avenues schools in major cities around the world, where students on each campus can increasingly benefit from virtual exchanges with young people from different cultures. They have already established a second school in Beijing, and there are plans to open in London. Students already have the opportunity to study in different countries through a program of 'Global Journeys'.[10]

The school's location could not be more ideal for highlighting the increasing necessity of this kind of education. A couple of subway stops down is Wall Street, the heart of the global financial crisis, which demonstrated so powerfully the interdependence of national economies and societies. Three stops over to the east is the United Nations Headquarters, home to the multilateral body that still represents more than any other the aspiration for global collaboration.

[9] www.avenues.org/   [10] www.avenues.org/en/nyc/global-journeys/

Avenues – and the learning goal of global competence more broadly – is caught between these two cultures: on the one hand, a tribe who use their knowledge of other cultures and economies daily to predict the rise and fall of companies and currencies, making billions of dollars in the process. On the other, the diplomats who seek through their skills to reach multilateral agreements, and pursue peace and stability. While the full purposes of these groups is in both cases not so straightforward, it is nevertheless the case that proponents of teaching global competence fall between these poles of the competitive and the collaborative, extractive and inclusive.

Despite its hefty price tag, the Avenues school tends more towards the latter culture – collaborative and inclusive. All students have to take 'The World Course', a global studies curriculum developed in collaboration with faculty at the Harvard Graduate School of Education. Students study questions such as 'how do new encounters change us?', and practise skills such as conflict resolution. The school also has a homestay program that supports regular visits from students from other countries, and an online discussion forum called 'Avenues OPEN' to encourage the exchange of ideas with students and adults in other countries.

In considering the goals of this kind of school, it is worth questioning what is really distinctive here. The execution may be more lavish, but are the purposes really any different? Teenagers studying history, geography or social studies in schools today are very likely to have to focus on different countries, and, while the numbers might not be what we would like, many students still study other languages to an advanced level. Their experience is arguably not that different then from students within 'The World Course', who still cannot learn in any depth about more than a handful of cultures or places during their time at school.

By going down that line, however, we miss the point. The most important knowledge entailed in global competence is not just having an awareness of several different cultures and types of societies. It is explicitly learning about the way that culture shapes our lives – our thinking, our values, our decisions. This is the knowledge that educators hope will be most transferable so that, when we engage in interactions with other people from different backgrounds, or make judgements about events happening in other parts of the world, we understand the need to interpret them through cultural lenses, even if we may not yet have all the relevant knowledge to do so. The inquiry-based approach of the World Course has this attitude at its heart: if we cannot know everything about our world, better to ask than to judge.

Avenues is currently just two schools, but it stands in a long tradition of independent schools raising their sights to the global stage. Over 50 years ago, in 1962, a group of educationalists inspired by the League of United Nations set to work establishing schools that would prepare young people to be public servants, entrepreneurs and national leaders, with a mind and spirit inclined towards 'international values'. These schools were to become the United World Colleges,[11] now a group of ten schools spaced around the world. More significantly, the United World Colleges were the birthplace of the International Baccalaureate (IB) programs, which now provide curricula and qualification structures for over 4,000 schools in 147 countries.

A central aspect of the IB diploma program , the culminating phase, is the Theory of Knowledge course. The course was originally modelled on analytic epistemology, but increasingly looks at the nature of knowledge in different cultures. 'Indigenous Knowledge Systems' form one of eight areas of knowledge. Students are inducted into learning about other indigenous peoples not just as external observers of their practices, but in terms of understanding their philosophies, values and long processes of knowledge accumulation.

The course and its popularity is a good example of how a much deeper understanding of the nature of culture can be taught explicitly in schools. It also draws attention, however, to long-running debates over the difference between fostering 'globalism', often associated with globalisation and a convergence of cultures, and 'internationalism', a greater inter-connection of people that keeps nations at the centre. The IB has long leaned towards the latter, with its notion of 'international-mindedness' and desire to adapt curriculum to individual nations.

These debates might seem like hair-splitting, but they illustrate the importance of being clear on goals and values. It is very difficult to make decisions about curriculum – what history and languages should we teach, who should decide – without having a clear sense of what is most valued. Is this about inducting students into a 'World Culture' to prepare them to take part in a global knowledge economy? Or is it about raising their awareness of the great range of practices and

---

[11] www.uwc.org/

knowledge they now have access to, and of what is particular and valuable about their culture in the context of such diversity? There is no one right answer here, but as Chapter 4 illustrated, the response that is untenable is to leave students unable to contextualise their place in an increasingly connected world.

Of course, the full extent of these decisions is not currently available to most schools. United World Colleges, for example, have access to considerable resources and are relatively unique in their student bodies: a wide variety of languages are nurtured among students and staff, and there is considerable emphasis on learning from other students. But other schools are demonstrating that it is perfectly possible to promote deep learning about other cultures and countries in the context of a public education system.

5.3 Beyond the Elite

The Academy of International Studies (AIS)[12] is a school-within-a-school at Independence High School, a long-standing institution of Charlotte-Mecklenburg school district, in North Carolina. AIS was founded with the support of the Gates Foundation in 2003, in a period when the foundation was investing heavily in the creation of small schools. With funds directed through the Asia Society, an NGO that has done much to nurture the notion of internationalism in US schools, Independence High School created AIS as a testing ground for new pedagogies that would develop global competence. This includes a strong emphasis on service learning, and completion of an international or internationally focused internships.

AIS has developed its own expansive vision of global competence. Their original curriculum design document[13] outlines a set of eleven 'global competencies' they want students to develop. These include: to develop multiple perspectives; understand the interdependence of systems; be capable of making ethical decisions; be proficient in English and one other language; understand complexity; achieve expertise on at least one culture and issue; and make healthy decisions for themselves and their environments. The list begins to bring the abstract concept of global competence into view, with a variety of

[12] https://sites.google.com/cms.k12.nc.us/indyais
[13] https://sites.google.com/cms.k12.nc.us/indyais

knowledge, skills and disposition. In addition, this vision of global competence entails all of the overarching learning goals the school has for its students. Just as Tyler Tingley at Avenues believes that knowing about other countries and cultures is central to being a good national citizen, for AIS global competence is interwoven with what it means to be educated.

As part of Asia Society's International Studies School Network,[14] AIS is involved in its work to try to assess global competence. The challenge of this type of network is in working out to what extent the practices of these schools are relevant to others – particularly others that have not made internationalism part of their mission. The danger of multilateral efforts to promote global competence is that any framework that could apply in any school is limited to rather abstract, content-less visions. It cannot address the many opportunities for learning that can arise from the specific contexts of schools. This is why it is so important that schools use their own initiative and context around which to shape their practices.

In the borough of Redbridge in Essex, around 200 miles away from the nearest United World College, students at Newbury Park Primary School[15] have a community that boasts almost as much cultural diversity. Pupils here speak over 30 different languages at home, and many students are the first in their family to be born in England. For over 10 years, the school has worked to make this community a resource for learning, recording children explaining to each other, and encouraging all children and parents to familiarise themselves with world languages and cultures through their 'Language of the Month' program. Newbury Park has been recognised both nationally and at the European level for its practice, and is a good school by all other measures. It is an example of what all schools could achieve – but each in their own way – by prioritising global competence.

5.4 Can We Really Do This?

In looking from Avenues to Newbury Park, it is hard not to focus on the dramatic differences in the opportunities available to their students. Even without concerns for the costs of providing international trips or

---

[14] https://asiasociety.org/international-studies-schools-network
[15] www.newburyparkschool.net/

cultural visits, the *time* required to invest seriously in developing global competence would put many schools off. Is it justifiable to focus on these challenges, when students might be 'behind' in their mastery of traditional subjects, or 'at risk' of not performing up to standard?

This dilemma is exactly why it is so important to address the question of purposes. If we stand back from our current education systems, we can acknowledge that, aside from the intrinsic value of gaining certain knowledge bases (which should not be ignored), a primary reason for ensuring that students learn up to a standard is to give them the same life chances as others. Our concern is, even by this measure, the goalposts are shifting.

In *The Global Auction*, David Ashton, Hugh Lauder and Phillip Brown write about the increased popularity of international schools among domestic elites.[16] In their research, they found that recruiters at multinational corporations look to these schools specifically when seeking employees. Our fear is that while government schools are doubling down on getting students up to a set of national standards, increasingly, elite schools have seen the tide turn and are rewriting the rulebook, preparing their students with an entirely different skillset, and the assumption that their future jobs might take them overseas, or at least be part of multinational professional teams.

With this as the competition, social mobility cannot be pursued by forcing state schools to spend all their time chasing a narrow set of national standards. This fact opens up the space for a debate about *what* knowledge is going to be most important for students in their lives. We do not suggest that there is any one answer to this, merely that knowledge of a diverse range of countries and an understanding of the role of culture in human lives and societies need to be more serious contenders.

Sustaining Learning for Sustainability

It would be irresponsible to describe the schools without acknowledging that this is hard work. Of all the shifts described in this book, the incorporation of global purposes demands the biggest breaks with traditional school practice. Finding time in a school day for students

---

[16] Brown, Lauder and Ashton, *The Global Auction*; see also *The Economist*, 'The New Local'.

to work on ecologies or learn deeply about another language and culture is not easy. And the timelines of this learning do not sit easily with the rigid rhythms of schools: a plant may not grow in the duration of a unit; the opportunity to progress with a language or understand another perspective may not occur in the time between tests.

Sadly, we have seen examples of wonderful initiatives that have not been sustained over time. This does not make the work any less valuable for those students who benefitted from it, but it does pose a challenge to the growth of practice that others can learn from. In Chapter 13, we examine how ecosystems for learning may sustain practice when individual schools cannot. But it is also vital to confront the underlying reasons why special programmes or optional courses often do not sustain. When learning towards the global goals is relegated to an add-on or option, it risks being sidelined as non-academic work. This is particularly a risk because this learning is often associated with ways of knowing other than western science, and is often best demonstrated through something other than writing. We should not be leaving it to individual students or parents to have to choose between what they see as 'academic' and competitive, and that which is most important to the future of our planet. Schools have historically taken the responsibility to decide what is 'core' for their students. We propose that ecological and inter-cultural learning has to be core.

Finding the Personal in the Global

Promoting global educational purposes is always going to be fraught with difficulty: schools have historically been about inducting students into a society, and even as the inter-connectedness of information and material fields increases, societies will retain local and national values and practices. What we have tried to show in this chapter is how schools can further an overarching global purpose in distinctly local ways. And indeed, if they do not, the goal becomes empty and meaningless for children and young people. As AIS put it in their motto, the goal is not for everyone to have the same knowledge, but rather 'a globally informed personal identity'.

Schools taking the lead in determining both the meaning and the implementation of global goals is particularly important when it comes to environmental protection: none of us know exactly what will be necessary to restore our planet's sustainable ecosystems, and the only way we will figure it out is by working concertedly in *real* areas, not prescribing abstract knowledge or skills at a multilateral level. Schools need to approach this challenge with a spirit of inquiry and close attention to their own place, and develop their own specific purposes and practices from there. This is exciting and inspiring work for both teachers and learners (and in this context the roles frequently interchange). And it can result in a quality and beauty of work from young learners that often teachers thought was not possible.[17]

Likewise with global competence, we must be careful not to allow the obsession with assessment to close down inquiry as to the range of knowledge and understandings that help people engage with each other across borders and cultures. The aftermath of COVID-19 has made this even more imperative, as the crisis gave oxygen to xenophobic tendencies. It is important to recognise that there are some concrete skills – such as perspective-taking and bias recognition – that we should be teaching and developing now. However, when the range of potentially relevant knowledge is so large, the most important aspects of global competence surely must be the disposition to inquire rather than assume. It is doubtful that one-off assessments can really test or incentivise the development of dispositions; instead, it is only when schools make it part of their mission and everyday practice that we will see this particular competency flourish.

5.5 Can It Ever Be Enough?

The educators we have met in this chapter are by no means alone. In the past 10 years, there have been a plethora of initiatives aimed at 'schooling for sustainability' or 'sustainability education'. Often this is fleshed out not only as having a sustainable impact on the environment, but in much richer terms to encompass also an understanding of the relationship between the individual and the global.[18] And just as more individuals have been trying to change their habits to reduce their environmental impact – eating less meat, turning off lights, using less plastic – more and more schools have instituted practices such as Meat

---

[17] For example: The Students of High Tech High, *Perspectives of San Diego Bay*.
[18] NCSL, 'The Journey of Sustainable Schools: Developing and Embedding Sustainability'.

free Mondays, recycling efforts, or energy audits.[19] Schools may strengthen their efforts by being part of networks with the same focus, such as the Green Schools Alliance,[20] Eco-Schools,[21] or the Sustainable School Alliance in the United Kingdom.[22]

We know, however, that it will take more than individual or even organisational behaviour change to limit emissions to a level that is sustainability for the planet. This fact has been brought home starkly by studies emerging of the impacts of COVID-19 lockdowns on energy usage. While one would assume that the near-elimination of driving, flying and recreation would result in a dramatic reduction in emissions across the board, the actual reduction varied widely. In the month of March 2020, CO_2 emissions in Paris, where most heating comes from nuclear-fuelled electricity, were down a huge 72 per cent. But in New York City, with a number of large fossil fuel plants in the vicinity, emissions were down only 10 per cent.[23] The implication is: energy usage is a structural problem. We can reduce our footprint by changing our individual behaviours, but the largest part of emissions depends on national policy and the nature of our national energy supplies.

For schools, this means that the key question about sustainability is not just what to do as organisations, but what to *teach*. Just as the history we teach in schools is often oriented towards understanding the risks that human pose to each other – through war, famine or genocide – so the science and geography we teach could be even more oriented towards understanding our planetary risks.

Educators are already demonstrating what's possible with limited curriculum time. In the United States, Kaleidoscope is an organisation that designs new curriculum units for high school students. Their Climate Policy course teaches students about the causes and consequences of climate change and the ways that we might tackle it through policy.[24] In addition, the course provides teenagers with a taste of the diversity of the social sciences, which many teenagers never meet in school. It is shaped around an introduction to the approaches of economics, political science, history, anthropology, geography,

---

[19] See, for example, programmes for schools trying to reduce their energy usage (for example, www.lessco2.org.uk/).
[20] www.greenschoolsalliance.org/   [21] www.eco-schools.org.uk/
[22] https://se-ed.co.uk/edu/sustainable-schools-alliance/
[23] McGrath, 'Coronavirus'.
[24] https://kaleidoscope.education/climate-science-and-policy

sociology and psychology, setting out in a single course what each those disciplines have to teach us about climate science and policy.

In countries with formal examinations, deviation from the prescribed subjects may feel too risky. But in the United Kingdom, SEEd (sustainability and environmental education) provides up to date resources for schools looking to teach more of the knowledge that students need in order to understand what it means for national and global systems to be more sustainable, including links to curriculum subjects.[25]

If we start talking about curriculum, however, how much can schools change without the support of government? There are certainly questions to ask about the time allocation given to different knowledge or subjects, such as why Biology tends towards the study of *human* health, and is often compulsory to a more advanced level than Geography. But the decision to guide students towards greater understanding of planetary risks and possibilities can be taken within schools, by teachers and department leaders, rather than government curriculum writers.

What do we mean by this? Let's think again of the example of History. A History curriculum might specify that all students needs to learn about a particular example of genocide. It is up to educators, however, whether we just teach students the facts or engage them in reflecting on these facts in particular ways, for example in the approaches developed by organisation Facing History and Ourselves.[26] Most teachers would agree, we think, that even if sticking to 'just the facts', it is impossible to teach a topic like genocide without entering into value judgements. We would propose that the same is true of teaching about our planet's ecosystems and our impact on them.

To clarify this debate, let's look at the alternative attitude. In England, the latest curriculum reform resulted in no formal place for teaching on sustainability and environmental education. Advocates objected and asked for explanation. Professor Bill Scott published correspondence from the Department for Education following his inquiry. A central part of this formal response reads:

[25] https://se-ed.co.uk/edu/resources/   [26] www.facinghistory.org/

the new programmes of study for geography and science cover this issue from key stage 3 [lower secondary] and focus on the key concepts in science and geography, rather than political, economic or social debates on this topic. In order for children to develop a firm understanding of climate change, it is essential that it is taught as a carefully sequenced progression, starting with the fundamental concepts and relevant background knowledge which underpin this topic.[27]

The position here is that we shouldn't focus on human responsibility until we can explain exactly why that matters. But as educators – even just as parents or fellow people – we know that this doesn't hold. We teach children to wash their hands long before we teach them the biology of microbes. We teach them to respect different attire or practices long before we teach them the histories of tolerance and intolerance. And we teach them that a family might have two mothers or two fathers before we explain homosexuality. When we know what is right, we know that we must teach it to our children before we can explain it all to them.

This is why we are interested in schools who are not afraid to make the health of the planet and the natural world part of their values. Considering the impact that we have on our natural environment, this needs to be become part of what we do in every aspect of our lives. This is not just about what we know, but about what we know to be important.

---

[27] Scott, 'Another Ministerial Stonewalling'.

6 | *Stronger Together*
Building Thriving Societies

Politicians need to broaden their focus from narrowly defined measures of learning and economic growth – both in practical and in rhetorical terms. However, this is not to argue that the issue of economic well-being should be ignored: on the contrary. The proposal is that it should get real.

Nations are comprised of communities, and an understanding of what will make for thriving communities in the future is therefore essential to underpin a redesign of schools' contribution. We have seen that a focus on GDP or social mobility is misplaced; these outcomes are too dependent on measurement issues and too influenced by the wider economy to be meaningful purposes for schools. However, to secure their own standard of living and contribute to a sustainable economy, young people will need to be well prepared to participate in the workforce – and one that is likely to look very different by the time they reach it.

The second argument here is that the precondition for thriving communities is reduced levels of income and wealth inequality, at least to a point where individuals can participate in society. And the key to reducing inequality and increasing equity lies in renewed forms of democracy. We will argue that while existing forms of democracy may, to some degree, have disappointed on this front, it remains the better alternative to its rival – revolution/autocratic control. But democracy could be strengthened and renewed. Therefore, the proposal is that the key future-focused learning goals for schools are as follows:

- *To equip learners to navigate a disrupted and uncertain landscape of work*
- *To prepare young people to reinvent a democracy that is participative, authentic and meaningful*

6.1 The Uncertain Future of Work

Although we have criticised the centrality of economic rationales as goals for learning, the importance of work (or the absence of it) in people's lives still must not be underestimated. What is crucial is that learning today must relate to the emerging world of work, not one that has already passed. The learning challenge for schools is to enable young people both to prepare for the reality of work today, and to start to encounter it in their own learning, so that they leave school confident in what they can offer, and how to create new opportunities in the future.

In the twentieth and early twenty-first centuries, the major determinants of increasing economic equality (or the 'rise of the middle class') were access to good employment opportunities and its evil twin, overall unemployment levels. Immense changes to the world of employment are widely recognised to be underway as a direct consequence of the technological disruptions set out in Chapter 3, along with a long-term trend towards flexibility in labour markets. These changes include more widespread part-time and self-employment, higher rates of job turnover, and more 'under-employment' and precarious work. These are currently in progress; they are not just vague possibilities among others in some distant future. The impact upon work as we have known it has been the subject of a raft of recent major analyses.[1]

The shifts driven by technology must be understood against their backcloth of globalisation, the connecting of virtually all locations in the world to one another through new flows of goods, raw materials, information, investment and people. In the late twentieth century, the early consequence was that localities – almost irrespective of their economic bases – learned to see themselves in a global competition. Steel workers in Wales grew to be conscious of the activities of their counterparts in China, and the relativities of trade tariffs. Workers in the United States auto industry directly competed with Japanese and German counterparts. Only the service industries were immune, though workers increasingly found themselves part of companies owned by international corporations. Globalisation has unquestionably contributed, first, to a levelling up of wages in low-income

---

[1] Schwab, *The Fourth Industrial Revolution*; Ross, *The Industries of the Future*; Manyika et al., 'Help Wanted'.

countries; and, second, to job insecurity and the rise of the 'precariat,' or that class of workers whose conditions are characterised by uncertainty and lack of security.[2]

For young people aged 16–24, the scourge of unemployment has been ubiquitous since the Global Financial Crisis of 2008. Among OECD countries, youth unemployment is still above 30 per cent in Italy, Spain, Greece and South Africa. In part, this illustrates again the futility of measuring educational progress in economic terms; there are obviously wider reasons why these countries have particularly high rates. But it also highlights that the production of 'skills' in the abstract cannot solve employment problems; none of these countries is lacking for qualified young people. Notwithstanding the prevalence of the human capital rationale for the purpose of learning, ironically education has done a pretty poor job of making strong connections to the world of work.[3] In recent years, efforts have been made to reach across that gap, recognising that to do so can bring meaning and relevance to learning.[4]

The COVID-19 pandemic plunged the world into a new period of recession, which some commentators claim will be the largest since World War II, and overshadows that of the Global Financial Crisis. At the time of writing, a reduction in global GDP of 35 per cent was being forecast. As a result of global lockdowns, businesses across the world were struggling for survival. In the United States alone, 30 million people were registered as unemployed in May 2020. The future of employment prospects for young and old alike look particularly bleak for decades ahead.

Further disruption will result from the impact of the technological developments broadly outlined in Chapter 3. The recession caused by the COVID-19 pandemic is itself accelerating the process of automation, as employers seek to drive down costs.[5] The penetration of robotics and artificial intelligence into labour markets will have profound consequences, and the question is how tomorrow's citizens can be prepared. In past revolutions, the introduction of technology led, in

---

[2] Standing, *The Precariat*.
[3] Mourshed, Farrell and Barton, 'Education to Employment: Designing a System That Works'.
[4] Hannon, Gillinson and Shanks, *Learning a Living*; OECD, *Getting Skills Right*.
[5] Gregory, 'UK Economy Headed for Record Contraction as Coronavirus Has Heavy Near-Term Impact'.

the short term, to the destruction of jobs (as the Luddites, who smashed the machines in the Industrial Revolution, feared); however, it resulted swiftly in the creation of new ones, and new sectors. Up until now that has been the pattern. However, economists are increasingly of the view that this is 'no ordinary disruption'.[6] While some projections of the potential of new job creation have tried to remain optimistic, overall the global share of productivity produced by labour (that is, human workers as opposed to technology) has fallen,[7] and job growth even in the high-skill professional and service sectors has stalled:[8] the replacement may not happen this time. Study after study demonstrates why. The increasing sophistication (and speed) of the technologies has expanded the reach of technological replacement beyond the routine, to more complex operations and tasks. In *The Second Machine Age*, Brynjolfsson and McAfee wrote:

There's never been a worse time to be a worker with only 'ordinary' skills and abilities to offer, because computers, robots and other digital technologies are acquiring these skills and abilities at an extraordinary rate.[9]

Brynjolfsson and McAfee went on to analyse three transfers changing the nature of employment.[10] The first is from human to machine, the potential implications detailed above. The second is from products to platforms: some of the biggest companies own no objects but run great platforms – for example, Uber and Airbnb. The third is from the core to the crowd. The core refers to centralised institutions, such as central banks or the 'Encyclopaedia Britannica'; the crowd refers to the decentralised, self-organising participants, be it bitcoin nodes that manage the virtual currency or contributors to Wikipedia. Each of these transfers fundamentally shifts the balance of power we have become used to in our economies – but where to exactly is not yet clear.

Technologies are creating a labour market in which there are no certainties, but in which the destruction of substantial numbers of existing jobs is a high probability, and in which many that replace them will demand a higher level of technological literacy. Academics have tried to quantify the potential scale of change by examining the

---

[6] Dobbs, Manyika and Woetzel, *No Ordinary Disruption*.
[7] Karabarbounis and Neiman, 'The Global Decline of the Labor Share'.
[8] Autor, 'Why Are There Still So Many Jobs?'
[9] Brynjolfsson and McAfee, *The Second Machine Age*, 11.
[10] Mcafee and Brynjolfsson, *Machine, Platform, Crowd*.

kind of tasks and therefore jobs that could be replaced by computer systems or robots. Using this method, Frey and Osborne estimated in 2013 that 47 per cent of jobs in the United States are 'at risk' of being automated in the next 20 years.[11] Telemarketers, accountants, sports referees, legal secretaries, and cashiers were deemed among the most likely of the job losses. Other estimates are even more urgent. Organisers of the World Economic Forum in 2016 predicted that 7 million jobs could go in five years, with women losing out the most.[12] Similar conclusions have been reached by analysis in the Bank of England. Their chief economist has repeatedly warned that automation poses a risk to almost half those employed in the United Kingdom, and that the new machine age would further hollow out the labour market, widening the gap between rich and poor.[13]

The evidence of the penetration of automation is already all around us. Hot on the heels of the introduction of driverless cars (for which regulations are being developed to enable their use on the roads of many countries now), in 2016 driverless truck convoys completed journeys across European borders.[14] A hardware store in San Jose, California has a retail associate robot named Oshbot.[15] Domino's Pizza in Australia has unveiled a pizza delivery robot in Brisbane.[16] The logistics and transport industries seem ripe for the next waves of disruption, but human services may not be far behind. A bartending robot named Monsieur is already on the market and NAO robots are being tried out as hotel and bank receptionists. A major development is the introduction of robots as companions and assistants to the old, especially in Japan, where the life expectancy of women is about to rise to 91 (and to 84 for men); so Japanese companies are building robots 'to reinvent the family,' such as 'Rosie' a 'female' (sic) nursing aid.[17] Robotic classroom assistants are now working in classrooms – and

---

[11] Frey and Osborne, 'The Future of Employment'.
[12] World Economic Forum, 'The Future of Jobs: Employment, Skills and Workforce Strategy for the Fourth Industrial Revolution'.
[13] Haldane, 'Ideas and Institutions – A Growth Story'; Haldane, 'Labour's Share'; Ahmed, 'Bank Warns on AI Jobs Threat'.
[14] Campbell, 'Trucks Headed for a Driverless Future'; Martin, 'Driverless Truck Convoys Cross Europe'.
[15] ABC News, 'SJ Hardware Store Uses Robot to Help Customers'.
[16] Holley, 'Domino's Will Start Delivering Pizzas via an Autonomous Robot This Fall'.
[17] Ross, *The Industries of the Future*.

children rather like them.[18] A robot can now be 'trained' by a human teacher how to interact well with children in three hours.[19] They are also working as 'buddies' aimed to support development for children with autism and Downs Syndrome.[20]

As these examples illustrate, while job replacement is a concern, not all outcomes of automation are negative. Over the next two to five years, the convergence of 5G, artificial intelligence, VR/AR, and a trillion-sensor economy will enable the mapping of our physical world into virtual space. While converging technologies slash the lifespan of Fortune 500 companies, bring on the rise of vast new industries and transform the job market, Web 3.0 will change how and where we work, and who we work with.[21] Again, the COVID-19 crisis has accelerated the process. Millions have become familiar with working remotely. The CEO of Microsoft observed that two years of digital transformation had been compressed into two months.[22] An international analysis of the potential long-term impact by the financial services giant PwC assesses that, overall, there is the potential to bring great economic benefits, contributing up to $15 trillion to global GDP by 2030.[23] But – as with most gains measured in the old metric of GDP – the benefits will spread unevenly. Greater productivity will not benefit all. They predict that 44 per cent of workers with low education will be at risk of losing out to automation by the mid-2030s.

Understanding these developments might seem like a futile exercise for educators: what can schools do about labour market turmoil or mass unemployment among former truck drivers? The purpose is twofold. First, it is simply to further highlight the need to expand the goals of public education beyond that of employment and skills; the pace of change in skill demands is too unpredictable and there are too many young people who may end up, like the 30 per cent in Italy and Spain, without employment but still needing to lead their lives in meaningful

---

[18] www.youtube.com/watch?v=iDoqaVL307I
[19] Cookson, 'Robot Trained to Be Useful Teaching Assistant in Three Hours'.
[20] Peters, 'This Cute Robot Is Designed to Help Children with Autism'; see also Huijnen et al., 'Roles, Strengths and Challenges of Using Robots in Interventions for Children with Autism Spectrum Disorder (ASD)'.
[21] Diamandis and Kotler, *The Future Is Faster Than You Think*.
[22] www.business-standard.com/article/international/microsoft-sees-yearlong-digital-transformation-happen-in-2-months-nadella-120043000184_1.html
[23] PwC, 'Will Robots Really Steal Our Jobs? An International Analysis of the Potential Long-Term Impact of Automation'.

ways. Second, it is to illustrate where trends are going. Automation, digitisation and flexibility all have potential upsides as well as down. The emerging generation has the potential to shape the future world of work to the benefit of the many, rather than the few, but to do so they need to be informed participants; the sooner they understand what they will be working with, the better.

The authors of *No Ordinary Disruption* argue that business leaders need to 'reset their intuitions' to take account of the unfolding reality, and accordingly think differently about their investments and decisions in the light of the knowledge of these disruptive developments already underway – not just dimly in prospect. Leaders of education systems, and practising educators, now need to do the same.

6.2 The Professions: Safe Havens for Employment?

The professions in many cases remain the default choice of high-achieving students, not least because, in addition to attractive rewards, they have been a safe option in terms of the vagaries of demand and indeed the impact of globalisation. Yet the indications are that this level of safety may be eroding.

In *The Future of the Professions*, Richard and Daniel Susskind set out how computerisation is penetrating the world of the professions.[24] They look at the roles of doctors, teachers, accountants, architects, clergy, consultants and lawyers and demonstrate that, once broken down by task, there is little of professional work that will not be capable of being done by a machine. Consequently, 'increasingly capable systems' – from telepresence to artificial intelligence – will bring fundamental change in the way that the expertise of specialisms is made available in society. The Susskinds shed no tears over this: they argue that in any case, our current professions are antiquated, opaque and unaffordable to too many.

Incursions into the fields of law and medicine serve as the shape of things to come. Millions of Americans have experienced robotic surgery, and, despite some scepticism about costs and safety, demand continues to grow.[25] The nature of robotic surgery is shifting from

---

[24] Susskind and Susskind, *The Future of the Professions*.
[25] Perez and Schwaitzberg, 'Robotic Surgery'; Schwitzer, 'New Questions about the $3B/Year Robotic Surgery Business'.

being little more than motorised precision tools to the testing of real robot surgeons, operating under the lightest of human supervision.[26] In law, algorithms can now select the most relevant cases for precedent faster and as accurately as junior lawyers and paralegals.[27] This capability is being scaled through tools such as ROSS, which uses IBM's artificially intelligent supercomputer Watson to take over the work of legal research.[28] In 2016 Deloitte predicted that 2020 would be a 'tipping point' for law firms in the adoption of technology, with 114,000 jobs in the United Kingdom's legal sector likely to become automated in the next 20 years.[29] Whether through self-fulfilling predictions or inevitable catch-up, as of 2019, law firms were talking of an 'explosion of innovation' in technology for the legal sector.[30] Whether such technology really increases affordability and access to justice, however, depends on how well it is used – and understood.

When it comes to the future of secure, high-paid jobs, the debate is the degree to which the disruption is confined to technology providing an enhancement to human capabilities (resulting in some net loss of jobs); or whether we are looking at wholesale replacement. No robots are due to argue a case in court anytime soon. But perhaps the very notion of 'profession' is becoming obsolete, giving way to a flexible set of skills and competencies required to handle a certain set of tasks. The implication for education is that the well-trodden path for lucky school students from academic high-performers through elite universities and into top professions may soon get more complicated. Already Silicon Valley has taken over Wall Street as a destination of choice for some young people in the United States, and there are equivalent changeovers in many countries round the world. But schools have yet to catch up with what this could mean: once we remove the need to demonstrate academic excellence for the sake of arcane professional gateways, we can start to think about a better range of ways these young people might spend their time in school – and beyond.

---

[26] Shademan et al., 'Supervised Autonomous Robotic Soft Tissue Surgery'.
[27] Susskind and Susskind, *The Future of the Professions*.
[28] Turner, 'Meet "Ross," the Newly Hired Legal Robot'.
[29] Croft, 'More than 100,000 Legal Roles to Become Automated'.
[30] Pooley, 'Lawyers' next Challenge'.

6.3 Are We Special?

With this debate, the search for 'human exceptionalism' has begun. What is it that humans uniquely can do that machines can't – and won't be able to? The specialists in studying this are Michael Osborne, a professor of machine learning, and Carl Frey, the director of the program on the Future of Work at the Oxford Martin School. The main conclusion of their work is that as technology races ahead, low-skill workers would need to reallocate to tasks that are non-susceptible to technology – that is, tasks requiring *creative and social intelligence*.[31] In collaboration with Hasan Bakshi of Nesta, they have looked at the creative industries and the extent to which they are more 'future-proof' to emerging technologies such as machine learning and robotics.[32] Summarising their review of the capabilities of new technologies, they conclude:

> ... machines can most successfully emulate humans when a problem is well specified in advance – that is, when performance can be straightforwardly quantified and evaluated – and when the work task environment is sufficiently simple to enable autonomous control. They will struggle when tasks are highly interpretive, geared at 'products whose final form is not fully specified in advance', and when work task environments are complex – a good description of most creative occupations.[33]

This is promising when everywhere, the creative industries are growing. As of the latest estimates, the UK creative economy accounts for 3.2 million jobs, bigger than sectors such as advanced manufacturing, financial services and construction.[34] The creative economies in the United States and Canada are likewise substantial.[35] In 2015, the first attempt to analyse the cultural and creative industries globally estimated that these sectors are a significant contributor to youth employment and are growing with urbanisation and rising middle classes.[36] These predictions are bearing out: global trade in 'creative goods' continues to expand,

---

[31] Frey and Osborne, 'The Future of Employment'.
[32] Bakhshi, Frey and Osborne, 'Creativity vs Robots: The Creative Economy and the Future of Employment'.
[33] Osborne, Frey and Bakhshi, 'Creativity vs Robots'.
[34] CIC, 'UK Creative Employment'.
[35] Nathan et al., 'Creative Economy Employment in the US, Canada and the UK: A Comparative Analysis'.
[36] EY, 'Cultural Times: The First Global Map of Cultural and Creative Industries', 18, 22–23.

even as other trade falls.[37] But where these sectors are already large, they are also increasingly closed shops for young people from lower-income families.[38] If the creative industries are to be a route to good employment and reduced income inequality, public education needs to improve the pathways to access for children of all backgrounds.

For now, it seems probable that humans will prevail in domains that involve more unanticipated factors. Artificial intelligence tends to solve problems methodically but the human brain is far better at making logical leaps of imagination. It is more intuitive, creative and better at persuasion. Similarly, caring and empathy are not computers' strong suits, and many jobs, currently primarily undertaken by underpaid women, rely on these skills and capacities – a theme that will be discussed in Chapter 10. Even here, however, the new generation of robot 'health assistants' and even 'pets' may also impact. As Harari points out, while robots may not be about to fall in love with each other, we may be quite capable of falling in love with them.[39]

The key questions for policymakers and for educators to ask are:

1. How can *all* learners be best prepared for societies and economies where digital technologies drive opportunities and developments?
2. What kind of tasks do human beings perform better than machines?
3. What kind of tasks do machines perform better than humans? What kind of knowledge and skills do humans need to shape and direct that computing power to productive ends?
4. How can people be best prepared to learn and relearn the skills to do *human* work, rather than be second-class robots?

A serious debate is needed about these issues by educators and by system leaders. It isn't happening yet.

6.4 What Are the Implications for Educators?

Everything that has been set out above concerning the oncoming disruptions suggests that higher and higher levels of learning are

---

[37] UNCTAD, 'Creative Economy Bucks the Trend, Grows Despite Slowdown in Global Trade'.

[38] Shorthouse, *Disconnected*; O'Brien et al., 'Are the Creative Industries Meritocratic?'

[39] Harari, *Homo Deus* and see the movie *Her* (2013) for an exploration of this idea.

imperative for communities to thrive, and reverse current trends of inequalities. But what this learning should look like remains an open question. There is no panacea, no formula that provides easy answers to how to prepare young people for their future. As the conveners of the World Economic Forum state:

The debate on these transformations is often polarized between those who foresee limitless new opportunities and those that foresee massive dislocation of jobs. In fact, the reality is highly specific to the industry, region and occupation in question as well as the ability of various stakeholders to manage change.[40]

So, we propose that an explicit learning goal for the future should be:

To equip learners to navigate a disrupted and uncertain landscape of work

The intention here is not to argue for particular curriculum designs or specific pedagogical approaches. It is rather to present the compelling evidence for 'thinking big' about education as Boroskova termed it; and challenging the assumptions on which education policymakers and practitioners make their decisions. There are no 'safe bets'; just informed judgement calls. But let no one charge that such risks should not be taken with children's education, for that is *exactly* what is happening now through inaction. What is being demanded of political and business leaders applies equally to education policymakers and practitioners: we need to 'reset our intuitions' and desist from clinging to the belief that the future will be like the past.[41]

Some indicators do, though, emerge from the mass of evidence. The pre-eminence of technology in conditioning many of the changes to come points to the centrality of a familiarity with the principles of automation and machine learning. This is not to say that everyone needs to learn advanced computer science and engineering (many people don't know their way around the engine of a car, but know how to drive one) – but these subjects would surely be good bets on where to expend energy. These subjects – often grouped under the acronym 'STEM' (Science, Technology, Engineering, and Maths) – are already the focus of a number of educational initiatives around the world. Currently, differential exposure to and mastery of STEM

---

[40] World Economic Forum, 'The Future of Jobs: Employment, Skills and Workforce Strategy for the Fourth Industrial Revolution', 8.
[41] Dobbs, Manyika and Woetzel, *No Ordinary Disruption*, 8.

subjects is a central reason why coming changes are likely to bring about even higher levels of inequality and social exclusion. In many countries, the take-up of STEM subjects has remained stubbornly low, as has the class and gender bias in access.[42] This may in part be because of insufficient reinvention of what STEM is.[43] Studies of US initiatives find that too many are not truly integrating the study of the sciences and technology and have little focus on engineering.[44] New ways need to be found to engage *all* learners in STEM to a more serious degree: the Pathfinders in Chapter 6 show that this can be done.

Nonetheless, doing so requires us to understand the underlying reasons for the low participation in STEM among young learners. The lazy default is that STEM is hard, and most kids just aren't smart enough. But the reality is that *all* children can engage meaningfully with the concepts and practices of STEM if they are given engaging and well-designed learning opportunities. Different approaches to making maths relevant, engaging and accessible are becoming available. And new thinking about the questions of 'Which maths and why?' are critically important.[45] The shortage of qualified STEM teachers is a huge problem. But that is only insurmountable if the 'school' is conceived of in the old paradigm. Settings where the boundaries are permeable between the community, colleges, businesses and, critically, the digital world, can deliver great engaging STEM education. These are learning ecosystems, beyond 'fortress school', and we explore this idea and practice in Chapter 13. The introduction of machine learning and coding into schools demonstrates this need well: most schools will never have the teachers who can acquire and update their knowledge in this area to 'teach' the most up-to-date skills and knowledge. But when teachers design the learning experiences for kids in partnership with others – organisations like not-for-profit Apps for Good[46] – they expand the pool of resources available for learning and engage many more students.

[42] STEM Women, 'Percentages of Women in STEM Statistics'; Cambridge Assessment, 'The International Popularity of STEM Subjects'; UNESCO, *Cracking the Code: Girls' and Women's Education in Science, Technology, Engineering and Mathematics (STEM)*.
[43] IET, 'Studying Stem: What Are the Barriers?'
[44] Council, NAENR, *STEM Integration in K-12 Education*.
[45] Wolfram, Conrad, 'Making Maths Beautiful'.   [46] www.appsforgood.org

Current institutional arrangements in secondary or high school mean that too many students are 'tracked out' (or streamed out) of serious study of STEM subjects before they have a chance to even touch on modern science. Rethinking the pathways through STEM subjects is a vital part of ensuring that all students are exposed to the ways of thinking in terms of probability and algorithms, systems and mechanics. There is great potential for pedagogical advance in the teaching of these ways of thinking, currently held back by lack of curriculum change that delays these topics until only the quantitatively fluent students are left. Governments are in a bind: they cannot dictate mass curriculum change without the pedagogical readiness in the workforce, but that will not develop while teachers are focused on old curriculum. To break this deadlock, schools (in partnership with willing partners) must take the first steps.

The effort to increase to 100 per cent the numbers of children who engage more meaningfully with STEM is not about dumbing down. It is for sure about equity in the new conditions of society that we face. But it is also about widening the pool so that there will be *more* youngsters for whom the magnificence and utter wonder of science and maths is revealed. And from this wider pool, even greater numbers can drive on to be the theoretical physicists, bio-engineers or researchers. It can be both.

And, of course, learning must not be confined to the STEM subjects. We have observed the monumental decisions which individuals and societies will need to take in response to continued scientific discoveries that push at the boundaries of what it means to be 'human'. To participate in making these decisions responsibly, *wisely*, will require an additional and complementary sensibility. It won't be enough for more young people to be better and differently educated in STEM. We believe that this makes the perspectives that arise from deep engagement with the arts all the more important. So we have to be thinking 'STEAM' and support the advocates of arts and humanities education who see these areas of knowledge downgraded and at real risk – an issue developed in Chapters 10 and 11.

6.5 Learners as Navigators

The final feature of the unfolding landscape of work is its uncertainty, volatility and precariousness. More and more workers will be freelance, portfolio, distance (perhaps across many geographies), and serially reinventing themselves to engage with new opportunities and industries. Therefore, the competencies (knowledge, skills, values and attitudes) of the social and business entrepreneur will be highly desirable, irrespective of whether one works within a company, collective or in self-employment; in the transforming economies or the newly emergent ones; or in the sharing, artisanal and maker economies.[47]

Navigating this new landscape will certainly entail the acquisition of the twenty-first-century skills identified and advocated by many writers, and now taught and practiced in many schools. Chapter 7 looks at the work of some schools who are doing this, not *instead of* knowledge acquisition, but as a part of it, with a *more clearly defined purpose*. And doing it moreover in the circumstances in which it counts most – namely, real-world settings.

6.6 Work and Equality in 'Post-Work' Societies?

Before we leave the subject of employment though, we must acknowledge that many writers and forecasters do see this 'no ordinary disruption', leading to a loss of jobs on such a scale that it becomes realistic to talk about widespread, structural permanent unemployment.[48] Should this come to pass in the next 50 years, renewed democratic processes will become even more imperative, because the need will be to devise new societal arrangements in order to prevent the formation of a permanently excluded underclass without any hope of employment, ever. The eminent economist, Robert Skidelsky, has proposed that the working week needs to be reduced as a means to spread remaining employment opportunities more broadly.[49]

We still live in a profoundly work-centred society. It is not only the primary means by which people meet their material needs but also a key source of status, identity and – for some – purpose. Engagement in paid work marks the passage to maturity. Lack of a job can be seen as a signal of failure, or even lack of character.

If societies choose to create jobs at any cost, however, the immense gains that might be derived from the increased productivity of

---

[47] Zhao, *World Class Learners.*
[48] Mason, *PostCapitalism*; Very recently this topic has been explored in full by Susskind, *A World without Work.*
[49] Skidelsky, 'How to Work Less'.

computerisation might well be lost. The trap will be if, fearing mass unemployment, millions of unnecessary low-skill jobs are created, much as the old Soviet Union used to do. The optimistic vision of the future is that new forms of productivity enable more and more people to experience *reduced* hours of work while maintaining a decent income.

It may be that we will need to recreate the way we exchange our productive human potential for the income necessary to meet basic needs – but also to create more, not less, equal societies. The solution may be to de-couple work from wages. Some countries are already starting to experiment with a 'citizen wage' or Universal Basic Income (UBI). There has been an explosion of interest in this topic around the world, not least in the aftermath of COVID-19, when in effect a number of states took over paying citizens' wages in schemes to offset the catastrophic effects of business closures.

Finland was the first to commence a sustained trial of UBI in 2016 and there are experiments in countries as diverse as Canada, Brazil, Mexico, Kenya and Namibia.[50] The results of the trial in Finland suggested positive impacts, but the jury is still out on whether this policy option is the solution to increasing automation and structural unemployment.[51] A 2019 study by researchers at the New Economics Foundation carried out on behalf of the union Public Services International sheds doubt on ambitious claims made for UBI, such as that it would help to reduce poverty and narrow inequalities.[52] The research reviewed for the first time 16 practical projects that have tested different ways of distributing regular cash payments to individuals across a range of poor, middle-income and rich countries, as well as copious literature on the topic. It could find no evidence to suggest that such a scheme could be sustained for all individuals in any country in the short, medium or longer term – or that this approach could achieve lasting improvements in well-being or equality. The research confirms the importance of generous, non-stigmatising income support, but everything turns on how much money is paid, under what conditions and with what consequences for the welfare system as a whole. UBI remains, however, a policy element in the

[50] Parijs and Vanderborght, *Basic Income*.
[51] McRae, 'Latest Report on Finland's Universal Basic Income Trial Says It Makes People Happier'.
[52] Coote and Yazici, 'Universal Basic Income – A Union Perspective'.

repertoire of political leaders who prioritise equity. Those who hold that goal as a priority but are still unconvinced by UBI as a solution, regard the dignity, meaning and purpose that works confers as a major stumbling block. This is why it is a crucial concern for education.

The implications of this for identity and for a sense of self and personal meaning – and therefore the implications for learning – are explored in Chapter 10.

6.7 Equity – A Precondition for Thriving?

The first point to note is that enquiring into what makes for a thriving society uncovers the interesting and perhaps surprising evidence that thriving societies are not a function of how wealthy they are. In their seminal study *The Spirit Level*, Wilkinson and Pickett used evidence from a wide variety of peer-reviewed sources on incomes and income-distribution, health and social problems to look at the question of what makes communities thrive.[53] Counter-intuitively, their work demonstrates clearly how a *society's well-being is not determined by its overall wealth*. Across 11 different health and social areas: physical health, mental health, drug abuse, education, imprisonment, obesity, social mobility, trust and community life, violence, teenage pregnancies, and child well-being, outcomes are significantly worse in more unequal rich countries. When it comes to thriving societies, then, increases in wealth appear to be counteracted by increases in inequality: societies with a larger gap between rich and poor are bad for *everyone* – including the well-off. (See Figure 6.1.)

The implications of this finding are particularly significant in the light of the entrenched conditions that create rising income inequality and increasingly polarise the fortunes of both people and places.[54] A 2016 review by one of world's leading experts on globalisation, Branco Milanovic, finds that while global inequality is falling, principally because of China's rise, the global top 1 per cent in income terms saw their income rise, between 1988 and 2011, by 40 per cent.[55] In terms of wealth, the global top 1 per cent own about 46 per cent of all wealth. Or to put it perhaps more starkly, eight men (sic) own the same

---

[53] Pickett and Wilkinson, *The Spirit Level*.
[54] Atkinson, *Inequality*; Piketty and Goldhammer, *Capital in the Twenty-First Century*; Cowen, *Average Is Over*.
[55] Milanovic, *Global Inequality*.

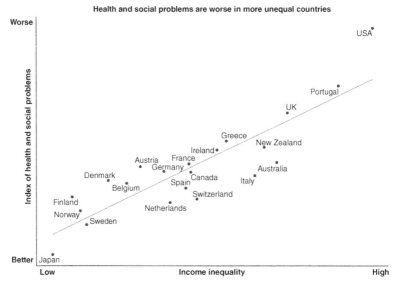

Figure 6.1 Health and social problems are worse in more unequal countries

wealth as the 3.6 billion people who make up the poorest half of humanity.[56]

Moreover, the great shifts noted in Chapter 3, especially in relation to technology, drive further in the direction of greater inequality, not less.

As Milanovic notes, very high inequality eventually becomes unsustainable. That is: unequal societies tend to be bellicose; wars are frequently one outcome.

He shows the intertwining of these economic developments with the political. The combined impact of globalisation, technological progress and the rising importance of finance leads to the emergence of plutocracy: a form of control that reinforces the tendency towards inequality. Analyses of the relationship between money and politics in the United States suggests a growing tendency towards plutocracy: Martin Gilens and Ben Page's study of policy decisions from the last 30 years indicates that new policies are more likely to follow the preferences of the top 10 per cent than the median income voter.[57] The wave of populist resurgence in the last decade, in response to these tendencies, now

[56] Oxfam, 'Just 8 Men Own Same Wealth as Half the World'.
[57] Gilens and Page, 'Testing Theories of American Politics'.

threatens some fundamental tenets of liberal democracies: open societies; gender and racial equality. The stakes are very high.

6.8 Democracy in Trouble

If addressing issues of inequality is a precondition of thriving, then a key lever is the active exercise of democracy. It is the imperfect but best of the available options. But the question in the transforming world is: What forms of democracy are now needed and what does this imply for learning?

The recent decade has been an interesting period for democracy. In a number of countries, electorates expressed their disdain for what became known as the 'political establishment' – which had been put in power by those electorates. Around the world, leaders have come to prominence on the basis of their 'anti-establishment' credentials.[58] Across Europe, new political parties gained profile, from both the left and from the right, that were *anti*-party. A prevalent sense of the alienation of electorates was palpable. History suggests that populist exploitation of this – while it has the potential to create regenerative change – is most likely lead to as yet unanticipated social upheaval.[59]

Perhaps we are at a staging point in the steady decline in the faith and belief people have in democratic institutions to make a difference to their lives or to the nature of the society they live in. It may be the age of 'democratic disappointment'. With very few exceptions, in democracies from the youngest (South Africa) to the oldest, scandals and revelations have revealed corruption, graft and manipulation in the institutions in which people used to have faith. In their research into democracy in 2018, the Pew Research Centre found that over half of voters from eight countries in Europe and North America said they were dissatisfied with how democracy is working.[60] Almost 70 per cent of Americans and French people say that their politicians are corrupt. Majorities in 7 of the 12 countries surveyed most dissatisfied with democracy said that in their country, no matter who wins an election, things do not change very much.

---

[58] TNN, 'Why Populist Leaders Are Shunning the Pundits'; Champion, 'The Rise of Populism'.
[59] Jordan and Mounk, 'What Populists Do to Democracies'.
[60] Kent, 'The Countries Where People Are Most Dissatisfied with How Democracy Is Working'.

This loss of faith in democracy is not without warrant. An important new study of US politics, *Democracy for Realists,* concludes that voters do not control the course of public policy, even indirectly.[61] Using a wide variety of data sources, the authors show that when parties are roughly evenly matched, elections often turn on irrelevant or misleading considerations such as economic spurts or downturns beyond the incumbents' control; the outcomes are essentially random, and not related to party performance or voter preferences. This situation is only exacerbated by the increasing potential for political parties to shape voter reality through social media.[62] While this phenomenon is known as 'fake news', it is perhaps more characterised simply as the rejection of objective reality as a basis for voter choices.[63]

Democracy cannot be defined merely by the power to vote, nor the rule of law. It must also include the active participation of people as citizens, in politics and civic life. By nearly every measure, Americans are less engaged in their communities and political activity than generations past.[64] Millennials are far less attached to organised politics, and have relatively low levels of social trust.[65] In the United Kingdom, alienation from the political system is strongest among those aged 18–24. Despite claims of a 'youthquake' in the 2017 election, turnout among this age group in 2015, 2017 and 2019 was under 50 per cent, and the lowest of all age groups.[66]

We should be deeply worried about this lack of participation – but not in order to buttress a set of inadequate and outmoded arrangements. There is widespread need for democratic renewal; a process that will involve citizens becoming involved in different ways in order to create a different form of polity. Can this 'season of democratic discontent' be turned into something positive? As Matthew Taylor of the RSA has put it:

To find ways of creating democratic processes and institutions that are fit for the 21st century, locally, nationally and internationally is a daunting, complex, long term challenge. But shouldn't we at least be looking?[67]

---

[61] Achen and Bartels, *Democracy for Realists.*
[62] Dice, *The True Story of Fake News.*
[63] Pomerantsev, *This Is Not Propaganda.*
[64] Campbell, Levinson and Hess, *Making Civics Count.*
[65] Pew Research Center, 'Millennials in Adulthood'.
[66] House of Commons Library, 'General Election 2019'.
[67] Taylor, 'Democratic Renewal, or Else …'

Young learners need to be a part of the process. So, a learning goal for thriving societies should be:

To prepare young people to reinvent and inhabit a democracy which is participative, authentic and meaningful

Most schools these days already make some kind of nod in the direction of 'creating active citizens', and in most countries 'civics' or citizenship education is part of a national or state curriculum. But the translation of these policies into practice has clearly not been enough to stem the tide of disillusion and disengagement with the active practice of democracy. Moreover, there is a plain disconnect between the aspirations that learners are introduced to in constitutions or political manifestos with their own lived reality.

The best citizenship educators know that the ultimate success of their endeavour cannot rely on the cognitive: just acquiring knowledge of the institutions, processes and traditions of the system within which one lives. Nor are opportunities to discuss and develop values, or to engage in volunteering in themselves sufficient. We have to start conceiving of democracy in education as something we co-create. And as something which is lived, and not just prepared for at some future date.

The good news is that there is now a strengthening field of innovation in the theory and practice of democracy, in which schools can participate. For example, NESTA, the UK innovation agency has its *Democratic Innovations* program, which is exploring the opportunities of blending digital and deliberative democracy; participative budgeting; transforming political engagement; citizens' juries and other alternatives to the structures and processes that have led to the current dysfunction.[68] Similar initiatives are pursued by GovLab in the United States.[69]

What does it look like when a school reinvents itself to put the values and processes of democracy (and new means to address them) at the heart of its own operation as an institution? What happens when, in addition to this internally facing practice, school communities become engaged with the wider community in which they live? What sort of learning happens then? Chapter 7 looks at the practice of schools doing just that, with inspiring and impressive results. They stand on the shoulders of many great traditions across the world, including the

---

[68] nesta, 'Democratic Innovations'.   [69] www.thegovlab.org/

Coalition of Essential Schools, established in the United States back in 1984, the Escuela Nueva model in Colombia founded in 1975 and the democratic schools of Israel, which grew through the 1970s and 1980s. The growth of these models and many others are starting to show that they can be the norm and not the beautiful exception. Their work would accelerate further and faster if their purpose became part of mainstream system narratives.

6.9 Democracy and Work: Still the Levers for Equality

This chapter has argued that thriving communities and countries need to address the issue of inequality more urgently than, and separately from, the creation of overall wealth if they are truly to thrive. The evidence shows that individual and societal well-being, and maybe even truly sustainable economic growth itself, depends on it.

The two levers to reduce inequality in the past have been spreading the dignity, improved personal prosperity and social mobility achieved by paid employment; and the democratic process, to ensure that the tools of the state are brought to bear on achieving equitable distribution of society's goods.

Of course this generalised statement masks a host of more detailed drivers. The five-year study *Inequalities in the Twenty First Century* (the Deaton Review) launched in 2019 by the Institute for Fiscal Studies in the United Kingdom will be asking some of the key questions around the nature and causes of inequality.[70] It will build on a range of research and scholarship such as Anthony Atkinson's *Inequality: What Can Be Done?*[71] How can policies that mitigate against inequality in the world (technological change, labour market institutions, family structures, globalisation, and indeed education systems themselves) be devised and implemented to attack this problem? Finding a way out of inequality is not a matter of individual effort, or personal agency, but of wider structural factors. Schools used to be viewed as engines of social mobility. It is recognised that they are not: for the most part, they reproduce the stratification of societies. However, if schools can address how their learners can become critical engaged citizens in the fullest sense, then it is possible that a different policy environment could be created.

[70] IFS, 'Inequalities in the Twenty-First Century'.   [71] Atkinson, *Inequality*.

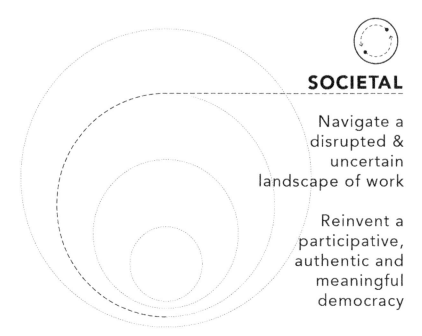

SOCIETAL

Navigate a
disrupted &
uncertain
landscape of work

Reinvent a
participative,
authentic and
meaningful
democracy

Figure 6.2 The societal level

We believe that the only way to address these is through renewed democracy. Milanovic's work draws out the incompatibility between ever-rising inequality and genuine democracy. Democratic processes are under increasing strain and focus – and that is good, because it is the precursor to renewal.

We recognise that there is a value base implicit in this stance. We do assert, unashamedly, that the values of liberal democracy underpin our approach. Just as there are some goals and values (for example, safeguarding the future of the planet and its biodiversity, and universal human rights) that are fundamental, so for us the liberal democratic concepts of freedom under the law; independent judiciaries; protection of the rights of minorities; the freedoms of the press, of individual speech and academic enquiry are all at the bedrock of truly thriving societies.

In Chapter 7, the work of pathfinder schools who have adopted this goal is explored: preparing their students to question assumptions, understand systems, and engage in political change.

7 | *Pathfinders for Thriving Societies*

A lot of people are looking for what the new model is supposed to be. I think what we really need are many, many different alternatives. ... In order to be effective, a school has to have a purpose.

Robin Lake, *Education Week*, June 2016

Robin Lake is Director of the Center on Reinventing Public Education[1] (CRPE), a research centre based in Seattle, Washington state. CRPE primarily studies the spread of charter schools: the US school type initially intended to bring innovation and teacher empowerment to schools in the United States. Charter schools have become contentious since the first policies enabling them were introduced in the 1990s, but in addition to issues about their overall impact, the spread of charters has created a debate about the way education leaders can define and design a school around specific purposes. And as some leaders become more conscious that their students are exiting into a world very different from the one they grew up in, these purposes are likewise starting to shift.

The previous chapter discussed how thriving at the societal level is undermined by increased income inequality, with every indication that this will become exacerbated by future trends. To successfully tackle inequality, schools need to engage with two future-focused purposes: to prepare learners to navigate a disrupted landscape of work; and to reinvent a more participative democracy. As outlined in the Chapter 6, we see these goals as intertwined because the evidence suggests that without a restructuring of our political economy the prospect of supporting oneself through good work will become increasingly scarce, no matter how prepared young people are. Rescuing our businesses and democracies from the threat of oligarchy is obviously not a task that can be laid at the feet of schools alone. But enculturating young people

[1] www.crpe.org

into lives as proactive citizens and workers is something that schools can do.

This chapter focuses primarily on US public schools in order to illustrate how educators are pursuing these goals in a context where questions of equity are an unavoidable part of any design. Inequities by race, in terms of access to well-resourced schools, remain a blight on the US public education system, matched only by inequities by class (wealth, income and educational background of parents).[2] American schools that set their eyes on the future do so at the risk of thereby ignoring and inadvertently perpetuating deep societal inequalities. The schools we feature here are ones that are trying to balance this tension, pursuing future-focused goals in a way that also addresses inequities, in any way they can.

Such schools are though by no means limited to the United States. Preparing learners for work post the 'fourth industrial revolution' is a goal of well-established schools such as the Australian Science and Mathematics School[3] in South Australia, or Connect Charter School[4] in Alberta. There are democratic schools all over the world whose core purpose is to create young people who are active participants with decision-making power.[5] To do this, however, most have had to establish as private schools, which inevitably rations their accessibility. Many other newer entrants could be added to this list.[6] In the United States, however, we see discernible signs of a significant new movement.

7.1 City as STEM-School

MC[2] STEM High School[7] in Cleveland, Ohio, was founded in 2008, as part of an initial wave of STEM-focused schools now spread thickly across the United States. As a city built on the back of manufacturing, Cleveland suffered major hits to employment in the late twentieth century, and was among the first US cities to focus intentionally on reinventing its landscape of work. In the early 2000s, the Mayor,

---

[2] Duncan and Murnane, *Whither Opportunity?*; Fahle et al., 'Racial Segregation and School Poverty in the United States, 1999–2016'; Reardon, Kalogrides and Shores, 'The Geography of Racial/Ethnic Test Score Gaps'.
[3] www.asms.sa.edu.au/   [4] http://connectcharter.ca/
[5] Education Revolution, 'Democratic Schools – Find a School'.
[6] For a full review see Hannon, Gillinson and Shanks, *Learning a Living*.
[7] www.mc2stemhighschool.org/

Jane Campbell, along with Cleveland State University and companies such as Intel began directing energies towards transforming Cleveland into a technology hub. MC^2 was founded amid this activity, capitalising on the willingness of local institutions and employers to support – both ideologically and with resources – a new kind of school.

MC^2 is an entirely project-based school, where subject learning is integrated into multi-disciplinary projects, each culminating in a 'capstone' where students design and build a product demonstrating what they have learned. The school was designed with the purpose of preparing students to be both competent in STEM *and* entrepreneurial. Every aspect of the design reinforces this purpose, including the timetable: students work on ten-week cycles, allowing for the completion of extended projects, followed by a short break. The synergy between time and learning design maintains motivation and momentum throughout the year.

What really sets MC^2 apart from other STEM schools is the way it situates students within work contexts – preparing them for lives that are likely to involve continuous learning as part of work. Classes are held not in a school building but at learning sites belonging to businesses, universities and the city of Cleveland. In their first year at the school, ninth-grade students are based at the Great Lakes Science Center, a science and technology museum and exhibition centre. Students study in the custom-built classrooms created on the ground floor, built with support from local foundations, surrounded by a culture of informal learning.

The following year, as tenth-graders, they transition to the Nela Park campus of General Electric (GE). Here, their year includes a five-week experience working with GE volunteers to develop and prototype (for now) a unique lighting fixture. Students form a 'business' of three to five students, and each receive dedicated sessions with their GE mentors covering each stage of the business development cycle, from understanding the science of alternative energy sources, to engineering a product and developing a marketing strategy. The support materials for the project are developed by the GE team and evolve each year. Students not only learn cutting-edge science and business operations, but also learn that this knowledge is continually evolving, and therefore the that the world of work is also one of learning.

Eleventh- and twelfth-grade students are based at Cleveland State University, preparing them to transition into their next phase of learning (whether there or at another higher education institution). The site is home to a FabLab, the model of a maker space developed at MIT, and here created with funds from two further Ohio-based foundations. Alongside their project-based classes, students in the final years can opt to take internships to explore career options, ranging from three weeks to as long as a year. The school's extensive links with local businesses means that every internship is supervised by a workplace advisor, and the school-based internship coordinator ensures that students are well matched and evaluates a student's reflective work to ensure that they are gaining value from their placement.

MC^2 is non-selective, and students are admitted by lottery from across the district. It is a Title I school, meaning that at least 40 per cent of the student body is eligible for free school meals (though this proportion has been as high as 85 per cent at the school). It prepares these students with contemporary knowledge and direct access to the world of work. Many other STEM schools in the United States are magnet schools, often selective entry requirements that reinforce a notion that knowledge of science, technology and engineering is suitable only for high-achieving students who will enter a narrow range of careers. Yet on the contrary, as described in the previous chapter, a STEM education is not just about ensuring a steady supply of top-end scientists, but about giving all young people the ability to understand the tools and knowledge that will shape their work lives – and increasingly the nature of our societies. This calls for a different vision of who STEM education is for and how it can be provided.

7.2 STEM – or STEAM – for All

When it comes to reducing inequality in education, schools have to promote this purpose not just in their curriculum and pedagogy, but also in their very design. Larry Rosenstock, founder of the now-renowned High Tech High schools in San Diego, created the schools first and foremost not to teach students to be problem-solvers, but to overcome high school structures that separated young people from opportunities:

At best our schools perpetuated race and class inequality. At worst, they promoted it, by tracking students by 'ability' and 'vocation', which in truth were a proxy for their skin colour and the education level of their parents.[8]

Rosenstock describes here the long struggle that the United States has had with realising the vision of comprehensive high school education. Where many countries separate young people into different learning opportunities at 16, 15 or even 10 years old, US high schools ostensibly offer the same learning opportunities to all. In practice, this is rarely the case: while explicit tracking (the allocation of students into academic or vocational pathways) has mostly phased out, de facto tracking still occurs through self-selection or gentle guidance into more and less demanding courses. Moreover, most 'lower tracks' are not truly vocational, but merely less demanding versions of the same general requirements. This practice is dangerous not only because it tends to replicate historical inequalities, but also because it prevents all students from experiencing an education that is rich in both academic and vocational learning opportunities.

High Tech High's design features – the class groups matched to just two teachers, the lack of hundreds of separate courses, the project-based pedagogy – were all developed to realise the vision of a high school that could achieve an education that combined 'head and hand' for *all* students. Equity remains a central priority for the High Tech High schools and is articulated as such as one of their four renewed design principles.[9] This principle represents the belief that to really reduce inequalities, schools have to be designed to do so from top to bottom.

Integrating the sciences with the arts and humanities is a central purpose of High Tech High, and is evident in the stunning work displayed all around the schools. As such, High Tech High is often called on as an example of the power of 'STEAM': a movement initiated at the Rhode Island School of Design to thread Arts and Design pedagogy throughout a science- and maths-heavy school

---

[8] Rosenstock, 'I Used to Think . . . That Traditional Public Education Was the Institution with the Most Promise . . .'
[9] High Tech High, 'High Tech High – About Us' The founding principles for High Tech High were: personalisation, adult world connection, common intellectual mission and teacher-as-designer.

curriculum. STEAM practices are flourishing in places such as the Da Vinci schools, Quest to Learn, and increasingly in school districts.

The spread of these one-offs is promising, but one of the distinguishers of High Tech High is that it has managed to grow a school model into a footprint of 12 schools, serving a significant part of the San Diego community. What does it take to provide high-level science, technology, maths and arts knowledge for *all* students, at scale?

7.3 Systematising STEAM

Directly west across the United States from Cleveland, just before the Rocky Mountains, is Denver, capital of Colorado. After being severely hit by the falling price of oil in the late 1980s, Denver has long since been attracting workers again, and in 2015 was *Forbes's* no. 1 place in the United States to build a career. In line with this growth, the city's school district has been trying to up its game, and is home to a wide variety of efforts – often politically contentious ones – to rethink public education.

One of these is DSST Public Schools[10]: a chain of seven middle and high school campuses with four more to open in the next few years. As a charter management organisation working closely with the Denver Public school district, DSST runs a group of inclusive STEM schools. Aligned with the theme of promoting learning beyond science and technology, two of the new campuses the network is set to open will provide enhanced opportunities to specialise in the arts and humanities.

DSST began in 2004 with one high school, the original Denver School of Science and Technology from which the chain takes its name. This school, now known as DSST Stapleton, remains the chain's highest performing, and has received national recognition for 100 per cent college acceptance rate. This success has not been achieved easily: the school has adopted a relatively traditional pedagogy that not all students warm to, but it is unrelenting in fulfilling its purpose of preparing all students for real scientific work. Irrespective of the student's level on arrival – and as an open-enrolment school many arrive with widely different levels of preparation in maths and writing – by the time they leave all students have studied pre-Calculus, participated

---

[10] www.dsstpublicschools.org/

in a trimester-long internship, and completed a year-long research project researching and addressing a local problem, culminating in a presentation of a tangible product, a 10–20 page research paper and an oral defence. Senior projects are completed in conjunction with one of two courses: biochemistry combined with the study of biotechnology, or physics combined with engineering. These courses are also structured around long-term projects of one or two months, where students are learning to work out a science problem from scratch. By the time they leave, students are prepared not just on paper but to apply and articulate the value of their knowledge.

To ensure that all students can tackle this demanding array of courses and assessments, the school has developed a mastery-based assessment system to identify exactly when and where students are struggling, and offers both online and early morning tutoring to help them catch up. They also offer carefully designed courses to engage students in the study of engineering and illustrate applied mathematics. The ninth-grade 'Creative Engineering' course is scheduled for longer periods each week than regular classes and is carried out in the form of projects. Through a partnership with nearby University of Colorado Boulder, the Engineering faculty visited in its early years to oversee the teaching of advanced engineering courses, preparing final students for guaranteed admission to CU Boulder's Engineering School upon reaching a fixed grade point average.

As a network, DSST stands out for its long-term vision. Supported by the Denver Public School District, they plan to open four more campuses, to ultimately provide education for 10,500 students across Denver. They are taking a niche model of education and trying to make it the new public school reality.

DSST, like MC², relies on partnerships with local institutions: these schools could not fulfil their purpose to prepare all young people for a new world of work – could not provide every student with an internship, high-level courses, or access to cutting-edge equipment – without support from local foundations, higher education institutions and employers. What does it take to grow an ecosystem for this kind of real-world learning?

Ecosystems from the Inside, Out

The Metropolitan Regional Career and Technical Center – known simply as 'The Met' – is a high school in the city of Providence,

Rhode Island, founded in 1996. It was created by Dennis Littky and Elliot Washor, who had been invited by the Rhode Island Commissioner of Education to create a 'school for the 21st century'. Littky and Washor built on their past work at Thayer High School in New Hampshire, where they had seen disaffected students completely re-engage with education once they were given real work to do. To develop this vision, they created a new NGO, The Big Picture Company, which would be able to support and foster the kind of roles necessary for a school to partner with local employers.

The Met today is the flagship of Big Picture Learning, a network of over 100 schools across the United States as well as in Australia, New Zealand, the Netherlands, Italy and Canada. As at MC^2 and DSST, students complete internships, but these take up to two full days each week and continue throughout a student's entire school career. To support this model, each Big Picture school team employs one or more 'Learning through Internships' coordinators, who create the contacts so that students can choose from lists of local organisations. The coordinators are responsible for developing relationships with key adults at each organisation who can work as mentors for students.

The Met has gone one step further in developing a school where students can directly learn how to create their own opportunities. In 2005, Littky met Bill Daugherty, a successful media entrepreneur working with the Network for Teaching Entrepreneurship. Daugherty was looking for a way to deepen the teaching of innovation and business in schools, and Littky was glad to benefit from his experience. They started a collaboration and Daugherty developed a curriculum, Entrepreneurship 360, to teach students all the necessary stages of starting a business. In 2010, Littky raised the funds to build a special-purpose Center for Innovation and Entrepreneurship on the Met site. Through E360, 20 start-ups have been founded right on site at the Met, and Met students have won numerous local and national entrepreneurship competitions.

E360 is just one example of how Littky and Washor have leveraged the profile of the Met to create an ecosystem that allows the school – and now five other Big Picture schools in Providence – to fulfil a purpose of linking students with real work and create future opportunities. Schools without that profile could do worse than look to the ecosystems being created outside schools, often by institutions that already have one foot in the future.

Ecosystems from the Outside, In

Carnegie Mellon is one of the most famous research universities in the world, known for its interdisciplinary programs and as a leader in key contemporary fields such as artificial intelligence, product design and renewable energies. Situated just three miles from downtown Pittsburgh, one of the largest cities in New York State, the university is also a key partner in the city's development of technology-based jobs.

A central hub for this activity is the Community Robotics, Education and Technology Empowerment (CREATE) Lab,[11] an initiative to support sustained engagement between the university and local groups. One of the lab's projects is to develop new kits and curricula that allow children to work with cutting-edge technologies. Researchers work with local schools to design tools that are easy to start using and then release them online in open-source formats. One of their early products was the Hummingbird kit,[12] which provides key pieces of circuit boards to allow learners to create robots using basic art supplies.

The CREATE Lab is part of Remake Learning, a major Pittsburgh-wide initiative supported by national foundations including the Macarthur Foundation. It is part of a new network known as LRNG, a group of cities across the United States working to create new ecosystems for learning based outside of schools or online.[13]

Remake Learning has spread from supporting small-scale projects on classroom pedagogy, to creating new frameworks in which whole schools can embrace new learning goals and purposes. In September 2014, the network convened to begin defining a new set of competencies to shape the learning pathways young people might follow through LRNG opportunities.[14] The competencies describe new areas of knowledge and skills, such as robotics, coding and gaming, media making, and indeed STEAM. The concrete definitions are supplements to a core school curriculum, defining the technical and ethical skills necessary to operate in a more technologically advanced society. They include a set of cross-cutting competencies, such as systems thinking and prototyping – skills now relevant for a variety

---

[11] http://cmucreatelab.org/   [12] www.hummingbirdkit.com/
[13] http://about.lrng.org/products/   [14] http://remakelearning.org/competencies/

of industries and sectors, and that can be taught explicitly, but that often fall through the cracks of traditional school curricula.

This initiative is just one example of how we might question the knowledge that is prioritised in STEM schools – and school more generally. In *Four Dimensional Education,* the authors look at what futures-awareness implies for curriculum selection and de-selection.[15] Their arguments for the replacement of certain areas of mathematics and science knowledge are strong and compelling, and should provide one foundation for the evolution of STEM education.

The collaborative process by which Remake Learning developed new competencies is an example of communities taking responsibility for the future well-being of their young people and their local economy. To see this kind of activity flourish on a larger scale, it will be necessary to curb a declining trend in the impact of democratic activity. This brings us to the second future-focused goal that we argue needs to become more central if we are to sustain thriving, more equal societies: to prepare learners to reinvent a more participative democracy.

7.4 Rebuilding Democracy

Practising democracy in unequal societies requires more than the conventional experiences of today's citizenship education. In the United States, there is a long – if still small – tradition of modelling schooling on democratic citizenship. The most famous and the model for many others is the Sudbury Valley School,[16] an independent school in Framingham, Massachusetts, established in 1968. Depending on how you choose to frame it, Sudbury Valley is either proof of the power of self-directed education, or proof that privileged children will do fine educationally whatever schooling they choose. We think it is worth taking seriously, however, that a community which focuses first and foremost on giving children freedom within a well-supported structure that requires them to take responsibility for preserving it, does seem to thrive.

Most 'democratic schools' are, like Sudbury, independent schools. But some have managed to sustain within public school system. This includes the 'school-within-a-school' at Brookline High School.

---

[15] Fadel, Trilling and Bialik, *Four-Dimensional Education.*
[16] https://sudburyvalley.org/

The school-within-a-school (SWS) is made up of 120 students who are part of the larger public high school. Unlike the rest of the school, SWS is run as a democratic community. Students have a weekly community meeting to deliberate on activities and matters of culture, and the offering of English courses is decided through a process of voting. Science and history follow common courses, although the history curriculum is more rigorously critical than one would find in many US high schools.

SWS was founded in 1970, a time that Dan Bresman, an English teacher and the current head of the program describes it, of 'Vietnam war era protests, the emergence of alternative ways of doing things, and a decentralised version of authority, and a group of students and staff who wanted to do something differently'. The approach has evolved a lot over the years, in particular in its decision to integrate closely with the main school. This does not require young people to give up the institutions of high school – sports, the cafeteria, additional electives. It has also helped it evolve from a program that attracted 'the burnouts, the smokers,' to one with a much more diverse reputation.

Students at Brookline decide whether they want to join the smaller community after their freshman year (year 10), and are admitted by lottery. A focus for the staff has been maintaining a group of students who are broadly representative of the school – they are conscious of the fate of many such 'alternate' programs in becoming either a tool of elite closure or a dumping ground. Keeping the size at roughly 120 allows for the whole community to fit in one room for the weekly community meeting, and is large enough that they can offer a full timetable of classes for 20–25 kids. Maintaining those class sizes is part of the key that keeps the programs low-cost and has helped to sustain it.

7.5 From Democracy to Social Justice

The self-described 'Democratic schools' label can be found across the world (Wikipedia helpfully has a list, by country). Most, however, are democratic in an inward-facing sense: students are highly participative in the running of the institution, and the defining feature of these schools is their promotion of student voice. Invaluable as this is, perhaps the more significant of the new pathfinders are those who also have an outward-facing orientation – and are more future-focused as a result.

The June Jordan School for Equity (JJSE)[17] was founded in 2003 as part of a parent-and-teacher-led movement to open a number of small schools within the San Francisco Unified School District, with a particular emphasis on reflecting the needs of their communities. The work of the school is oriented towards developing students into active members of their society, including learning to identify and remedy societal injustice. Like DSST, June Jordan is an open-enrolment 'college prep' school. The school population is majority low-income (in terms of being eligibility for free lunch) and the school has the second highest college eligibility rate in the state). But all coursework is designed to expose students to tools and experiences to make them 'agents of positive change'. Students study an ethnic studies curriculum to develop their ability to take multiple perspectives and integrate their knowledge of history, arts and social science. Class assignments take the form of projects that culminate in oral presentations to parents and community members.

Students then learn to demonstrate their commitment to justice in real action. All eleventh and twelfth grade students commit to weekly community-based internships every Wednesday afternoon. In parallel with work-based internships, these involve students learning what it means to improve their community, and take responsibility for the well-being of those around them.

Project-based learning or pedagogies, such as youth participatory action research,[18] are not the only way of engaging in civic action through schools, but they offer pedagogical frameworks that help teachers and students take the first steps. Kiran Bir Sethi, founder of Design for Change, an international movement of teachers and students completing design thinking projects in their communities, believes that offering a framework is a crucial first step: 'Schools get the relevance, but the "how to" is the biggest challenge'.[19] Sethi and others have done the work to create tools that teachers find useful and useable, from one-week starter projects to entire year-long design

---

[17] www.jjse.org/
[18] For example, Duncan-Andrade and Morrell, *The Art of Critical Pedagogy*.
[19] Interview with Sethi, May 2016

thinking curricula. They are ready for the schools who want to make change.

7.6 A Drop in the Ocean or Making Waves?

All of the schools featured in this chapter are taking steps to prepare young people for a future that will make new demands on them and on their societies. Interestingly, there is something of a divide between schools that major on entrepreneurialism and STEM, and those that promote democracy through literature and history. This difference across the disciplines reflects a curriculum balance that often remains tacit in other schools: that science is for those who are career-oriented, while English, or more generally literature, is a subject for identity development and exploration of diversity. What this means for the development of students who gravitate towards one or other of these areas – often on the basis of early facility with reading or maths – or those who do not immediately flourish at *either* – is an important question. There is no question that subjects – disciplines – are needed as a grounding of curriculum and pedagogy, but they can go onto shape much more than that. Even innovative schools can struggle to break out of their categories.

More and more are trying, however. Just in the United States, there are numerous other small schools that offer young people a chance to learn how to create value from their ideas, and take charge of their futures. Some new ones have benefitted from the XQ 'Super Schools' initiative, funded by Lauren Jobs.[20] Many more longstanding ones are associated with the Expeditionary Learning network and the work of Ron Berger.[21]

Around the world, there are flagship innovation schools in the Netherlands, Spain and Beijing.

Many of these schools are small independent schools, or state schools that attract only an ambitious minority. If only a small number of children are prepared quite differently for the future – prepared to take and create opportunities, see the system and make change – then we will be creating a new source of inequality, in addition to those that already persist.

---

[20] xqsuperschool.org   [21] Berger, *An Ethic of Excellence*

As Larry Rosenstock emphasises, schools have to recognise that to contribute to reduced inequality, it is not enough to refine one pedagogy and do the best to teach the students who are in front of you: in too many countries, a history of tracking or streaming means that considerable structural changes are necessary if *all* students are going to have access to the abstract knowledge *and* real-world experiences that prepare them to thrive in a disrupted work landscape. To successfully place equity at the centre of public education, *we need to more directly design around future-focused goals.*

The other thing we learn from looking at these schools is that even a well-designed school cannot do it alone. To prepare students to thrive in disrupted societies, all these schools rely on an ecosystem of partners to provide students with that crucial ingredient: the unpredictability of real-world experiences. No amount of classroom study can match experiences such as internships, community service, and employer-led projects for developing confidence and resilience to handle oneself in unfolding circumstances. *All* students are going to need those experiences, so *the work of building learning ecosystems needs to accelerate now.*

The good news is that the number of social entrepreneurs (often young teachers who want to contribute in a different way) available to facilitate and populate these networks (in the way that LRNG is doing at scale) is growing by the day. Organisations such as Teach a Man to Fish in Guatemala, Nicaragua and Honduras,[22] Hive Learning Networks and communities in 13 cities from Toronto to Mombasa,[23] *Bairro Educador* (The Educating Neighbourhood) in Rio de Janeiro[24] and many others are becoming a part of the thick learning mesh we need. What we need to do now is broker the connections and make every school part of a learning ecosystem that comprises more than just schools. We return to this subject in Chapter 13.

---

[22] www.teachamantofish.org.uk/enterprising-schools-network
[23] https://hivelearningnetworks.org/
[24] www.cidadeescolaaprendiz.org.br/projetos/bairro-educador-rio-de-janeiro/

8 | The Interpersonal Purpose
Growing Strong Bonds

With the advent of social robots, for the first time we will share our planet with an intelligent alien species. Rather than descending from Alpha Centauri, the aliens will be the products of our own wealthiest corporations, all destined to monetise us with the same vigour as today's internet. The social robots are coming, and they will unleash both celebration and anxiety.

Illah Nourbakhsh, Professor of Robotics at Carnegie Mellon University[1]

For many, perhaps most, people, a thriving life depends on the capacity to form and sustain interpersonal relationships of different sorts: from the most intimate and long term, to the pleasures and supports of friendship, to the amicable co-existence with neighbours. The quality of relationships with other people – family, friends, lovers, co-workers – is at the heart of whether life is satisfying or not. There is now strong longitudinal research evidence to support this intuitive sense. The Harvard Study of Adult Development has tracked 724 men for over 75 years and studied the quality of their lives.[2] Begun in 1938, it is the longest and most comprehensive study of its kind in the world. The director of the study summed up the findings of the research with refreshing simplicity:

The clearest message that we get from this 75-year study is this: Good relationships keep us happier and healthier. Period.[3]

But this is not often conceived of as a *learning* issue. If the good life is built with good relationships, is it to be left to chance and intuition? Surely it is genuinely a learning challenge too. Therefore, we suggest that to thrive at this level entails learning the following:

---

[1] Nourbakhsh, 'Fears and Joys of a Life with Social Robots'.
[2] harvardstudy, 'Harvard Second Generation Study'.
[3] Waldinger, 'Transcript of "What Makes a Good Life?"'

- *To develop loving and respectful relationships in diverse, technologised societies*
- *To engage with, and learn from, other generations*

Before turning to the role that schools should have in this space, let us examine more deeply the implications of the key shifts identified in Chapter 2, as they relate to interpersonal relationships.

8.1 Technology-Shaped Relationships?

One of the findings of Chapter 2 was the penetration of technology into ever more aspects of our lives at a pace that is accelerating as artificial intelligence (AI) develops, communication networks become ever faster and more ubiquitous, and devices mediate more of our interactions. The COVID-19 shutdown and resulting self-isolation rendered millions dependent on technology to maintain social connection. The more than 1 billion young people between the ages of 15 and 24 in the world today are the most connected and mobile generation the world has ever seen. It is estimated that 71 per cent of 15 to 24-year-olds in the world today are online.[4] In the United Kingdom, the regulator Ofcom has highlighted that children under the age of 11 have signed up for social media accounts, even though there is supposed to be a minimum age imposed by the social media companies.[5] An analysis of the Millennium Cohort Study in the United Kingdom found that girls spend far more time using social media than boys, and also that they are much more likely to display signs of depression linked to their interaction on platforms such as Instagram, WhatsApp and Facebook.[6]

It is a fine paradox that in an age when, at one level, young people have become connected as never before in history – with all the scope that brings for the development of thick and diverse social networks, and inter-cultural awareness – there are grounds for concern about the quality of interpersonal relationships as a result.

Are we substituting 'connecting' for true attention? Simone Weil wrote that attention is the rarest and purest form of generosity. However, as many increasingly prefer a text to a conversation

---

[4] UNICEF, *Children in a Digital World*.
[5] Young, 'Social Media Being Used by Growing Number of Children under 11 despite Age Limits'.
[6] Kelly et al., 'Social Media Use and Adolescent Mental Health'.

(checking in without getting too entangled), we retreat from the emotional work of being really present.

8.2 Empathy – The Casualty?

A serious concern is for the development of *empathy*. We use this term colloquially to mean imagining what another person is feeling, but the formal definition usefully distinguishes two parts: the ability to recognise another person's thoughts and feelings ('cognitive empathy'), and the ability to respond with an appropriate emotion to those thoughts and feelings ('affective empathy'). A study linking self-reports to genotyping has concluded that, while there is an element of heritability, empathy is largely a developed trait.[7] As was evidenced in Chapter 6, some argue that it is one of the few human features that distinguish us from robots. Moreover, the development of empathy is absolutely at the heart of the reduction of violence. And it can be *learned*.

Yet there is growing evidence to suggest that empathy may be a casualty of the hyper-connected age. No longer are technological tools simply shaped by humans: the tools are shaping us. Psychologists are reporting a sharp drop in empathy levels among college students.[8] Some researchers suggest that we are living in a 'narcissism epidemic' – enveloped in a culture of self-obsession.[9] Increasing numbers of ever-younger children engaging with screens rather than playing with others gives rise to a fear of a Mowgli generation, raised by technology not humans. An interesting variant is how voice-controlled technologies may influence interactive styles.[10] Parents are starting to notice their children imitating the way they bark orders at their voice-based system controlling the lights, room thermostat, stereo and so on. We are not used to being polite to gadgets.[11] Perhaps we will need to become so.

---

[7] Warrier et al., 'Genome-Wide Analyses of Self-Reported Empathy'.
[8] Konrath, O'Brien and Hsing, 'Changes in Dispositional Empathy in American College Students Over Time'.
[9] Twenge and Campbell, *The Narcissism Epidemic*.
[10] Rudgard, '"Alexa Generation" May Be Learning Bad Manners from Talking to Digital Assistants, Report Warns'.
[11] Though technology companies are eager to help us; Alexa now has a 'polite' mode that prompts the speaker to say please. See Thompson, 'May A.I. Help You?'

Of course, there have always been moral panics about the young and their fascination with new technology. Similar fears were expressed about TV (but that does not mean they were wrong). However, the difference today is both the ubiquity and extremity.

Humans are ever more wedded to their devices – 'always on'. Many now log on before they roll out of bed; compulsively check their devices throughout the day; and commune with their screen as the last thing they do before sleep. Data from the OECD PISA results (on student attitudes) show a significant proportion – in some countries up to 80 per cent – of 15-year-olds 'feeling bad' if they were not connected to the Internet.[12] In the most recent of a series of global surveys of mobile phone use carried out by the consulting firm Deloitte, almost 40 per cent of adults in the United Kingdom felt they were using their phone too much. The Pew Research Center drew on a nationally representative sample of 13–17-year-olds in the United States and found that 54 per cent said they spend 'too much' time on a phone.[13] Researchers are currently debating whether 'problematic' use of mobile phones and the Internet amount to addiction[14] and gaming addiction is already recognised as a clinical condition.[15] It is too soon to say how these data will be effected by the transfer to technology of social interaction during the time of the pandemic.

This sense that technology is not just ubiquitous but irresistible is unique to our time and, as we have seen, may intensify with wearables and implants. Interestingly, however, in some contexts smartphone ownership is plateauing and even decreasing – albeit from highs of 97 per cent among 18–24-year-olds.[16] Apps are now available to track phone usage and help people to cut down. The same Pew study in the United States found 52 per cent of teens reporting that they were taking steps to cut down on phone use. Young people are already showing signs of wanting to resist the dominance of technology over their lives – and with good reason.

---

[12] OECD, 'PISA 2015 Results (Volume III) Students Wellbeing', 23.
[13] Jiang, 'How Teens and Parents Navigate Screen Time and Device Distractions'.
[14] Panova and Carbonell, 'Is Smartphone Addiction Really an Addiction?'
[15] NHS, 'Children Treated for Computer Gaming Addiction under NHS Long Term Plan'.
[16] Deloitte, 'Plateauing at the Peak the State of the Smartphone', 5.

8.3 The Dark Side of Connectedness

Scepticism about phones reflects a growing feeling that devices are getting in the way of rather than facilitating good connections. Studies on cyberbullying highlight the effect of online versus offline interaction on empathetic concern and bystanding.[17] While cyberbullying has in many ways just replaced the bullying between youth that has always occurred, the medium means that bullies – and victims – are typically experiencing the activity while physically separated, suggested that cyberbullying is both experienced and perpetrated as a more individual act, with increased potential to cause anxiety.[18]

But it is access to extreme images that gives the greatest concern for the future of human relationships. Pornography is now easily available to all, and it is an extremely vigilant parent or carer who can ensure that their child cannot access it. Research indicates that that around 40 per cent of boys in England aged 14–17 regularly watch pornography; and one in five harbour extremely negative attitudes towards women.[19] Similar data are found for the United States;[20] in Australia, one study indicates that the *average age* of first-time exposure to pornography is 12.2 years.[21]

We should also be clear that we are not talking here about a 'mere' extension of 'lads mags'. The images available are extremely dehumanising and frequently violent. They celebrate the degradation of women and normalise sexual aggression. A growing body of research suggests that young people suffer serious negative impacts from a hyper-sexualised culture.[22] There is intense pressure to conform to expectations deriving from porn, leading to grotesquely dehumanising behaviours, which young people find difficult to understand how to resist. As one research study of young people's attitudes captured it:

---

[17] Barlińska, Szuster and Winiewski, 'Cyberbullying among Adolescent Bystanders'.
[18] Kowalski, Limber and Agatston, *Cyber Bullying*.
[19] NSPCC, '40% of Teenage Girls Pressured into Having Sex'; Rallings, 'Youth and the Internet: A Guide for Policy Makers'.
[20] DeAngelis, 'Children and the Internet – Web Pornography's Effect on Children'.
[21] Pratt, 'The "Porn Genie" Is out of the Bottle: Understanding and Responding to the Impact of Pornography'.
[22] Collins et al., 'Sexual Media and Childhood Well-Being and Health'.

'he's the stud and she's the slut'[23] For girls, the exposure to porn also sets up unrealistic and oppressive expectations of how they should look and feel during sex.[24]

8.4 *Literally* Technology-Shaped Relationships ...

One further twist to the degree to which technology is entering the space of our intimate relationships is that of the sex robot market. There has been a market in sex toys/dolls perhaps immemoriably. However, with the introduction of AI and advanced production techniques, it is now possible, and highly affordable, to purchase a sex robot that is in a very different category to its toy forebears. These anthropomorphic robots, with facial and voice recognition, exquisite silicone 'skin' and faces designed with the features of classic movie stars, now offer the possibility of creating a sexual 'relationship' beyond the entirely physical. Purchasers/participants even have a name: digisexuals. The option is there to opt out of sex with humans altogether. The market is aiming for mid-price, mass sales; and is thought to be a valuable one. The implications of this for cultures where women already struggle to avoid objectification can only be guessed at; but they are not positive. This development does not further the cause of promoting human intimacy and empathy.

This discussion of technology's impact on the development of empathy and nurturing human relationships should not omit the positive aspects, and the possibilities that technology offers to be used to the opposite effect. According to this more optimistic view, communications tech can be used either to destroy or to create empathy. Again, there is a choice. Storytelling websites can and do highlight the pain and the experiences of others to precipitate connection and support.[25] Linkages through Skype can bring home and make tangible to young people the direct experience of those in fundamentally different circumstances. Some social scientists argue that, if technology is part of the cause of the decline in empathy, it can also become part of the

---

[23] Zero Tolerance, '"He's the Stud and She's the Slut" Young People's Attitudes to Pornography, Sex and Relationships'; see also Valenti, *He's a Stud, She's a Slut and 49 Other Double Standards Every Woman Should Know*.
[24] Orenstein, *Girls & Sex*.   [25] Manney, 'Is Technology Destroying Empathy?'

solution. Virtual reality (VR) creators claim that there is the potential for VR to create the ultimate form of immersive empathy.[26] The development of virtual reality technologies for this purpose is already well under way. Google now houses an 'empathy lab'. Stanford's Virtual Human Interaction Lab (VHIL) explores – among other things – how VR can be applied to improve everyday life, such as in the areas of conservation, empathy and communications systems.[27] Putting on a VR headset, one can be transported to 'live' the experience of losing a job, a flat and go to living on the streets and feeling vulnerable – even experiencing gut fear as a threatening figure looms on a night bus. It can enable imagining what it feels like to meet racism face to face, far more powerfully than through say a novel or a film. This is an emotional and disturbing experience. It is not surprising that VR is already being used in schools, for purposes including developing understanding across cultures.[28] These uses are in their early stages, but as with any medium, VR is more likely to benefit educators and young people if we can understand how it works and be part of shaping what is created.

Empathy can be learned. But the *challenges* to empathising are only becoming greater: we are needing to empathise across more and more boundaries; in contexts where we cannot see each other face-to-face; and when we may have encountered information about 'the other' specifically designed to set us against them. We cannot assume empathy as a given, but need to actively foster it. We believe that this is a task important enough to warrant a place in schools.

8.5 Our Ageing Species

The case for making proper space for learning empathy in schools, as the foundation for strong relationships, is strong. If we think about the quality of relationships across a full lifespan in the years ahead, the demographic trends suggest a further challenge. We saw in Chapter 3 that urbanisation is a major demographic trend impacting the future of our species. A second major such trend is ageing.

---

[26] Milk, *How Virtual Reality Can Create the Ultimate Empathy Machine*; Bertrand et al., 'Learning Empathy through Virtual Reality'.
[27] https://vhil.stanford.edu/ See also: www.oculus.com/vr-for-good/
[28] www.lyfta.com/about

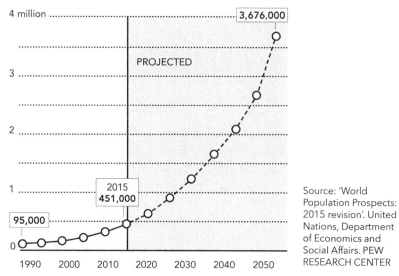

4 million

3,676,000

PROJECTED

3

2

1

2015
451,000

95,000

0

1990   2000   2010   2020   2030   2040   2050

Source: 'World
Population Prospects:
2015 revision'. United
Nations, Department
of Economics and
Social Affairs. PEW
RESEARCH CENTER

Figure 8.1 Centenarian population. Source: UN DESA, 'The World Population Prospects: 2015 Revision', Report. New York, NY: United Nations Department of Economic and Social Affairs, 29 July 2015. world-population-prospects-2015-revision.html. PEW Research Center.

The challenges facing ageing societies, at a time when the family is less likely to be a stable continuous entity or geographically close, are becoming more apparent. The speed with which public health systems and improved medical techniques have extended life is extraordinary – and that is set to increase. Globally, life expectancy at birth is projected to rise from 71 years (70 years for males and 72 years for females) over the period 2010–2015 to 77 years in 2045–2050 and to 83 years in 2095–2100.[29] That of course masks big differences amongst high- and low-income countries. Globally the number of persons aged 60 or above is expected to more than double by 2050 and more than triple by 2100.

In addition, the number of centenarians will increase eight-fold. See Figure 8.1.

To put this in perspective: between 30 and 50 per cent of all babies born in the United States and the United Kingdom in 2016 will live to be 100. Data from more than 30 developed countries shows that since

[29] UNDESA, 'The World Population Prospects'.

1950 the probability of surviving past 80 years of age has doubled for both sexes.[30] In a recent study, *The 100-Year Life*, researchers from the London Business School (LBS) show that in high-income countries, it is more likely than not that a baby born today will live to be 105.[31] Of course, this extrapolation from trends disregards possible 'critical disruption' arising from other phenomena – for example, climate change, or new uncontrollable pandemics.

We have touched elsewhere on the societal challenges such longevity throws up. The LBS study suggests that, if turning 100 becomes the new normal, this will precipitate 'a fundamental redesign of life'. This would move from the stages of education-career-retirement to something much more fluid. Otherwise the dependency ratio of economically active persons vs. the inactive will grow, making the financing of all public services, in addition to the increased costs of elder health and social care, highly problematic; as would be the viability of many pension schemes. The trends in the increase in Alzheimer's disease are very concerning, although there is considerable promise in new gene-related treatment paths. However, it is the inter-relational dimensions of this future that are of interest here.

8.6 Thriving as We Age? Relationships Are Key

Today's learners are likely therefore to live longer lives; but the ability to thrive through old age diminishes sharply. Quite aside from health and wellness issues, the pattern is that relationships slip away and loneliness and isolation ensue.[32] It is these that are widely experienced as the most negative aspect of a life history. An important research finding is that inter-generational contact is probably more effective in combating loneliness than contact with one's own age group, though peer friendships are important too.[33]

Today, as societies glimpse the beginnings of this shift in the human lifespan, old patterns are starting to disappear. People aged over 65 are working longer, digging into their equity and pension pots to support an active lifestyle (and probably signalling the end of the 'inheritance generation'). But care for those who eventually become unable to do so

---

[30] http://news.bbc.co.uk/1/hi/health/8284574.stm
[31] Gratton and Scott, *The 100-Year Life*.
[32] AgeUK, 'Loneliness and Isolation Evidence Review'.   [33] AgeUK.

for themselves is in transition. The family as a care unit is increasingly under strain – through geographical dispersal, two-partner careers, and multi-generational responsibilities. Japan is a relatively conservative society, with continuing stronger family ties than many in high-income societies. It is (nearly) the planet's oldest society (beaten only by Monaco, in effect a retirement community). Of its elderly population, an estimated 4.6 million people suffer from dementia, and studies find that the share is rising.[34] By 2025 there will be 7 million, unless a medical breakthrough emerges. Most live at home, putting an enormous strain on relatives.[35]

We have a set of choices when we consider these trends. Many of them are political and financial: what resources will the state put into future elder care (and expect individuals themselves to provide)? But how will such care be organised in the future? For many this could amount to the undignified fate of 'joining the infantilised and catatonic denizens belted into their wheelchairs' described by Atul Gawande in his book *Being Mortal*. Gawande focuses on the medical and social service decisions to be made, but notes the cultural implications:

In a sense the advances of modern medicine have given us two revolutions: we've undergone a biological transformation of the course of our lives and also a cultural transformation of how we think about that course.[36]

Surely though there is a *learning* dimension too: how can we create learning experiences that diminish the divide between the generations and recreate a value in inter-generational exchange? Can organised learning build ways to incorporate elders into the learning experience; and support structures of friendship and connection?

An alternative choice could lie in the creation of robot caretakers – again, a space in which Japan is unsurprisingly in the lead. Its eldercare robots are being tasked with helping the elderly move rooms, keeping tabs on those likely to wander; and providing entertainment through games, singing and dancing.[37] Maybe this will form an important dimension of how ageing populations will be cared for. But will they – and will the younger generation – be thriving if that is the totality of it?

---

[34] Asada, 'Epidemiology of Dementia in Japan'; Okamura et al., 'Prevalence of Dementia in Japan'.
[35] Henson, 'Dementia Crisis in Japan'.   [36] Gawande, *Being Mortal*.
[37] Ross, *The Industries of the Future*.

As Sherry Turkle, Professor and Director of MIT's *Initiative for Technology and the Self* has written:

It's not just that older people are supposed to be talking: younger people are supposed to be listening. We are showing very little interest in what our elders have to say. We are building the machines that will literally let their stories fall on deaf ears.[38]

We sow the seeds of our future in schools. If we want to have a thriving old age, we need to set the foundations for inter-generational learning early. As we will see in Chapter 9, schools can foster the practice of learning from our elders – and helping elders to learn from the young. But we can only really reap the social, emotional and *knowledge* benefits if it can become a more explicit and central part of what schools are for.

8.7 Relational Implications of the Future of Work

The future of work as described by those mapping out the next disruption, or the '4th Industrial Revolution', throws up the question of what distinguishing human characteristics will enable us, not only to find or create satisfying work, but also to ensure that it is humans and not machines in the manager's chair. As Alec Ross puts it:

Tomorrow's labour market will increasingly be characterized by competition between humans and robots. Either the human is telling the robot what to do, or the robot is telling the human . . . .[39]

Machines and now computers have acquired – and therefore enhanced – many of our capacities in the physical and cognitive realm. There remains the affective and relational realm.

Let us take first the professions: relational aspects of law, medicine and finance. Personal judgement and adherence to a code of ethics were things that set professionals in these domains apart. To some degree, these can now be programmed in. But there is also the all-important personal interaction: the best experts know how to anticipate their clients' concerns, find the right words, make the right connection.

---

[38] Turkle, *Alone Together.*   [39] Ross, *The Industries of the Future.*

Like many who have thought about these areas, Daniel and Richard Susskind in *The Future of the Professions* also come up with that quality that seems uniquely human: empathy. Stripping the human interaction out from other aspects of professional work, they suggest that there may be a role for full-time empathisers who can deal with the deeply interpersonal work, which computers cannot handle.

Any quest for the uniquely human, however, can lead to some disturbing realisations. One is that machines just might become better at empathising than people are – if one is looking at 'cognitive empathy' as defined above: recognising a person's emotional needs and adjusting behaviour accordingly. There is now work going on in 'affective empathy' (experiencing the appropriate emotion to those thoughts and feelings). And 'affective' computing (the work of machines that observe humans and analyse their emotional state) is already an established branch of the science, as the Susskinds note. This entails a form of AI that can recognise, interpret, process and simulate human affects. It is empathy of a sort: but only if empathy is defined in such a behaviourist way. Nussbaum speaks of the 'development of the narrative imagination' (the ability to understand the emotions and wishes of another person).[40] What appears to matter when empathy is at work is the impact on the subject, defined by perspective-taking, empathic concern and personal distress. Is it feasible to speak of computers as having feelings at all, including concern and distress?

This is not an argument for resisting or denying change. As Daniel Susskind, points out:

The purpose of the professions is not to provide people with 'personal interaction'. It is to solve problems that people do not have the wherewithal to solve themselves. It just so happened that, in the 20th century, the best way to do this involved face-to-face interaction with other human beings. But in the 21st century, if we find more affordable and accessible ways of doing so, we should embrace them rather than reject them.[41]

Nevertheless, some areas of work are indeed precisely about providing personal interaction. These include jobs in personal care, nursing, policing and, we would argue, teaching – all circumstances where humans are working with others who are vulnerable or transitioning.

---

[40] Nussbaum, 'Education and Democratic Citizenship'.
[41] Susskind, 'Robot Doctors and Lawyers?'

As the Susskinds acknowledge, we want a human being to have reflected on, perhaps even agonised over, decisions and advice that matters to us. In another analysis, *Humans Are Underrated*, Geoff Colvin suggests that it is useless to try to beat computers at their own game, and that any job relying entirely on the grey matter will be in jeopardy.[42] What makes people special, according to Colvin, is their inbuilt propensity for social interaction. We work well in groups – communicating, collaborating and, yes, empathising. Our best hope lies in what makes us most different from the logic-processors.

This overview of the implications of future developments for thriving at the interpersonal level leads to the conclusion that the *learning goals* at this level should be:

- **To develop loving and respectful relationships in diverse, technologised societies**
- **To engage with, and learn from, other generations**

8.8 Implications for Educators

Learning how to form and sustain thriving interpersonal relationships of course is a central function of the family.[43] But one of the rationales for mass schooling – especially in the face of de-schooling, 'disintermediation', or home education movements – has been the task of socialisation. This, however, has tended to be less about learning to form positive and respectful relationships, and more about the transmission of a particular culture: in essence, learning how to conform to a given society's norms and expectations.[44]

Naturally, there are differences across communities and sub-cultures both about the appropriateness of schools playing any role in the children's development in the area of interpersonal relationships and about the value frames surrounding it. But these are not immutable, and can shift over time. At their weakest, the statements to be found in many schools expressing their value systems assert some cultural expectations: variants of '*we all treat each other with respect*'. At their

---

[42] Colvin, *Humans Are Underrated*.
[43] Even in those societies which experimented with collectivised forms of child-rearing, for example, the kibbutz. See Aviezer et al., '"Children of the Dream" Revisited'.
[44] Saldana, 'Power and Conformity in Today's Schools'.

most sophisticated they strand through a school's DNA, such as at High Tech High:

Relationships. HTH schools foster relationships of trust, caring, and mutual respect among students and families; among colleagues; and between students and adults. Elements of school design that help to build such relationships include small school size; small classes; student collaborative work; advisories; home visits; team teaching; teacher collaborative planning time; parent communications; social-emotional learning strategies; and restorative discipline practices.[45]

Daily prolonged contact with a wider group of non-related, possibly more diverse, peers is seen as a good in itself, as it is the ground where exposure to the needs and expectations of others can lead to better social adaptation. This was the dimension of schooling most missed by learners when schools shut down across the world during the pandemic. Schools are known to be powerful contexts for gender socialisation:[46] whether this is a positive or negative contribution is a matter for debate. Schools that take care to help children to encounter and respect non-traditional family structures as a normal part of life play an important role in widening children's perspectives on relationships.

As schools evolved to shift the peripheral ('pastoral care') agenda to the core ('well-being'), curricular approaches have emerged that position these issues in the *learning* space. A recent review of work devoted to the idea of 'well-being' charts the evolution of the concept and its emergence in practice.[47] The objective of 'well-being' covers the issues and challenges both at the interpersonal level, considered in this chapter, as well as those at the intrapersonal level, discussed in Chapter 10. It was again the Delors report, with its inclusion of the aims of *learning to live together* and *learning to be* which 20 years ago began the debate. Subsequently, the discourse has shifted away from the notion of well-being supporting the ultimate outcome of knowledge acquisition, towards a more reciprocal relationship: one in which well-being is an important objective *in itself*, and aspects of which can be learned.

---

[45] HTH Design Principles 2.0 Draft 23 May 2016
[46] Bigler, Hayes and Hamilton, 'The Role of Schools in the Early Socialization of Gender Differences'.
[47] Awartani and Looney, 'Learning and Well-Being: An Agenda for Change'.

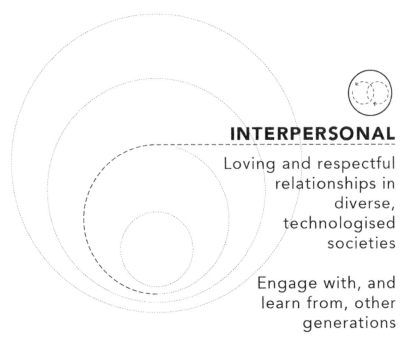

INTERPERSONAL

Loving and respectful relationships in diverse, technologised societies

Engage with, and learn from, other generations

Figure 8.2 The interpersonal level

In the United Kingdom, the movement around Social and Emotional Aspects of Learning (SEAL) emerged. SEAL was defined as:

a comprehensive, whole-school approach to promoting the social and emotional skills that underpin effective learning, positive behaviour, regular attendance, staff effectiveness and the emotional health and wellbeing of all who learn and work in schools.[48]

The program sought to emphasise the importance of relationships in both social and academic learning. The balance between the two is a delicate one, and arguably has shifted too heavily towards academic outcomes.

We are now witnessing important innovation in this space, as well as the retrieval of modes of learning that had been lost. New

---

[48] DCSF, 'Social and Emotional Aspects of Learning for Secondary Schools.'

organisations such as Karanga[49] and the Yale Centre for Emotional Intelligence[50] have inserted a new dynamism into the space, through research and advocacy. These move issues of interpersonal thriving from the periphery back to the core. Chapter 9 discusses some inspiring examples.

[49] https://karanga.org/   [50] www.ycei.org/

9 | *Pathfinders for Thriving Relationships*

This experience has reaffirmed ethics of care, relationship – it's pedagogical love. When people feel that you really love them, even adults, they will try things that they didn't think they could do.

Kim Ondrik, Principal of Mill Bay Nature School[1]

Mill Bay is located in the Cowichan Valley on Vancouver Island, about 50 minutes from British Columbia's provincial capital of Victoria. In 2017, with a growing population of residents, the school district needed to open a new elementary school. The district superintendent, Rod Allen, wanted to use the opportunity to create an environment where children could connect with British Columbia's most evident resource: its natural ecosystems. The natural land of British Columbia is important for both economic reasons – logging, fishing and tourism remain major industries – but also to its people and cultures. The First Nations of British Columbia are slowly regaining their strength after decades of suppression. Their respect for the land and understanding of the complex relationships between natural and human ecosystems are gradually seeping through many communities and sectors.

To help create the Nature School, Rod hired Kim Ondrik, founder of a school-within-a-school in British Columbia's Okanagan Valley that had developed and strong culture of connection both within the school and with the wider community. Rod asked whether Kim wanted to create a school – and a school community – from scratch. The school opened on the site of a former elementary school that had been closed for years. In the first year, there were just a handful of classrooms and a large, open field behind. Taking over the gymnasium, Kim and the team of founding teachers created a community circle where all students gather.

[1] Interview with Kim Ondrik, November 2019

Mill Bay's new school has 'nature' in its name – and kids do spend a large amount of their time outside, investigating their natural world – but the school is first and foremost about relationships. Both the teachers and the students, who are all early elementary age, are constantly having to push boundaries. They are learning how to do unfamiliar things in unusual spaces. Without the habitual structures of a school they are pushed to think about what will be best, what they should do. They are pushed by guides such as Tousilum, their elder-in-residence, to think about the role of education in reconciliation between indigenous and settler communities and between humans and the earth. All of this requires immense trust. Without other touchstones around, they can only lean on each other. This has its benefits pedagogically. As Kim describes, in trying to develop their practice in a new context, they as teachers have to constantly remind themselves to focus on what is in front of them:

It's so conditioned to go to curriculum – 'they're supposed to be here' – but becoming attuned to children has to be there first. It's professional development in situ – how do you become more attuned to children, while you yourself are growing.

Could schools help us all become more attuned to each other and, in being so, grow?

9.1 The Real Work of Schools

As research now clearly confirms what our intuitions might have suggested, namely, that 'good relationships keep us happier and healthier', then learning to develop them must rank high in the list of learning goals.[2] Chapter 8 argued that the conditions of the future make this ever more challenging. Yet still, not all are agreed about the importance of this goal.

Richard Weissbourd, a lecturer at the Harvard Graduate School of Education, has recently carried out a large-scale survey of adolescents in schools and their teachers and parents. Weissbourd and his team found a startling disparity in the way that adults and adolescents perceive the purpose of school. While both parents and teachers are likely to rank it as very important that students are growing up to be kind and caring people, the adolescents judged that adults' priority was

---

[2] Havardstudy, 'Harvard Second Generation Study'.

for them to achieve academically. In focus groups following the survey, the researchers came to understand students' perspectives: everything they heard and saw in schools celebrated working hard and doing well. Helping others was seen as optional – something that could be left to nice people.

The findings stoked a movement among schools and parents concerned to turn this message around, now underway as Making Caring Common.[3] It caught the eye of Carmela Leornardi, Principal of Huntington High School, who found that she was just one of many principals who saw this problem as part of a much bigger breakdown of communications in the values imparted in schools.

9.2 Prioritising Empathy

Huntington High School is a large comprehensive high school based on Long Island, in New York state. Like many US suburban high schools, it does not have the socio-economic challenges of some of its urban counterparts: the local school district is well resourced, and few students suffer from material deprivation. A few years ago, however, staff became worried that students were showing increased signs of anxiety: not just small stresses relating to adolescence and exams, but crippling anxiety. In addition, more and more students seemed to have difficulty engaging with other people.

Leonardi was worried that the school was suffering from an empathy gap. Students were focused on academic matters and on pursuing individual goals, and too many other dimensions of life were being ignored.[4] She heard about Making Caring Common aimed at schools struggling with the quandaries of bullying, moral education and discipline in the context of contested values and online/offline interactions. Leonardi took part in an early convening, and encouraged her successor, Brenden Cusack, to attend the follow-ups. Cusack took the mantle with pleasure, and began working to make the school first and foremost a caring and empathic community.

A key motivator for this work was that Cusack and his team found similar patterns to the original MCC survey when they used the questions in their school:

---

[3] http://mcc.gse.harvard.edu/   [4] Hough, 'Get Under the Hood'.

We as adults feel we have a caring environment, and the kids know that we care, but they also know that we care about their academics, and perhaps they think we don't always care as much about the whole of their being. But we do; in the faculty that's very apparent in all the conversations I have: behind the scenes we are always thinking about their wellbeing. So, finding ways to make them know that became the focus.[5]

One of Cusack's main concerns was to create changes that would be felt right across the school. He has seen some success by galvanising student concern through one-off events, but believes that these initiatives tend to have a 'half-life' – 'by the end of the year they start to dissipate'. To create a more consistent way of communicating values with students, he instigated a simple innovation called 'Text of the Day'. Using a basic phone app (remind me) students can sign up to receive a daily text, sent at 7am each morning, and no more than 140 characters. Initially, all the texts were quotes that Cusack himself found. He then encouraged students to submit their own texts, receiving about 200 responses, from which he has since selected. These included links to pages with student work, expanding the range of ideas and feelings communicated across the school. Staff likewise submit quotes, and on unique days such as 9/11 the daily text featured a link to a video made by students. Through a small innovation that was not too time consuming, Cusack found it had a significant impact on the quality of conversations he had with students. Moreover, by bringing an element of depth and reflection into the school each day, in a format that students can choose when they engage with, the daily text changed the tenor of relationships in the school.

Cusack highlights a particular moment when he realised how much had changed when a student put forward as a text a link to a video message about the way that transgender experiences and rights are addressed in schools.

This was to me a great opportunity to showcase not just the student's beautiful video work, but also her message on how we treat transgender students and their identity and how they fit into our school population. To me that strikes right to the heart of empathy, where this is becoming a vehicle to show kids that they all matter, that we are all part of the blue devil collective.

[5] Interview with Cusack, May 2016.

Online, it is evident that many other young people are capable of similar bravery in speaking out. But their actions to instigate change or share their stories can have different effects when sent out into a faceless ether, sometimes with unintended and even tragic consequences. Huntington demonstrates the value of hosting these actions within face-to-face communities, both to increase the likelihood that they are received in an open-minded spirit, and to ensure that other students who would not otherwise seek out these messages are forced to engage with and consider perspectives very different from their own. Rick Weissbourd describes this as 'expanding our circle of concern': when an issue of identity is presented to us not in the abstract but in the form of a person with particular experiences and feelings, we are much more likely to respond empathically and to subsequently consider people who might previously have been 'other' as part of our community.

Cusack takes every opportunity to expand the collective circle of concern at Huntington – including his own. When approached by a student looking to raise awareness of a fundraiser for an eating disorder charity, Cusack offered her a whole-school assembly – a considerable offer in US high schools, which unlike in some parts of the world do not hold daily or even weekly morning assemblies. The gamble paid off and the student's presentation was met with a hugely warm response by her peers, including prompting several students to come forward seeking help for the same disease she suffered.

Making Caring Common is seeking to share the ideas of schools such as Huntington and support other schools to gradually shift their culture to create school communities that are compassionate and foster stronger new relationships. Along with this general goal, the movement has spawned specific projects focusing on two issues that seem to pose considerable challenge to the goal of developing strong, healthy relationship: digital media, and expectations around sex.

9.3 The Future of Sexual Relationships

In looking at digital technology and romantic relationships as twin challenges, Making Caring Common is not alone – it is a combination explored by films such as Jason Reitman's *Men, Women and Children* or documentaries such as Beeban Kidron's *InRealLife* – but it is relatively unique in school circles. For the most part, sex education remains something dealt with in a few science lessons, while online safety is shoehorned into assemblies, homeroom or citizenship classes – wherever school can find time to shoulder another agenda. Yet if we look at the research on adolescents, it is the meeting point of these domains – the Internet, and sexual relationships – that preoccupies most of their time. It might be argued that it has always been the case that teenagers at school spend more time thinking about sex than anything else, but contemporary research shows that the way they are thinking about it and the distorted or confused expectations carry huge potential of damage for both boys and girls.

Sex education of the past is simply not equipped for a generation that is all too often perfectly clear on the nuts and bolts, but lacking in any opportunity to consider the emotional and ethical aspects of sex. This situation prompted Sharon Lamb, a professor at University of Massachusetts, to create Sex and Ethics,[6] a free, downloadable curriculum for instigating discussions about all the complexities that come with sexual relationships. The content of lesson units ranges from debating pornography from the perspective of J. S. Mill's utilitarianism, to whether human rights dictate that we should or should not condone masturbation for all. Lamb is emphatic that for young people today, there is no putting the genie back in the bottle: for example, 'abstinence curricula' have been found repeatedly to only raise the risk of teenage pregnancies. Instead, as adults our responsibility is to encourage students to weigh the full range of consequences of sexual relationships, and begin to counter their other sources of information – predominantly male-centric porn – by emphasising issues such as mutual respect, trust and mutual pleasure.

Few state education systems have taken steps to make comprehensive sex and relationships education an entitlement for all children – the Netherlands being one exception. But at the school level, there are an increasing number of teachers who recognise that many young people have no trusted adults in their lives beyond their parents and their teachers. If we do not start taking issues of sex and ethics seriously in schools, we are leaving un-countered information sources that corrupt what should be the most human and fulfilling aspects of our lives – the very heart of thriving. We should seriously question any reason given for looking away from this learning purpose.

[6] http://sexandethics.org/

9.4 Integrating Empathy

Sex education may seem like a very specific topic to underpin a central learning goal, but fundamentally it is about learning respect and empathy.

Vishal Talreja is the co-founder of Dream a Dream,[7] an organisation working in Bangalore and across India to develop the life skills of children and young people who grow up in slums. Their methods have developed over 20 years of observing these children as they relate to others, complemented by the burgeoning research field on how conditions of adversity inhibit child development, as well as their own research using measures of life skills. Talreja believes that empathy is only learned when children have an opportunity to witness it: unless they see adults listening to each other, caring for each other, they will not value those actions. Talreja describes how this struck him particularly sharply in conversations with some of his own young staff, who have come to work for Dream a Dream after taking part in the programs as children.

The boys were saying 'if she doesn't cook well for me I'm going to beat her up ...' That's all they've seen. ...What adult facilitators bring into this is the possibility of a different choice. They have to role model that. So these 20 young people who work with us see nurturing relationships between couples. They see relationships where the man is cooking, or helping out with cleaning, and the woman is sitting down and having a chat.[8]

Even the young people who had chosen to work for Dream a Dream – who clearly had a social conscience – were not able to display caring behaviour beyond what they had seen. In recent years, Dream a Dream has become much more concerted about the way it coaches teachers and volunteers as role models for the children and young people with whom they work.

What really happens in the program is role modelling empathy, role modelling listening; you role model eye contact. It becomes social conditioning almost.

Over the past two years, Dream a Dream has been working with 2,500 teachers on a pilot of a training programme, aimed at developing

---

[7] http://dreamadream.org/our-strategy   [8] Interview with Talreja, May 2016

teachers to support the holistic development of their students, including those who have grown up in conditions of great adversity. To do this, they aim to develop teachers into being a place of security, from which anxious children take the risk of new experiences. The adults who can do this, they observe, are those who focus on empathy, care, validation, listening, trust, and non-judgement: what they describe as 'being'.

The programme's activities focus on helping teachers recognise their own strengths and uniqueness, building their confidence to be role models. They prompt teachers to map out their lives and tell the story of their childhoods, re-connecting them with the experience of being a child and helping them to empathise with students.

9.5 Organising for Relationships

For schools that place particular value on interpersonal development and relationships as learning goals, developing the ability of teachers to empathise with students becomes a central part of what they do. This is nowhere more the case than at XP School[9] in Doncaster, in the north of the United Kingdom. XP was founded in 2012 and adapts core principles of the Outward Bound movement as well as learning from schools such as High Tech High in the United States Their central metaphor is that of sailing: students form a 'crew' of fellow students and a teacher. Developing relationships starts with the staff: as part of induction, new staff take part in a week-long 'outward bound' and complete a project together, mirroring the experiences that they will then be working to create for students. The school's official inspection report attests to the strength with which this culture pervades the school, praising students who are 'impeccably behaved … kind, generous-spirited and aware of the needs of others, both at school and beyond.'[10] A parent comment sums up how this behaviour is created:

XP is fantastic. They treat each crew member [pupil] as an individual and cater to their individual needs. They work as a team and do things together as crew to build relationships and conquer problems and fears, helping everyone to grow.[11]

---

[9] www.xpschool.org/   [10] Ofsted, 'XP School', 1.   [11] Ofsted, 4.

It is hard to think what could be more important for young people's development than developing these kind of caring, supportive bonds for each other. Good behaviour – so often the goal of schools – and restrictive behaviour do not have to go hand in hand. XP shows that it all comes down to relationships.

9.6 Learning to Listen before Acting

Role modelling is a powerful way of developing empathy, but equally some schools have developed explicit processes that teach the art of listening, engaging and feeling with others, before leaping to judgement or action.

Design for Change is a movement that began at the Riverside School in Ahmedabad, India. Kiran Bir Sethi founded the school, frustrated by what she saw as a shallow and meaningless curriculum at all the schools available to her son. With a background in design and a consciousness of the many social challenges facing India, Sethi could not fathom how students could go all the way through school without learning the techniques and dispositions to start tackling these problems. With initially just a small group of children, she started a school that would have social responsibility at its heart, spending considerable time on teaching children to care for one another and their community. The centrepiece of the curriculum was action projects oriented towards taking on some kind of social problem.

To scaffold these projects, Sethi developed a simplified version of design thinking, involving just four steps: Feel, Imagine, Do, and Share. The approach was so successful that Sethi thought it must be something that other schools could do, and created the Design for Change Challenge – a week-long event where schools or individual teachers lead their students through the Design for Change process, and produce a project that they then submit to an international competition.

The Design for Change process all starts with putting oneself in others' shoes and thinking about an issue from different perspectives. Children start by brainstorming the challenges that concern them most. In one year these ranged from forced marriage, to the experience of deaf children, to simply not having a football to play with. Classes of children then use the 'feel' stage to consider what kind of response will be most effective, learning to think in different ways about needs and wants. They then work through a systematic process to come up with responses. In Benin, a 17-year-old used D4C to create a street play and petition drawing attention to forced marriage practices. Sixth-grade children in Portugal learned sign language so they could tell stories to deaf classmates. Five-year-olds in Cameroon worked out that they could make footballs from many different materials that would be just as good for playing with.

As well as learning to think carefully about people's feelings and needs, Design for Change also support interpersonal development by directly enabling new relationships. As part of the challenges, students may form new relationships on multiple levels: among classmates they work with, with adults in their local community as they develop an idea, and, in some cases, with children from other countries as they take part in the international convening. There are now several national and local challenges that culminate in similar convening, bringing together children from different schools to learn about the ways they have been reaching out to others.

Design for Change is now in its seventh year, and working in 40 countries. From the one-week challenge they have developed a longer, year-long curriculum, as well as several other guides and resources to help teachers implement the Design for Change process as part of particular projects, courses, or in after-school clubs. In several countries – India, Mexico, Chile and Peru – there is support from government and large numbers of public schools are participating in Design for Change challenges.

As evidenced in Chapter 4, in a world where daily interactions are increasingly across cultural boundaries, being disposed to question our own unconscious biases must be treated as a central competence; and it can be taught and developed as a habit. We are all susceptible to making snap judgements – indeed, we are programmed to do so – but the more we are aware of this tendency the more we can learn to step back and familiarise ourselves with different perspectives and experiences before proceeding.

9.7 Lifting the Age Limit

It is not only across cultural boundaries that we struggle with empathy and seeing past our differences. We might all be able to recall an experience of being in a hospital or nursing home, unsure how to act around people whose internal selves we cannot imagine. Without the aid of family ties or memories of younger selves, very old people can seem alien to us, sharing no cultural touchpoints and seemingly with their experience of life narrowed. Furthermore, we now know that, in the future, there will be many more old people than ever before.

Yet in some parts of the world, the young and very old engage regularly, seeing each other as natural learning partners. Arihia Stirling, the Principal of Te Kura Maori o Nga Tapuwae in Auckland we met in Chapter 4, describes how the school has been working gradually to restore the learning relationships that are central to Maori education.

In our traditional education system, it was the grandparents who did the educating – the parents would be working. This was a treasured relationship; the most valuable lessons the kids could receive. ... But pakia (white) society dislocated us from the elders. It was tougher for parents. Now though we see that the revitalization of language and the protocols of our culture depend on and rest with our elders [so] we are more urgent about this in schools. We have 2 days a week where older people are very involved and where they are supported. On one, the elders come into the library, have their cup of tea, spend time with the years 1–6. On Thursdays, the 14–16 year olds go in twos to the elders' flats; they are 'buddied'; they do their shopping with them, hear their stories; kids have a 'foster' grandparent. Kids love it – no-one opts out, though they can.[12]

This form of relationship is well understood by Maori who are working to restore it in their schools in New Zealand. In other parts of the West, the dominance of 'white' culture makes this harder. But there are schools that are trying to break through and make inter-generational learning a mainstay of public education systems.

Leading this movement are two doctors, Peter and Cathy Whitehouse, who moved to Cleveland, Ohio, where Peter founded the University Alzheimer Center at Case Western, and began finding different ways to approach the disease. He began to write about the ways that people with dementia can still live with purpose given the right environment. Meanwhile, Cathy was working with children with behavioural difficulties and observing the way that teachers and students often interacted in unsocial ways in classrooms. The Whitehouses began wondering about a school that would address both their challenges: where children would develop socially and emotionally through interaction with old

[12] Interview with Arihia Stirling, May 2016

people, including those with dementia, who would in turn get valuable interaction.

In 1999, the Whitehouses created the first Intergenerational School[13] on a site at a Fairhill Partners nursing home in Cleveland. The Intergenerational Schools are now a group of three charter schools in Cleveland, Ohio, for students from kindergarten up to grade 8, or age 14. The schools are extremely high-performing and have received national attention. The Whitehouses now speak and write about 'intergenerativity', re-conceiving ageing as a source of vitality and life.[14]

In 2010, another care home provider, Judson Smart Living[15], initiated a co-habitation program for students at the local Cleveland institute of Music (CIM). Graduate students at CIM can now opt to live for free in the local retirement community accommodation, in exchange for providing concerts and music lessons as part of the homes' cultural planning. The program has recently expanded to include undergraduate students from the Cleveland Institute of Art, and students at Case Western Reserve University. The living option is very popular with students, who receive advice, cooking lessons and friendship from their co-habitants.[16]

Other examples of bringing the old and young together indicate a string of successes.

At Grace Living Center in Jencks, Oklahoma, kindergartners spend their first years of school in the company of elderly residents. The local elementary schools note that these students arrive particularly well prepared in their reading and languages skill. In Seattle, the 'Intergenerational Learning Center'[17] is a nursery school housed in a retirement home, which in 2013 became the subject of a documentary film, *Present Perfect*. In Invermere, British Columbia, the Columbia Garden Retirement Village is, twice a week, home to the kindergarten class of Eileen Madson Primary School,[18] who carry out crafts and reading activities with any residents who choose to join in. This collaboration was directly inspired by the Grace Jencks Living Center,

---

[13] www.tisonline.org/tis/
[14] George, Whitehouse and Whitehouse, 'A Model of Intergenerativity'.
[15] www.judsonsmartliving.org/
[16] Attoun, 'Students and Elders Share Camaraderie'.
[17] http://washington.providence.org/senior-care/mount-st-vincent/services/child-care/
[18] www.sd6.bc.ca/emps/

when the superintendent's wife, a kindergarten teacher, read about the Jencks story and pulled some strings with the British Columbia Ministries of Health and Education to get her class into Columbia Garden.[19]

Some of these programs have developed extensive practices to ensure that both students and the elders are getting the most from the engagement. At Grace Jencks, curated 'shared study' scaffolds interaction between small groups of kindergartners and elderly individuals, ensuring that they have something to do that will build vocabulary, or develop manual skills. Moreover, the school actively prepares the young children for interacting with elders. At the start of the school year, teachers lead children in thinking about some of the experiences these people have been through, and in understanding some of the struggles they have.[20] In other words, they help them empathise.

Unfortunately, school models that bring together the generations are more unusual as students get older, but some examples buck the trend. A number of secondary schools around the world are home to senior centres, as part of the trend towards community schools that flourished in the 1990s and early 2000s as a way to try to generate new revenues for schools. Mostly, these are just co-habitation situations, but some schools make it an opportunity for learning and building relationships.

The Senior Citizens Center at Boone Grove High School is maintained by final year students who opt for the multi-disciplinary course 'Project Care'. The course has been in operation for 20 years, with about 25 students taking part each year. The young people coordinate activities such as board games and exercise classes, and learn about running a business, while developing relationships. Students in the past have commented on how spending time socialising with the elderly is a welcome break from classes. Indeed, as we detail in Chapter 10, evidence suggests that interspersing social and physical activities into the school day aids learning. Nevertheless, it can be difficult to create time for courses such as Project Care when students are under pressure to pack their schedules with specific academic classes. But as their course

[19] Hammer, 'Kindergarten in a Retirement Home Proves a Hit with Young and Old'.
[20] www.edutopia.org/grace-learning-center-prekindergarten-community

guide says, Project Care is both a way to 'make amazing memories with wonderful people' and 'a plus to add on a resume.'[21]

The success of institutions such as the Intergenerational School and Grace Jencks – both in terms of the academic and social development of the young, and the social and mental well-being of the old – illustrates the huge potential of models that bring together the generations. It is disheartening that despite this track record, these types of partnerships have been spreading at a very slow rate. This may change as elderly care becomes even more of a social challenge, but our argument is that it should be schools who are the instigators of these partnerships: not only for the short-term skill development of their students, but to lay the foundations of societies that will foster inter-generational empathy and relationships, which will well serve us all. The demographic changes that lie ahead suggest that this is necessary and urgent.

9.8 Making Time for Relationships

From the psychology of early childhood attachment to the conclusions of life course studies of the old, it is evident that the ability to relate to other people forms a bedrock of our well-being. The examples here illustrate how schools can flourish as micro-societies when they look hard at their core purposes and create the time to focus on caring, empathy and learning from others.

Creating time is one of the most important things that school leaders do. No one understands this better than Maurie Abraham, Principal of Hobbesonville Point Secondary School in Auckland. Visiting the school when it had recently opened in 2015, and again in 2017, the school's timetable covers the walls in Abraham's office – and is made up of post-its. Each term the staff gathers to reconsider how the structure is working and what will allow for them to fulfil the majority of what they want to offer within the limits of staffing. By being flexible not just on the allocation of students to classes but also the length and size of classes – including using co-teaching – they can provide a great amount of depth and specialisation even in a growing school.[22] How they use the time is guided by 'die in the ditch' principles: linked

---

[21] Boone Gove High School (BGHS), 'Course Descriptions: Multidiciplinary Course Offerings'.
[22] For an account of one of their early timetable meetings, see: Abraham, 'Principal Possum', 18 May 2015.

learning – across subjects and to real-world questions; co-construction of learning contexts – bringing students into decision-making about courses; and collaboration – meaning building time in for teachers to work together.[23]

The key lessons from these examples are two-fold. First, creating this time takes leadership: when school leaders make caring a priority, and think carefully about ways to communicate this priority, it can completely change the culture of the school and the type of interactions teachers and students make time for. Second, it takes some work to prepare both adults and children for powerful relationships. Bringing people together – whether that be young children and elders, teachers and students, or students and their community – has much more potential if time is taken previously to prepare groups to be open, inquiring and empathetic with each other.

For Vishal Talreja, a focus on relationships is not only about securing our individual thriving, but also that of our societies:

There is a dearth of leadership – the education system in India is highly conformist; it does not nurture leaders who respond with empathy or care.

Chapter 5 discussed how an attitude of inquiry is the only approach that can hold up in societies that are becoming ever more culturally complex. When we add to this the challenge of our generations drawing further apart – both literally as fertility is delayed, and metaphorically as life experiences diverge; it has never been more important that we develop a disposition towards caring for others, however different from us they may seem. Empathy takes a step beyond inquiry, and asks more of us. It is something that can be developed, modelled and spread. If we cannot do this, we lose our best hope of thriving both individually and collectively.

---

[23] Abraham, 'Principal Possum', 16 January 2017.

10 | *Me, Myself and I*
Towards the Thriving Self

In many ways, the pivotal shifts in the three domains – environment, technology and human evolution – come together most profoundly in learning challenges related to the *intrapersonal* level. This chapter focuses on issues confronting post-millennial learners in terms of inner thriving: personal meaning, purpose, identity and inner peace.

This is about attaining a secure sense of the self: one that enables the growing adult to know who they are, and at the same time retain the fluidity to respond and adapt as the world unfolds itself. It is in contrast to the fragile, brittle or uneasy self. This is part of the business of *learning* – it is not just a question of good luck, genes and family circumstances.

Some of the challenges at the intrapersonal level encountered by young people today are of course those intrinsic to the human condition – rehearsed by philosophers for centuries. But the conditions of postmodernity mean that we now confront a bewildering array of expectations, prescriptions, claims and demands. Navigating them has become deeply challenging – few just sail through. In 1994, Robert Kegan dissected the degree to which we are ill-equipped to face these demands in his book *In Over Our Heads*.[1] As we enter the Anthropocene age, with inherent risks of our further alienation from nature, we are encountering new and hitherto unknown challenges that are making the task of developing a secure sense of self even more complex. Consequently, we are required to rethink our foci and emphases for schools in the future.

So thriving in this space will entail learning to:

- *Attain a secure sense of self and identity, with sources of personal nourishment and renewal*
- *Learn responsibility for personal physical health, fitness and well-being*

What are the distinctive issues that arise at the intrapersonal level as a result of future changes?

---

[1] Kegan, *In Over Our Heads*.

10.1 The Contemporary Mental Health Challenge

Mental health problems have become a leading concern across the world. According to the Global Burden of Disease study, the largest international study of health around the world, mental disorders and substance abuse combined were the biggest cause of non-fatal illness worldwide in 2010, contributing nearly 23 per cent of the total global disease burden. The authors of the study that was published in *The Lancet* concluded that:

In view of the magnitude of their contribution, improvement in population health is only possible if countries make the prevention and treatment of mental and substance use disorders a public health priority.[2]

The World Health Organization predicts that within 20 years more people will be affected by depression than any other health problem.[3] Some writers have referred to the impact on mortality as 'deaths of despair', not correlated with levels of wealth or prosperity, but more with lack of hope for the future, or optimism.[4] Of course, the causes are multiple and complex: the quality of our relationships, food, sleep patterns, economic circumstances and multiple other factors may contribute.

Poor mental health among young people is particularly concerning, affecting an estimated 10 to 20 per cent of the youth population globally.[5] Moreover, this rate is rising in many contexts. In the United States, rates of depression and psychological distress have increased by more than half in the past decade among 12–24-year-olds, against no corresponding rise in adults.[6] In its 2018 annual youth survey of 30,000 Australian young people, Mission Australia found that mental health was the top issue facing Australia in the eyes of people aged 15 to 19. In the United Kingdom, children's mental health charities report a steady increase in the number of young people

---

[2] Whiteford et al., 'Global Burden of Disease Attributable to Mental and Substance Use Disorders', 1575.
[3] BBC News, 'Depression Looms as Global Crisis'.
[4] Graham, 'American Optimism, Longevity, and the Role of Lost Hope in Deaths of Despair'.
[5] WHO, 'Child and Adolescent Mental Health'.
[6] American Psychological Association, 'Mental Health Issues Increased Significantly in Young Adults over Last Decade'.

seeking help with serious mental health issues.[7] Commentators argue that the stresses of schooling currently are serious contributors to the problem.[8] While the funnelling of societal pressures through high-stakes exams or tests is not a situation that schools create, it is a reality that requires a response. The uncertainty and instability experienced by many young people during and in the wake of the 2020 pandemic can only have exacerbated the problems.

10.2 Environmental Degradation and Loss: The Cost to Our Souls

However, what of the effect of the increasing disconnect between young people and the natural world? We have noted that sapiens has now become an urban animal, with accelerated migration patterns to towns and cities. One effect of this is to detach young people from any sense of being a part of and connected with nature.

Chapter 4 reviewed the evidence around climate change, resource depletion and the sixth extinction in the context of the consequences for humans' capacity to thrive on earth – in the physical sense. There are clear consequences for an educational agenda that currently consigns these issues to the margins. However, here we look at the psychological impact of these trends and pose the question: what impact is environmental degradation having on us in terms of our mental and spiritual well-being? Is this a challenge that learning could address or ameliorate?

The consequences of detachment from the natural world have been observed in multiple ways. One is in the concept of 'nature deficit disorder', set out by Robert Louv in his 2010 book *Last Child in the Woods*.[9] Louv has proposed that a number of problems flow from the fact that fewer and fewer children spend time outdoors, and fewer still in wild or natural environments. The term 'nature deficit disorder' is not meant as a medical diagnosis, but rather as a shorthand description

---

[7] YoungMinds, 'Young People's Mental Health Statistics'; CYP Now, 'NSPCC Reports Rise in Children Seeking Mental Health Support'; Siddique, 'Mental Health Disorders on Rise among Children'.

[8] Tait, 'Causes of Growing Mental Health Problems Sit Largely within Schools'; Stone, 'Over-Focus on Exams Causing Mental Health Problems and Self-Harm Among'.

[9] Louv, *Last Child in the Woods*.

of the human costs of alienation from the natural world. Perhaps we are contributing to that when the business of learning compounds the sense of detachment from the natural world by shutting learners indoors for 90 per cent of their time inside school buildings.

The impact of that alienation is seen as attention deficit disorders (ADD) and depression. There is already strong evidence to suggest that exposure to natural settings is effective in addressing ADD.[10] Furthermore, mental health organisations are attesting to the power of reconnecting with nature to address depressive illness.[11] Research published in *Nature* in 2019 showed that just two hours a week spent in nature boosted both mental and physical health – for all age groups.[12] Moreover, this didn't need to entail exercise: it could simply mean sitting in a beautiful natural place. What if, instead of looking to counselling and therapy when problems manifest themselves, the learning lives of young people included as a matter of course sustained engagement and *being* in the natural world before the disconnect becomes too wide or unbridgeable? Again, in the crucible of insights that emerge from the 2020 pandemic, we find that the loss of free access to open spaces caused a kind of desolation; so too the precious opportunities to engage with nature again provided profound solace.

Another consequence of environmental degradation is a particular kind of sadness – described provisionally by researchers as *solastalgia*.[13] Australian researchers looked at the impact on people as they observed their familiar environment impacted by climate change.[14] Australians described their wrenching sense of loss as they watch the landscape around them change. Familiar plants failing to grow; gardens lost; birds gone. It is suggested that this is a new type of sadness, similar to being displaced – except that you haven't moved, the environment has.

---

[10] Kuo and Faber Taylor, 'A Potential Natural Treatment for Attention-Deficit/ Hyperactivity Disorder'.
[11] Bragg and Atkins, *A Review of Nature-Based Interventions for Mental Health Care*.
[12] White et al., 'Spending at Least 120 Minutes a Week in Nature Is Associated with Good Health and Wellbeing'.
[13] Albrecht, '"Solastalgia". A New Concept in Health and Identity'.
[14] Connor et al., 'Environmental Change and Human Health in Upper Hunter Communities of New South Wales, Australia'.

10.3 Technology's Apotheosis: Where Does That Leave Our Identity?

As outlined in Chapter 3, technology's tipping points lie in:

- the evolution of AI to rival/supplant humans' cognitive abilities
- the automation of hitherto 'safe' areas of work in 'no ordinary disruption'
- hyper-connectivity – humans' experience of being (at some level) globally connected and 'always on'
- the potential merger of technology with the body, as implants overtake wearables.

Of the multiple psychological implications of these developments, we select just two to consider in terms of their implications for learning: the future of work's place in our identities, and the 'end of silence'.

10.4 Self and the Future of Work

Chapter 6 laid out the implications of the next waves of disruption in work, as they not only continue to hollow out the middle layers of the labour market but also penetrate many aspects of the professions, from data search and analysis to advising and prescribing. We also saw that Generation Y are already creating new economies, including the sharing, artisanal and maker economies. But we have to take seriously the possibility of a substantive reduction in the overall volume of employment available in the next 30 years. Of course, no predictions can be conclusive; human inventiveness will doubtless give rise to new forms of work and value exchange. However, what is certain is that the robots and machine learning programs to replace human tasks *are in production now*, and where they are more efficient, they will supplant. Even in China, where labour costs are relatively cheap, many employees fear replacement.[15]

As outlined in Chapter 6, there is no clear recipe to 'robot-proof' a career plan. But the aspect to consider here is not what this shift means for employability, but what it means for a sense of self and purpose. The prospect of far less work being available, and potentially

[15] Wong, 'Workers in These Countries Are Most Scared Robots Will Replace Them'.

widespread structural unemployment or under-employment, should lead us to think about how we are preparing young people to organise their work in terms of the most precious resource mortals have: our time. As we saw in Chapter 6, this has led some to propose mandating a shorter working week. As the economist Robert Skidelsky put it back in 2013, when first setting out this idea:

If one machine can cut necessary human labour by half, why make half of the workforce redundant, rather than employing the same number for half the time? Why not take advantage of automation to reduce the average working week from 40 hours to 30, and then to 20, and then to 10, with each diminishing block of labour time counting as a full-time job? This would be possible if the gains from automation were not mostly seized by the rich and powerful, but were distributed fairly instead. Rather than try to repel the advance of the machine, which is all that the Luddites could imagine, we should prepare for a future of more leisure, which automation makes possible. But, to do that, we first need a revolution in social thinking.[16]

Unquestionably, a radical rethink will be required to adjust to this emerging reality. Right now, economic systems require people to work to make a living (unless they are one of the few who can rely on personal wealth, inherited or previously earned). But this is based on the assumption that economies can create jobs for all who need them. This assumption will break down if the marginal cost of human time gets too low to make work worthwhile. Chapter 6 referred to the experiments being conducted in societies that are already thinking ahead to possible solutions, among them, universal basic income (UBI). While this policy remains at the proof of concept stage, the key question it raises is about at what point – in our lives, as our incomes increase, or as our societies develop – we value time over money.

Of course, rationally, these developments should be welcomed, along with the possibility of divorcing a society's overall prosperity from the level of human labour it currently entails. This genuinely holds out the prospect of more balanced lives, with more time for family, relationships, productive projects, creativity, culture, engaged democracy – which is what J. M. Keynes predicted (prematurely) 85 years ago.[17] This relies, however, on the distribution of that

---

[16] Skidelsky, 'Rise of the Robots'.
[17] NPR, *Keynes Predicted We Would Be Working 15-Hour Weeks. Why Was He So Wrong?*

prosperity with some regard to equity. The alternative is that it leads to a huge and permanent underclass, with all the instability that entails.

Whichever direction it goes, we must consider the intrapersonal implication of this possible forthcoming shift, and the challenges it poses for education. Getting a job and securing a paid future have long been held out as the core motivators within the schooling system. But more than that, our work identities have often defined us. Not least, this has led to the sense of invisibility or non-personhood that many women experienced in undertaking the role of homemaker or principal carer. What happens to the self when it cannot be defined by a job, skillset, or corporation?

Work has been the key source, not only of income, but of status. This situation has only become more acute in higher-income countries, leading to what Daniel Markovits describes as a 'the meritocracy trap' where people feel the consistent need to prove themselves in terms of their educational, and then their employment, achievements.[18] When children are asked what they want to 'be' when they grow up, the question actually means what job they want to do. The implication of analyses of the future of work is that it is the wrong question. Perhaps the question should become: *Who and how do you want to be?*

10.5 The Lack of Silence

If one source of finding 'wholeness' or inner peace is to be found in reconnecting with our natural environment, another is the capacity to shut out the 'noise' of everyday life, and look inward to one's own being. In different traditions and cultures this may be conceived of as meditation, mindfulness, spiritual practice, or forms of prayer. It entails deliberately removing oneself from the multitude of stimuli that assail us (and that preoccupy, delight and disturb us) to listen to the 'small voice within'. It is irrelevant whether one holds to any religious or even spiritual belief system. The evidence is mounting that some form of 'mental silence' affords clear benefits in terms of mental health.[19]

---

[18] Markovits, *The Meritocracy Trap*.
[19] Manocha, Black and Wilson, 'Quality of Life and Functional Health Status of Long-Term Meditators'.

The ubiquity and penetration of the communication technologies have for many young people brought with them an empowering sense of connectedness hitherto unknown. This is to be celebrated. In many ways technology empowers young people as never before in history – albeit that schooling has come nowhere close to realising the potential this provides.[20] However, this connectedness has a downside, especially in the context of the amount of time people are devoting to online activity.[21] It curtails the space for silence, reflection; that process of 'getting in touch with oneself'. But this is a process that can be learned, intentionally. One of the great challenges, therefore, in the face of technology's apotheosis, is to provide young people with the tools (perhaps even the permission) to attend to this dimension of their development.

And is it ironic that there's an app for it? Mindfulness training apps are now plentiful and during the self-isolation phase of the 2020 pandemic took off at scale.[22]

10.6 Thriving Bodies: Contemporary Health Challenges

The more visible challenge to our thriving is the set of chronic and growing threats to physical health that afflict humans, notwithstanding the stupendous improvements in medical science, public hygiene and welfare systems. Health is increasingly understood in positive terms as the pursuit of well-being, rather than the treatment of pain and disease when it arises. Most chronic diseases are now behaviour-related. Depending on what weight we place on the complex genetic and environmental factors that determine behaviour, we might call them self-induced. Diabetes and heart disease (and it appears, some types of cancer) correlate highly with obesity, lack of exercise and smoking. We are more at risk from obesity than of starvation. These diseases are all the more tragic because they feel avoidable.

Health systems can now treat these conditions, and indeed prolong life; but the quality of such life is largely down to individuals. And naturally enough, these diseases are also highly correlated with

---

[20] Price, *Open*.
[21] For the United States, see Richter, 'Always on'; For the United Kingdom, see annual Ofcom reports: Ofcom, 'Online Nation: 2019 Report'.
[22] https://thenewdaily.com.au/life/wellbeing/2020/04/15/coronavirus-mindfulness-smiling-mind/

depression; it is much more difficult to rescue oneself from poor physical and mental health than to avoid it in the first place. When combined with the data on longevity, it is imperative – not least for the viability of healthcare systems already under immense strain – that young people learn to support their own health in a positive and life-affirming way. Modifiable lifestyle behaviours, such as sleep, moderate to vigorous physical activity, and screen time, are associated with physical, social, and mental health outcomes in adolescents.[23] But the research suggests that few adolescents are actually meeting the guidelines that have been drawn up around these factors.[24] There is an acute need for young people to be equipped to take responsibility for their own health (mental and physical) over time. This is urgent.

10.7 Our Evolving Selves: Longevity and Enhancement

Of the futures trends, maybe the most likely (barring even more catastrophic pandemics or asteroid strikes) is the increased longevity of humans. The lifespans now anticipated, as set out in Chapter 8, throw up interesting challenges for managing the self over timeframes that humans have never previously enjoyed.

Increasingly long lifespans will smudge the boundaries and may well erode altogether the notion of 'retirement', which even in the first decade of the century became less clear-cut. Among others, pensions experts are the keenest to bury it: the burden of old-style pension schemes is no longer bearable, it is claimed. More people in any case are earning in the insecure 'gig economy' and sharing economy (AirBnB, Lyft, Taskrabbit, Postmates) where pension schemes do not exist. Therefore, where and if they can, people are tending to work longer but in more flexible ways. Not least, it is observed that continuing to engage in some form of work well beyond what used to be 'retirement age' is a contributor to better mental and physical health. The imperative will be to become self-managing, enabled individuals with a strong sense of personal identity and agency.

Finally, multiple forms of enhancement and augmentation are likely to be available through advances in genetic engineering,

---

[23] Pearson, Sherar and Hamer, 'Prevalence and Correlates of Meeting Sleep, Screen-Time, and Physical Activity Guidelines among Adolescents in the United Kingdom'.
[24] UCL, 'British Teenagers Don't Hit 24-Hour Movement Guidelines'.

pharmacology, bioengineering, cybernetics and nanotechnology. This will no longer just be a question of acquiring say a new kidney, or lung to improve health. Human enhancement technologies (HETs) are moving beyond the restoration of health into the sphere of advancing human capabilities. The enhancement might be physical, cognitive, affective or cosmetic. Some of course are available now: sales of cognition-enhancing supplements exceeded US$1 billion in 2015. But this is nothing to what lies in store. Brain interface technologies that allow people to modify their cognition and develop neural connections to other humans point towards the emergence of a collective consciousness.[25]

Technology could soon (by which is meant within decades) be permanently implanted in our brains. Brain implants already exist to treat Parkinson's and clinical depression. Hundreds of millions of dollars have been poured into the next generation of brain implant research and development, such as Elon Musk's *Neuralink*.[26] The goal of such brain-computer interfaces (BCIs) is to massively enhance processing capacities. Thus, it is not about pitting AI against humans. Rather, it's about creating the merger of humans and AI.

10.8 Personal Identity: Who Are We?

Whether it is 5 years away or 5, the continued development of *mental* human enhancement obliges us to consider its impact on *personal identity* – that strong sense of self, constituted by a set of attributes that makes a person uniquely themselves.[27] This is what enables persons to integrate experience and find coherence; and it also enables a sense of self-esteem. There is intense debate in the field about the implications of HETs for personal identity.[28] Moreover, it takes us into the deepest of philosophical waters – notably, what has been known has 'the Hard Problem': that of the nature of consciousness itself.[29] It is impossible to know where these paths will lead, or at what

---

[25] Naam, *More Than Human*.
[26] For an explanation by Peter Diamandis, the founder of XPRIZE, see Diamandis, 'Merging Mind with Machine'.
[27] Ball, *How to Grow a Human*.
[28] Brey, 'Human Enhancement and Personal Identity'.
[29] Philosopher David Chalmers first described consciousness as 'the hard problem' in 1994. For coverage of that event and an update on how the science and philosophy has developed, see Horgan, 'Flashback'.

pace. It is also difficult to discern what impact they are likely to have on human psychological well-being. But even aside from these fast-approaching technological advances that challenge the idea of human identity, there is any case a powerful argument to be made that right now, issues of migration, indigeneity in post-colonial societies, migration and mixed race, and gender fluidity pose acute questions about identity to young people. School needs to be a place where they can securely explore and examine them.

10.9 Implications for Educators

The first step for leaders and practitioners in education is to recognise the relevance of these shifts for education's goals and its practice. Specifically, at the level of the intra-personal, the learning challenges arising now are:

- *Attaining a secure sense of self and identity, with sources of personal nourishment and renewal*
- *Learning responsibility for personal health, fitness and well-being*

It is the task for twenty-first century educators to design the experiences that address these challenges. There are now some great models, both emergent and established. And some are ancient. The deep principles of indigenous people's approaches to learning are resurgent, as indigenous educators themselves refresh and adapt them for modern conditions.[30] Such principles prioritise the *'well-being of the self, the family, the community, the land, the spirits and the ancestors'*[31] and in their practice locate learning firmly in the framework of connection with the earth and spiritual well-being.[32]

The demands of a hyper-technologised society may seem to point in the direction of a curriculum that privileges STEM. However, learning how to attend to an inner life calls for the intentional inclusion, in a serious fashion, of alternative ways of understanding the world. Insisting that learners are entitled to engage with various art forms will probably become more difficult to sustain, just as it becomes more

---

[30] See, for example, First Nations Education Steering Committee (FNESC), 'First People's Principles of Learning'.

[31] FNESC 2015, ibid.

[32] Rosborough, Halbert and Kaser, 'Aboriginal Enhancement Schools Network: Walking Together in a Spirit of Respect and Inquiry'.

critical. In many schooling systems across the world it is observed that the arts are under threat, retreating in the face of a culture of 'performativity' that does not value the nature of the experience the arts provide.

Furthermore, there is only so much time in school. But it will become all the more important that learners have access to experiences that genuinely develop their creative capacities – not just to solve problems, but also to experience beauty for its own sake in many art forms (because humans relate differently to them). The important thing here is the purpose (among others) of nourishing the inner life, in a noisy, distracted world. A powerful source of inner thriving is to become a maker and creator, not just a consumer – whether of art or technology.

Humans come into this world without a handbook about their body that gives clear instructions about its care and maintenance. Many of us take years to learn what kinds of diet suit us best: what we need to exclude or include. Similarly finding out what forms of physical exercise really suit you – as a unique individual – can sometimes be a long (unaccompanied) journey: and some people never find it, to their physical detriment. The schooling years, if refocused on thriving, could transform all that. Imagine a Learners' Entitlement, in which students had guaranteed a learning journey that enabled them to understand their own body, its particular needs, strengths and weaknesses. And it could also guarantee that they could practise and adopt the right kind of habits to support their own vigorous health. Two 40-minute PE classes a week just won't hack it. Educators who are now pursuing more personalised approaches to physical fitness (including many more choices, such as yoga, dance, tai chi or circuit training, as well as team or individual sports) see a very different response from young people when they find the right track for them.[33] This has to be seen as part of an integrated whole. Each of us has at least one major life project: to ensure a thriving healthy body and mind, upon which all else depends.

An element of this learning journey is forming our relationship with food. Again, this is not just a question of the quality of school lunches (though that should not be ignored). It extends to the personalised process of each child learning his or her dietary needs and particularities; and learning, too, how to source good food to meet them. Experience in growing, preparing and savouring healthy food as a

[33] OECD, 'Making Physical Education Dynamic and Inclusive for 2030'.

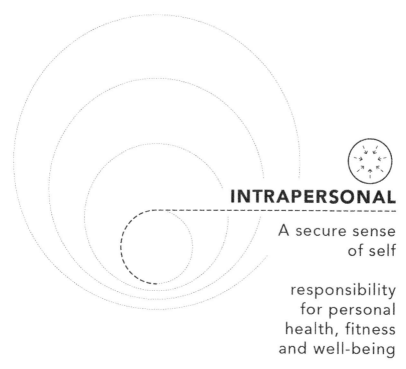

INTRAPERSONAL

A secure sense
of self

responsibility
for personal
health, fitness
and well-being

Figure 10.1 The intrapersonal level

child is a great protective against the addictive qualities of ubiquitous and all too 'fast' food.

The development of physical and mental health is often now subsumed into contemporary frameworks for the furtherance of well-being. These frameworks have become stronger as well-being is increasingly understood as enabling the experience of life in a full and deeply satisfying way: not just the pursuit of 'happiness'. There is a multiplicity of programs, with the trends favouring an emphasis on young people's agency, capabilities and strength-based approaches.[34] In addition to the professional efforts to re-centre on intrapersonal well-being, there are encouraging signs that civil society is becoming proactive. From philanthropists and social entrepreneurs to philosophers, we see a profoundly important ecosystem for learning arising in

---

[34] Awartani and Looney, 'Learning and Well-Being: An Agenda for Change'.

this field. From these sources, educators can derive useful frameworks. *Project Thrive*, for example, by the not-for-profit Dream a Dream, suggests a powerful map of intrapersonal thriving, based on a series of pedagogical processes: expression nurturance; affirmation; non-judgement; sharing; reflection; re-definition; acceptance; and finally, empowerment.[35]

With such partners as these, schools can successfully address these future-related challenges. Chapter 11 discusses some examples.

[35] Dream a Dream, 'Project Thrive'.

11 | *Pathfinders for the Thriving Self*

What can *schools* do to help learners find the space to develop their own sense of self, one that is more secure in its existence in a physical world? As suggested in Chapter 9, one source of such a space is literally spatial – spending time in nature.

11.1 The Great Outdoors – Ever Greater

The importance of spending time outdoors is increasingly apparent in the accumulating evidence of its benefits for mental health, especially in terms of reducing anxiety and managing attention deficit disorder (ADD). Indeed, spending considerable time outdoors is valued by many schools around the world, where children learn to see forests as classrooms or 'mountains as teachers'.[1] In parts of northern Europe, the tradition of *Wäldkindergarten* – woodland nurseries – is increasingly popular, so that children can spend their formative years outdoors. The Mill Bay Nature School is another beautiful example, where children can be outside for the majority of the day and where much of their learning is focused on understanding how to observe, investigate, infer and wonder about the natural cycles around them.

Yet these set-ups are much less common as children get older, and it is increasingly unlikely that children get time outdoors unsupervised, where they might most benefit from what the natural environment provides. Multiple studies have found that children in rich countries today spend much less time outdoors than previous generations.[2] A 2016 representative survey of parents across the United Kingdom found that three quarters of children spend less than 60 minutes

[1] http://sd10.bc.ca/mountains-as-teachers/
[2] Children & Nature Network and IUCN, 'Children & Nature Worldwide: An Exploration of Children's Experiences of the Outdoors and Nature with Associated Risks and Benefits'.

outdoors each day – less than the requisite minimum for prisoners.[3] This lack of exposure may be related to a growing rejection of the outdoors altogether: an earlier three-year project led by the University of Essex found that only one in five children in the United Kingdom showed a 'connection to nature', in terms of their attitude to being outside, animals and the environment.[4] A recent representative study of adolescents in the United States finds similar levels of distaste for the outdoors due to inconveniences such as bugs and heat.[5] Other research has found that time diverted to academic study, health and safety legislation, and parental fears – all well-intended – are unintentionally depriving the young generation one of of the best-known consistent, reliable routes to well-being.[6]

A repeated finding of the above studies is that young people's attitudes to the outdoors can change dramatically through experiencing more of it. Both the UK and US polls find that children who had had 'a personal experience in nature' were twice as likely to prefer spending time outdoors. Some secondary schools are taking steps to ensure that children can have these experiences.

St Cuthbert's School is an all-girls school in Auckland, New Zealand. Students put themselves under considerable pressure to achieve academically; some years ago, teachers became worried by reports that girls who excelled through school were then suffering breakdowns in further education or work, unable to cope with life outside of the steady cycles of striving and achievement. New Zealand has a strong tradition of valuing outdoor space – many schools have partnerships with outdoor centres – but St Cuthbert's wanted to take this one step further to ensure that all students could have an extended experience that really developed their identity and resilience. In 2008, working with outdoor educators John and Christine Furminger, they created the Kahunui campus, an outdoor site located in the rural expanse of the Bay of Plenty, 100 miles south of Auckland.[7] Over

---

[3] Carrington, 'Three-Quarters of UK Children Spend Less Time Outdoors than Prison Inmates – Survey'.

[4] RSPB, 'Connecting with Nature: Nature with Finding out How Connected to Nature the UK's Children Are'.

[5] The Nature Conservancy, 'Connecting America's Youth to Nature'.

[6] Moss, 'Our Natural Childhood'.

[7] https://staging.stcuthberts.school.nz/senior/kahunui-our-remote-campus/

the course of each school year, the year 10 students, aged 14–15, rotate through the campus with each group of 25 spending a month on the site.

The 28 days are constructed as a rite of passage, where the girls learn to look after themselves, living in households of eight and doing all their own cooking, cleaning and budgeting. Lessons continue with teachers onsite, but additionally, each day students take part in outdoor challenges and in learning how to look after the Kahunui site. A key challenge is the 'solo', spending six hours alone in the bush from evening into night. Girls practise with 'mini solos' – getting used to being alone outdoors.

Student responses to the experience are recorded in *The Kahunui Times*, an informal newspaper created after the trip. Many girls reflect not on specific activities, but on how their interior life has changed:

Before Kahanui, I would tune out of deep conversations and not give much input. Throughout the course of the month I have become more self-aware, found my good points and other parts that need changing. I feel that I now contribute to 'deep' discussions and open up more.

I know I'm not the only one who feels that we have gotten to know that girl in the mirror, and had time to reflect on who we have become during our stay at Kahunui.

I have become motivated to make the most of every minute of every day. I am more confident of my own abilities and more confident to speak my mind and share my ideas. Most of all, Kahunui has taught me to be myself.[8]

This expanded capacity for thought, self-reflection and a sense of identity is what we might hope that all students get from school. But we should not under-estimate how hard it is to develop these capacities when bombarded by others' thoughts, others' opinions, others' judgements about who we are and what we are worth.

Christine Furminger, co-director of the campus, describes its value in terms of the space it provides for identity development:

Kahunui is really about those quiet times by yourself reflecting on things you have done and not done, sitting with nature and experiencing the closing of the day and the beginning of the night.[9]

---

[8] 'Kahunui Times: Intake 6'.
[9] www.stcuthberts.school.nz/wp-content/uploads/2013/07/Intake-6-2008.pdf

11.2 Refracting the Self

Nature provides just one of the environments where people can reflect, connect and develop new sources of meaning in the hyper-connected world. The other – the human equivalent – is the arts. Fine art, applied arts and performing arts all feature to some extent in schools around the world, but in many contexts they are at risk. In the United States, for example, during the era of No Child Left Behind, the proportion of elementary schools offering drama and dance quartered, to the point where fewer than 1 in 20 elementary schools featured these arts.[10] In 2012, in two fifths of US secondary schools there was no requirement for arts courses to graduate – something that may change as the arts are once again reinforced by new federal accountability require-ments.[11] Likewise, in England the arts were left out of the 'English Baccalaureate', a set of qualifications that all students are encouraged to take from age 14, disincentivising schools from focusing on any arts courses or experiences. In some other countries, however, the arts remain a fundamental part of the curriculum at least until age 16: in Australia[12] and Scotland,[13] for example, curriculum reforms in the past decade have reinforced a central place for the arts throughout general education.

Stipulation in curriculum frameworks or accountability require-ments is one thing, but it leaves considerable range in provision and the question of whether students are introduced to the power and potential of the arts. It can be difficult, in short lessons carved out from competing demands, to create environments where artistic prac-tices are opportunities for exploring, inventing and affirming the self.

This is not a problem for Campbelltown Performing Arts School,[14] in Sydney, Australia. Campbelltown is impressive in many ways – it is a state school where only 40 per cent of students are selected based on audition and the other 60 per cent arrive from local elementaries. Carefully designed learning and teaching means that students are quickly inducted into a community of confident learners, often working independently or in small groups to maximise the depth of

---

[10] NCES, 'Arts Education in Public Elementary and Secondary Schools'.
[11] Arts Action Fund, 'ESSA (Every Student Succeeds Act)'.
[12] www.acara.edu.au/curriculum/curriculum.html
[13] www.educationscotland.gov.uk/learningandteaching/curriculumareas/index.asp
[14] http://pc.cpahs.nsw.edu.au/

all students' learning. Stacey Quince, the school's principal, sees the performing arts focus as critical as students become more confident in themselves and the elasticity of their abilities by being able to see their progress and stretch in their chosen field – aided by a well-developed portfolio assessment system and peer feedback both in person and through video tagging.

There are many social practices where young people can learn what it means to improve, but arguably the arts, and in particular the performing arts, are especially appropriate for supporting identity development in the stage of adolescence. As Quince explains:[15]

teenagers are incredibly vulnerable and susceptible to social humiliation, but the Arts allow them to explore new concepts, be provocative, make mistakes and try on new personalities with minimised risk.

The opportunity to take risks with identities as well as to learn the power of communication gives Campbelltown students a poise and collectedness unusual in teenagers, and which is apparent on any visit. As society offers us ever more images of who we might be, the opportunity to gradually learn more about who we *want* to be, is a hugely valuable one.

11.3 Finding Silence

Campbelltown's arts specialism creates the time for students to explore different identities and sources of meaning, just as the physical space at Kahunui provides a dedicated environment for developing self-knowledge. In regular school environments, this space to escape and root our own ways of thriving might seem impossible to find. But new possibilities are appearing.

One of these is the growth of mindfulness in schools, supported by organisations such as Inward Bound[16] or the Mindfulness Foundation.[17] Mindfulness is, on the one hand, a set of practices with its roots in Buddhist meditation; it also refers to the form of consciousness that can be called on at will by experienced practitioners. There is already a body of evidence that mindfulness or meditation can improve

---

[15] Interview with Stacey Quince, May 2016   [16] http://ibme.info/
[17] www.mindfulnessfoundation.org.uk/

health outcomes in adults[18] and impacts emotional well-being and empathy.[19] More recently, researchers have turned to studying its impact in schools.

In Chicago, in 2015, the US Department of Education funded a $3 million trial of mindfulness as an approach to improve academic outcomes in 30 high-poverty elementary schools. The research is being led by Professor Amanda Moreno and is expected to report imminently.[20]

Meanwhile, in England, the health and science foundation the Wellcome Trust has provided £6.4 million to fund a randomised controlled trial of mindfulness training in English secondary schools in a large-scale project.[21] Researchers are working with almost 6,000 students aged 11–14, while other strands of the study are testing optimal approaches to mindfulness training with teachers, and investigating relationships between mindfulness and executive control. The large scope of the project, called MYRIAD (Mindfulness and Resilience in Adolescence), is allowing researchers to capture a fuller landscape of student experience, with measures for the culture of a school, mindfulness in classrooms, attainment, and also teacher well-being.

As an endeavour, MYRIAD is focused less on boosting academic achievement and more on mental health. Central to the rationale is the idea that mindfulness and improved executive control can enhance well-being across an entire continuum – from the troubled and the floundering to the cruising or flourishing. As Willem Kuyken, director of the project, states, 'If we can work with executive control in this way we can move the entire distribution to the right – we can achieve greater thriving for everyone'.[22] After the initial two-year trial, researchers will follow children in the study for seven years, with the goal to add follow-ups in their early thirties.

---

[18] Goyal et al., 'Meditation Programs for Psychological Stress and Well-Being'.
[19] Schonert-Reichl et al., 'Enhancing Cognitive and Social–Emotional Development through a Simple-to-Administer Mindfulness-Based School Program for Elementary School Children'; Davis, 'What Happens When Mindfulness Enters Schools'.
[20] See the work of Erikson Institute, 'Amanda Moreno, Director, Child Development Program'.
[21] Wellcome Trust, 'Large-Scale Trial Will Assess Effectiveness of Teaching Mindfulness in UK Schools'.
[22] Interview with Willem Kuyken, May 2016.

The outcomes of these trials will be of be of great interest for those seeking to support children's mental health and personal thriving in schools. Meanwhile, some schools continue to practise mindfulness as part of their culture and philosophy. Meditation has been part of some cultures for over 2,500 years, and individuals who practise it are clear about its value. From their feasibility study, Kuyken and his colleagues are already observing the way mindfulness can shift the way that both adults and children experience silence:

Mostly in schools, silence is used almost punitively. But in these schools, silence is experienced differently: silence enables the students and staff to 'settle' like the sediment in a pond.[23]

UCL Academy, a secondary school in north London that is taking part in the study, has also found that the benefits can be as important for teachers as students. All their students and staff now take part in a six-week mindfulness course upon joining the school. The course is led by geography teacher and mindfulness trainer Paula Kearney, using a mindfulness curriculum called .b (dot be),[24] originally developed by three school teachers. Students and teachers are then given opportunities to practise throughout their time there, with 'mindfulness moments' in classes, and a dedicated silent room that can be used at any point during the day. Kearney emphasises that the practice 'is not a religion and is not airy-fairy-hippy. Our intention [is] to give students access to a set of tools and techniques which they may – or may not – wish to make use of'.[25]

The school's Principal, Geraldine Davies, is more forthright that the practice is something that they want to promote, and that helping students 'find a place where they could find inner peace and space' is an important thing for schools to do.

I've always been interested in what secular schools could do to encourage a sense of spirituality, to explore what it is to be human and to work with the whole person and not just the cognitive.[26]

Mindfulness is just one part of the school's approach to developing student's sense of self. All students take part in an extra-curricular

---

[23] Interview with Willem Kuyken, May 2016.
[24] https://mindfulnessinschools.org/
[25] Interview with Paula Kearney, May 2016.
[26] Interview with Geraldine Davies, May 2016.

'Self-Directed Learning' program that includes a variety of clubs and activities, ranging from fitness to gender-specific 'empowerment' sessions. Options to spend time on 'learn what you love' or 'make change' allow students to develop their own interests with dedicated support from the school. Students record how their learning is developing them in mind, body, heart and spirit; the school makes clear that each of these dimensions should be treated with equal importance.

11.4 Identifying Purpose for *Yourself*

It is one thing to have control over our mind and body, but it is another to work out what we really want to do with ourselves – what uses to put our lives to.[27] The more open we believe the future to be, the more we might want to allow students to exercise personal agency in finding their place in it.

In the heart of Victoria, the capital of the Canadian province of British Columbia, one school is placing *student* purposes at the heart of their practice. The Pacific School of Innovation and Inquiry (PSII) was founded in 2013 by Jeff Hopkins, formerly a teacher and then superintendent in the Gulf Islands school district. After years of discussing limitations of current school models with colleagues, Hopkins decided that the only feasible way to enact them was to start a small independent school that could work outside the system, working with a team of teachers who were prepared to be in a constant state of iteration, and with students and parents who had signed up for something different.

PSII is certainly different. While students are still required to think about graduation requirements, meeting these is secondary to the goals of learning to work independently and developing their own interests. To do this, students spend the majority of their time working on projects, which they develop either independently or in small groups over the course of a term or more. Students work closely with their teachers to ensure that each project idea will require them to study a number of required areas of the high school curriculum, and develop a plan for how they will learn that material. Much of this might be through learning from teachers – there is plenty of explicit teaching in the school, including in modules developed by the teachers, which aims to expose students to interests and knowledge areas they may not

[27] Damon, *The Path to Purpose.*

otherwise choose – but it might also be through online courses, YouTube videos, or simply studying books. The message that Jeff is most keen to convey is that for students with good access to technology and materials, and the right social environment, there should be no limits on what they can learn.

Walking into PSII, the first thing one notices is the well-stocked book shelves; the books range from Aristotle and Kant to computer science guides and technology books. A life-size model brain and a Shakespeare bobble head adorn higher shelves. The students do not lack inspiration. Next to this is another shelf full of shoes: each morning the students take off their outdoor shoes, and put on slippers. It is partly a practical move to keep the carpets clean in the repurposed spaced they have inherited, but also a sign that they are entering into their second home. Student workspaces are tidy but many are surrounded by pictures cut out from magazines, slogans and hand drawings, as if the scrawlings traditionally kept to the back of teenage notebooks were being allowed out onto the walls.

While Hopkins and his teachers feel that they are very much still learning and improving the model, students already seem to be thriving. In an early visit, a group of girls compared their experience at PSII to their previous schools, talking quite openly about how anxious and unhappy they had been. But a smile quickly broke through as they spoke of PSII. As one said, 'We're all just ourselves here'.

11.5 Too Much for School? Expanding the Boundaries

Hopkins and his colleagues are working hard to demonstrate what is possible in schools within the bounds of public regulations, but across the other side of the world, another group of educators believe that to really help young people find their own space and thrive one has to create new time and space beyond schools.

In Delhi-6, the historic, bustling heart of India's capital, a new learning space is growing in the classrooms of a state secondary school. The school, an all-boys institution that during the day is filled with students studying for their certificate exams, for three hours each afternoon is transformed into 'the Creativity Adda'.[28] In Bengali, *adda*

---

[28] http://shikshantar.org/innovations-shiksha/creativity-adda/creativity-adda

means a type of intellectual exchange, typically used to describe meetings of young bourgeois intelligentsia. The Creativity Adda takes this notion and opens it up to a wide variety of activities, but maintains the notion that intellectual and holistic growth can be a social exercise.

Around 40 children attend the Creativity Adda each day, directing themselves into one of its five hubs: an organic farm and slow food academy; a media academy, a design lab and makerspace, a music and dance studio, and a sports and fitness centre. Each one is facilitated by adults who are not formally qualified as teachers, but have expertise in the particular area. Age groups are mixed, and both boys and girls attend. A short film created by students in the media hub shows both young and teenage boys happily engaging in cooking with food grown in the school garden.

Children can decide where they want to learn but are encouraged to treat each space as an opportunity for self-development. The facilitators ensure that they are always working on new things. The aim is to nurture intrinsic motivation, mastery of new creative skills, and self-awareness. As Ashish Tiwari, one of the co-founders, says: 'Building a culture of dedication and practice is important'.

Tiwari and the other founders like to call the Adda an 'unschool'-within-a-school: where usually children in Delhi schools have no choices about what they study, and study a curriculum that still reflects some of the country's colonial past, at the Creativity Adda students can develop more diverse talents and explore different kinds of careers. Alongside the five hubs, the Creativity Adda invites a wide range of people to come through and work on projects with the children, introducing them to domains such as robotics, animation, toy making and theatre.

The Creativity Adda is supported by Shikshantar, the people's Institute for Re-thinking Education and Development, founded by former UNESCO officials Manish and Vidhi Jain. The institute grew from observing the limitations of models of education and development that pulled only in one direction: towards an unsustainable model of development. While the Adda is still new – starting formally only at the start of 2015 – through the Institute Manish and Vidhi are working to ensure that the children can convert the skills and interests they develop at the Adda into ways of life. Manish and Vidhi have created contacts with over 300 organisations, primarily NGOs, who are willing to offer initial placements for young people without a formal degree. They are calling the program, 'Healing ourselves from the Diploma Disease'.[29]

11.6 A New 'Phys Ed'?

Most schools would agree that they have an important mission to help their students thrive physically – in their bodies – as well as academically and socially. Physical education is a part of most school curricula around the world, but as we saw in Chapter 10, it has not been enough to counter-act changes in our eating habits and environments and forestall what the World Health Organisation (WHO) describes as a global epidemic of obesity. Very few children today meet what is considered a healthy level of exercise – an hour of physical activity per day. Across all OECD countries, fewer than one in three children meet this benchmark, and in over half of these countries it is fewer than one in five.[30] The OECD has periodically surveyed physical activity in 11-, 13- and 15-year-olds, and in adults. In almost all OECD countries, levels of exercise fall from age 11 onwards and at age 15, the number reporting taking part in adequate activity is around the quarter that of the older population.[31]

Lack of exercise undermines not only our physical but also our mental health. Dr John Ratey, a psychiatrist and professor at the Harvard Medical School, has spent his career studying the relationship between exercise and mental health. Having worked with children with ADD, Ratey repeatedly saw how increased exercise was an effective way of managing the condition. Consequently, he began studying the benefits for all children. He was drawn to the case of a particular school, Naperville Central High School, in Chicago. In the early 1990s the school's PE coordinator, Paul Zientarski, had instituted a change to its PE program to promote exercise as a life-long activity, rather than focusing on competitive sports few young people sustain after leaving school. Ratey found that introducing a fitness class in the first period of each day had a variety of positive impacts on the participating groups (including improved literacy scores).[32]

[29] Purohit, 'Social Innovators of Udaipur: Interview with Vidhi Jain'.
[30] International Child Development Centre, *Child Well-Being in Rich Countries*.
[31] OECD, 'Health at a Glance 2019: OECD Indicators', 76–79; OECD, 'Comparative Child Well-Being across the OECD'.
[32] Ratey and Hagerman, *Spark*.

The impact on test scores is a notable reminder of the connections between physical and mental thriving, but the most important question about the 'New PE'[33] is to what extent it lays down the foundations for lifelong physical health. It certainly tries to do so by allowing for a variety of activities that combine enjoyment of games with attention to maintaining one's personal fitness. Students learn to play competitive sports, but rather than spending time on large games where many hardly move, New PE is all made up of small three- or four-a-side games of different sports, where students have to move constantly. Alternatively, students can choose to exercise on workout equipment, initially just a few stationary bikes that the school purchased. Students all use heart-rate monitors and compete on how long they can keep their heart rate up during a session. This way, each student competes against their own fitness, rather than on aspects such as speed or skill, which can reward certain body types over effort. And the emphasis is on enjoyment and pleasure. Students need to 'learn' their bodies: in the future, they are likely to need to care for them for a very long time. Whereas old approaches emphasised team membership and success in competition (excellent in themselves), the future-oriented approach incorporates personalising the experience to find the right path for each individual.

11.7 Finding Space for the Unquantifiable

Looking beyond diplomas is a real challenge for schools when, for the taxpayers or parents paying for them, certificates and qualifications are the currency that is supposed to signify a job done. Nonetheless, many people share the feeling that schools must pursue some goals that are immeasurable and un-assessable. Even Donald Kamentz of Character Lab, a research organisation that relies on measurement, believes that it has its limits:

It is now so hard to escape everything being measured, and there is kind of feeling that things that were innocent and pure and supposed to be about true formation and growth are no longer. People are trying to sort out ways to quantify all aspects of learning, but one might make the argument 'why do we need to do that?[34]

---

[33] http://sparkinglife.org/page/naperville-central-high-school
[34] Interview with Donald Kamentz, June 2016.

Howard Gardner, founder of the theory of Multiple Intelligences, and more recently author of *Truth, Beauty, and Goodness*, believes that schools' practice can transcend measurement and assessment only when schools really place their ideals and values at the heart of what they do. Two places that he believes manage this are Colegio Monserrat in Barcelona and the schools of Reggio Emilia, in Northern Italy.

Monserrat and Reggio Emilia are both examples of the power of commitment to a mission and vision. Both are completely committed to whole-person education, and both place emphasis on children – from as early as they begin to talk and walk – being entrusted to *be* themselves, to express feelings and learn to manage and take responsibility for themselves. The schools' level of commitment to this mission means that they have altered both their structures and practices to promote it, and in doing so have become role models for other schools. Reggio has already become a model that rivals Montessori for its popularity in nursery and primary education. Monserrat is likewise gaining increased international attention.[35]

Approaches can also start with the educators' sense of self. In the Netherlands, a new development programme aimed at developing a cadre of innovative school leaders and teachers begins with a phase focused on 'know thyself', on the basis that educators cannot form strong learning relationships with students and be confident in where they are leading young people until they feel confident in their own sense of self.[36]

11.8 Promoting Purpose

In PSII, the Creativity Adda, Monserrat and Reggio Emilia, we see the value of having a sense of purpose, both as a school and as individual teachers and students within it. This is not to suggest we ought to be converting all young people into zealous missionaries, but more to propose that schools have a role in introducing students to the *idea* of purpose: to the possibility that they might develop what used to be called vocation (or calling), and the recognition that even if the

---

[35] Leadbeater, Charles (2016). *The Problem Solvers*.
[36] www.denederlandseschool.nl/

meaning in our lives is entirely self-made that makes it no less sustaining, important and real.

As this book has shown, there is no shortage of problems to solve in the world, people to relate to, or places to be cherished. The notion of creating silence and space at the centre of schools is not meant to block these things out, but to allow the time for children and adults to become open to them. Otherwise we spend so much time in a quest to reach our goals, we miss discovering what is being lost along the way.

12 | *Agency*

A Key Outcome for Learners

This is a movement led by young people across the globe. We're not just looking for an excuse for a day off school or college; we're standing up for the future of our planet. Why should we study for a future that is being taken away from us?[1]

Striking school student

No one will forget 2020 for the global shutdowns in the wake of COVID-19. But we must also remember that it was in 2019 that global events first brought schools to a halt, as young learners in their millions became vocal and visible about their needs for a changed system of education. The Students' Climate Strikes, which occurred on every continent, made stunningly apparent how passionately young people feel about the specific issues of the climate emergency and extinctions, and their political leaders' wholly inadequate response to it. But they also demonstrated that students wanted to have a say in what they learned and how – so that they could make a difference. Education is not doing one of the critical jobs they need it to do for them.

This book has focused on re-examining the overall purpose of learning today. Put another way: what is the job that we want education to do? Asking that question in the light of what is known both about our future, but also about our present, leads to the learning goals that we have set out. These goals are either neglected altogether or marginalised in most schools.

This neglect naturally has implications at the individual level, but we have not focused here on the specific outcomes for learners in the sense of frameworks of knowledge or skills. There are many such models, and they frequently underpin approaches to curriculum.[2] We believe

---

[1] Laville and Watts, 'Across the Globe, Millions Join Biggest Climate Protest Ever'.
[2] These include Fadel et al., 'Four-dimensional Education'; New Pedagogies for Deeper Learning http://npdl.global/makingit-happen/deep-learning-progression;

that such frameworks are secondary to establishing a renewed sense of the purpose of education in the world today; we also need to look beyond individuated outcomes in order fully to re-imagine the education the world needs. But if there is one individual outcome that is both under-developed and critical to achieving thriving in a transforming world, we believe that it is *agency*. That is what those students striking from school were both displaying and demanding.

12.1 What Is Agency?

There is a common-sense understanding of what agency is. 'A free agent.' 'Agent of one's own destiny.' 'An agent of change.' These all entail ideas of autonomy and action-orientation. But this is not a notion that is often applied to young learners. Now, it needs to be.

This is because without a belief in their power to impact their own future and that of the broader world, learners will be condemned to passivity: to the view that not much can be done. A lack of a sense of agency, or powerless, itself leads to negative consequences: at the individual level, lack of motivation, indifferent decision making, depression; at the collective level, passive, unengaged citizens.

Student agency is at last becoming an increasingly important concept in education, both as a goal and as a process. Articulating agency as a goal, psychologist and education scholar Helen Haste has suggested that a 'competent human' is self-sufficient, able to focus attention and plan, has a future orientation, is adaptable to change, has a sense of responsibility, has a belief that one can have an effect and is capable of commitment.[3] In the light of the holistic approach that we have suggested is now essential, perhaps the emphasis should be more on inter-dependence than on 'self-sufficiency'. We propose as a slight adjustment therefore that *learners who have agency are purposive, reflective, invested and action-oriented*. This is about not just taking control of one's own life but recognising one's responsibility as a human actor at a time when the average human has never had more power.

It is important to distinguish this idea of agency from much weaker notions such as 'choice and voice'. These are laudable aims, and undoubtedly lead to students being more engaged. But we need now

The Graduate Performance System (Asia Society) Graduation Performance System. http://asiasociety.org/graduation-performance-system/ and many others.
[3] Haste, 'Ambiguity, Autonomy and Agency'.

to move beyond engagement. What these objectives leave out is the transfer from teacher to learner, at crucial points, of a degree of control and ownership; and they leave out too the propensity to action which agency confers. As the OECD put it in its Framework for Education and Skills 2030:

It is about acting rather than to be acted upon, shaping rather than to be shaped and choosing rather than to accept choices decided by others ... It assumes the possession of a sound self-concept and the ability to translate, in a responsible way, needs and wants into acts of will: decision, choice, and action.[4]

The emphasis on 'responsible' is important: unthinking, uninformed activism is not a part of this agenda.

Drawing these views together, agency means:

- developing goals (personal and social)
- initiating action towards those goals
- reflecting on and regulating progress towards those goals
- belief in self-efficacy.

What this means for practice depends on how we interpret 'goals;, and this is turn will vary greatly with the age and context of learners. But the key point here is that this should include goals that young people themselves are creating. This does not mean picking them out of thin air at will, but, with the support of teachers and other knowledgeable adults, working out what they care about, what is meaningful, and what they can do about it.

We should not underestimate how radical it is when schools create space for children and adolescents to develop their own sense of agency. In many countries, schools are under immense pressure to prepare students for demanding standardised assessments. These assessments serve valuable purposes in education, not least trying to ensure some floor of equity, but when they are poorly calibrated to local capabilities or their purpose is poorly communicated, they distort school practice and foreclose opportunities to focus on other goals.[5] Understanding what agency is and why it is so important is a key step to restoring balance.

---

[4] OECD, 'The Future We Want'.
[5] Koretz, *The Testing Charade*; Gerdin and Englund, 'Contesting Commensuration'.

12.2 Agency and Culture: The Importance of Context

The concept of agency is central to the overall objective of thriving. In reflecting on this, however, it is important to be aware of how the concept has different meanings and connotations in different cultures – if indeed there is a term for it at all in the relevant languages. In some languages there is no direct translation for the term 'agency' and it is equated with related but not identical ideas around 'student centred' or 'independent' or 'active' learning. But apart from the difficulty of making a clear translation of the term itself, more fundamental cultural differences are critical to adaptation in different contexts.

These differences centre on the relationship of the individual to the group. At the heart of this is the degree to which harmony, compliance and conformity are valued above creativity and individualism. In Japan, for example, the notion of the individual is derived from relations within a community: the community is primary. In some Western traditions, one might say that communities are derived from relations among individuals who choose to associate: the individual is primary.[6]

There are implications of these considerations for 'agency', as both an education process and outcome. There may not be a universal formulation, relevant to all contexts, that captures the underpinning ideas in 'agency'. It may be that practical illustrations, cumulatively, may be the best way to communicate and develop the concept. And sensitive account needs to be taken of any cultural context within which it will need to evolve, without necessarily adopting the view that any historical cultural view is incontestable. Upcoming generations – both east and west – are raising questions about the value frame their society has bequeathed from times that are now gone.

12.3 Agency as Outcome as well as Process

The processes that schools can adopt to foster agency are becoming more sophisticated and codified. In terms of outcomes, it is useful to think about the levels and also the domains in which agency becomes

---

[6] Steinemann, 'Student Agency in Asia: Educators' Perceptions on Its Promises and Barriers'.

Agency as an *outcome* - at many levels...

	moral	political	economic	creative
individual				e.g. artistic expression
collaborative			e.g. new enterprise creation	
collective	e.g. acting against human rights abuse	e.g. adopting a green energy policy		

Figure 12.1 Agency as an outcome

applied. Leadbeater notes that a person with agency might apply it in a variety of different ways.[7] His ideas suggest the matrix as shown in Figure 12.1:

This aligns with the *Education 2030 Framework* insistence that agency is not just a personal or individual quality: the OECD work emphasises the equal importance of *co-agency* (with peers, teachers, family and community). The cells in the matrix illustrate the spaces in which persons can manifest their agency in free societies. The third level – the collective – is where most people experience a sense of impotence. Without practising or experiencing agency at the other two levels, it is unlikely that an individual could engage in the third. Perhaps this gives a kind of map to enable educators to think about the kinds of experiences they might design to promote agency as a constituent of thriving.

Before exploring more closely what learner agency looks like in practice, it is worth examining the relationship between it and key learning outcomes: competencies.

12.4 Agency and Competencies

The linkage of competency and agency is important. The OECD *Framework for Education and Skills 2030* initiative, introduced in Chapter 2, insists on the value of thinking in terms of competencies

[7] Leadbeater, 'Education 2030 – Conceptual Learning Framework: Background Papers'.

as focal outcomes: defined as knowledge + skills + values + attitudes.[8] All four are needed now to satisfy the criteria for a fully rounded education. It avoids the sterile 'skills' vs 'knowledge' trap. And competencies apply just as much within disciplinary knowledge (science, history, maths and so on) as they do in cross- and inter-disciplinary domains.

Going a step further however, the OECD initiative extends these ideas about competencies to advocate for the need to include three 'transformational competencies'. These are particularly related to the challenges explored in this book. They are:

1. creating new value (innovation)
2. taking responsibility and
3. coping with tensions and trade-offs.

What do these 'transformational competencies' mean? Briefly, they mean:

Creating new value is about the knowledge, skills, values and attitudes of innovation and entrepreneurship. Individuals who acquire it are doers, makers, creators, people who add to the stock of possibilities in the world. Previously, the elements and qualities that comprise innovative individuals and societies have been a by-product, not an intentional outcome, of education systems. Worse than that, they have sometimes arisen *in spite of*, not as a result of, schooling systems. It is striking how many entrepreneurs and innovators dropped out of school or were failed by it. It is a competency that is urgently needed for the making of a better world. The notion of innovative competency embedded in the *Education 2030 Framework* again stresses values and attitudes in addition to skills and knowledge. The values and attitudes dimension is of extreme importance. Innovation in and of itself need not be a good.[9] There needs in addition to be an ethical and value-sensitive contextualisation of the products and processes created. Thinking about what they would mean, for good and possibly ill, is also a central component.

Taking Responsibility. At the core of taking responsibility lies the capacity of self-regulation: the ability to control emotions, thoughts and behaviours such that individuals stay focused, especially when things get difficult, unpleasant or tedious. Dozens of scientific studies

---

[8] OECD, 'The Future We Want'.   [9] Yamanaka, 'Creating New Value'.

point to self-regulation as perhaps the single most robust predictor of success, happiness and psychological well-being, as well as the absence of emotional and behavioural problems during adolescence and young adulthood.[10] 'Taking Responsibility' however also entails the preparedness to step up; to shoulder leadership; to be counted and to count. Reflecting on the trends and opportunities set out in the previous sections, it is immediately apparent how vital this competency is in the big picture of challenges we face.

Coping with tensions, dilemmas, trade-offs. In the transforming world described in previous chapters, balances need to be struck between equity and freedom; autonomy and solidarity; efficiency and democratic processes; ecology and simplistic economic models; diversity and universality; and innovation and continuity. This entails integrating seemingly contradictory or incompatible goals as aspects of the same reality. It means recognising that in complex conditions there may be more than one solution or solution method. To be prepared for the future, individuals have to learn to think and act in a more integrated way, taking into account the manifold inter-connections and inter-relations between contradictory or incompatible ideas, logics and positions both in short- and long-term perspectives. In short, they have to learn to be systems thinkers. For any learner, the ability to understand, respond to and influence the possibilities that these conflicts create will be fundamental to their own life-chances and their prospects of influencing the world taking shape around them.[11]

All of these three 'transformational competencies' are of relevance when one starts to consider how and in what circumstances agency can be exercised.

12.5 What Does Agency Look Like in Practice?

If we think only of the level of the school as an enclosed institution, then one can perhaps think of learner agency being exercised in at least three domains (see Figure 12.2).

Voice and leadership are spaces in which most schools today are different to schools, say, 50 years ago. No longer do students expect to

[10] Steinberg, 'OECD Transformative Competencies 2030: Taking Responsibility.'
[11] Bentley, 'OECD Transformative Competencies 2030: Coping with Tensions, Dilemmas'; Kyllonen, 'Inequality, Education, Workforce Preparedness, and Complex Problem Solving'.

Agency as a set of processes...

Ownership
Teaching and
learning processes
that build self
efficacy

Leadership
processes that give
students opportunities
to lead the direction of
change

Processes that increase
student influence over their
learning environment
Voice

**Agency within
the school**

Figure 12.2 Agency as a set of processes

have to tolerate complete voicelessness and powerless when they are in school. At the lowest level, almost every school has some kind of school 'council', which might deliberate on issues that teachers allow them to consider. Their views may be just advisory; or in some instances they may have decision-making powers. This has generally been over marginal matters about how the school runs: uniforms, lunches and so on. That is good as far as it goes. So too are efforts to have student voices 'heard' at the system level, in the shape of Student Representative Councils for districts.[12] Many governments now support the movement (not least because Article 12 of the United Nations Convention on the Rights of the Child (UNCRC) says that children and young people should have a say in decisions that affect their lives) and issue guidance and support materials.

Then there are schools that offer serious opportunities for their learners to show leadership in the school's direction of travel. This is most overtly the case at some of the newer schools we have met. At the

[12] Lister, 'How Can We Meaningfully Include Students' Voices in Schools?'

Nature School in Mill Bay, students as young as five and six have been involved in decisions about the organisation of furniture, and the layout of their many outdoor spaces. More importantly, they are involved in a daily basis in creating the school's norms. In the large 'circle' time that at first started each day, and then phased into biweekly gatherings, children were invited to share how they were feeling about their experience at school and 'problem-solve' together. As Kim Ondrik, the Principal describes it, the extra time and effort they spend on this work is all worth it because, 'these children are helping to create something'.

Giving young people more control over their school does not necessarily mean involving them in governance or management decisions, but can just mean allowing them to feel that it is their space, too. We should not underestimate how unusual it is for young people simply to be to be able to *move* where and how they want in a school. Sudbury Valley, the early democratic school we meet in Chapter 6, takes this trust very seriously and poses no restrictions on student movement. An adolescent describes their first impression of this as revelatory:

The very first time I walked in here for my admissions interview, one of the most powerful things I saw was kids walking anywhere they wanted to. Some people were on the basketball court, and then they would walk to the swings, or kids would walk between rooms. That felt really powerful to me because... being able to move where you want to, independent of other people, has a big effect ... You can do what you want, you can also go where you want ... It felt really powerful to me.[13]

Sudbury lets students choose all of their own learning, which is not something that all schools would consider appropriate or desirable. But this perspective highlights that in many contexts, even just allowing students to move when they need to – to go to the bathroom without asking – feels radical. There are trade-offs in creating this kind of school community, where young people are trusted to move on their own. In some contexts, the risk may be too great. But it is worth considering what the real risks are and how they compare to students not developing a sense of responsibility for themselves, their space and their learning.

---

[13] Sadofsky, 'What Is "Agency"?'

Finally, and coming closer to authentic notions and practice of agency, is where learners are enabled to exercise real decision-making about their own learning journeys, beyond the mere selection of options from a set menu, like consumers. The COVID-19 shutdown revealed starkly where schools had already enabled learners to exercise agency in this regard: such learners did not feel at sea in the same way that students who had been used to being closely directed on a daily basis did.

This level of agency can be expressed through the pursuit of themes and issues in project-based learning; or through the selection of personalised programs of study. There are now so many pioneering schools in this space, it is invidious to select one: but the work of the Norris Academy in Wisconsin illustrates the practice well. Norris is a public school, 93 per cent of whose students are economically disadvantaged.

By focusing on four interwoven diagnostic assessments, learners at Norris Academy explore their unique identities through the lenses of academics, citizenship, employability, and wellness (physical and mental). These assessments form the foundation for tracking future growth as the learner develops their knowledge, skills, and dispositions toward learning. During the 30-60 days of self-reflection and exploration, learners engage in "mini explorations" that immediately introduce them to open-walled experiences within the broad disciplines of Skill Trades, STEM, Business, and Creative and Community. They are able to develop a master plan to accelerate their growth and development as lifelong learners. And, if learners have already identified their passions before setting foot in the school, they can head straight to the makerspace to work on individual and collaborative pursuits. When the creative gears start churning inside each learner's head and the individualized learning paths are established, learners take their newly developed agency and begin advancing their self-accountability in dynamic ways.[14]

This is an exemplar of the growing practice of control over a student's own learning.

Of course the now well-established practice of integrating internships into a learning journey provides a powerful platform for the acquisition of agency in this sense. The work of Big Picture

---

[14] https://education-reimagined.org/wp-content/uploads/2017/11/Pioneering-46_ FINAL.pdf

Learning,[15] operating right across the United States and in many other countries, has pioneered this practice, which is a part of their '10 Distinguishers' (or learning design principles). Big Picture Schools aspire to operate authentically across all the spaces of the Venn in Figure 12.2.

It should not be thought though that the practice of assisting learners to acquire deeper ownership of their own learning can only be exercised with older students. The work of schools in New Zealand, supported by *Infinity Learning*[16] shows otherwise. Children as young as six are helped to construct 'Learning Maps', charting how and where they learn and assisting them to formulate learning goals and plans as to how to achieve them. The method deploys the knowledge base around learning-to-learn.

Nor is agency a notion that is just relevant to privileged kids in elite institutions. The very reverse is the case. *Project Thrive* of Dream a Dream[17] in India shows how the development of agency is at the heart of enabling kids in the greatest adversity to thrive.

It is fundamental that 'agency' can become a powerful tool that will help young people build the capacities to overcome their own adverse circumstances, catch-up to their development milestones and at the same time leapfrog into a future with purpose, creativity, empathy, responsibility and social consciousness. It helps young people become Change-makers.[18]

12.6 Agency beyond the School Walls

To experience agency in its fullest sense means looking beyond the confines of the school to one's wider life. Embedded in family, community and society, what is the scope for young learners to practise agency and explore how they can make a difference in the wider world? 'Real world' learning is not just about the physical location of learning; it is also about how that learning is grounded in and affects the real world, and how individuals can become involved and effective.

Outward-facing schools, schools that are not afraid to support their students to engage in real-world issues, are no longer rarities. These are schools whose students do not need to go on strike to insist that their

---

[15] www.bigpicture.org/ [16] http://infinitylearn.org/
[17] https://dreamadream.org/
[18] Talreja, 'Student Agency: The Impact of Adversity', 52.

learning engages with the major issues of our time. Among our path-finders we saw the work of the June Jordan School for Equity (JJSE), where students study a curriculum focused on social justice alongside their other subjects. This focus spills over into their real-world activity. School students from JJSE featured on local news for taking a five-hour round trip to visit a 17-year-old refugee from Afghanistan who had been detained by the US Immigration and Customs Enforcement (ICE), instead of taking their end-of-year trip to Santa Cruz, and decided to leave an open chair at their graduation to symbolise his detainment (though he was not a student of the school).[19] They subsequently raised $25,000 to bail out their fellow teenager.[20]

The Pacific School of Innovation and Inquiry (PSII) is another place where school activities regularly spill over into the 'real world'. The PSII twitter feed is continuous evidence of this.[21] It is not surprising that is was a PSII student, Finn Greischer, who followed Greta Thunberg's lead and led the organisation of school climate strikes in British Columbia.[22] But students also demonstrate that there are ways to impact the world beyond activism. In the same month at the climate strikes, a PSII student, Mady Hoosen, was a winner of her city's first 'Dignity on the Streets' poetry competition, to reflect the lives of homeless indigenous people in Victoria.[23]

British Columbia is a place where some of the most interesting examples, practices and resources for promoting learner agency are to be found. One such example is Farm Roots, in the Delta school district. Founded by teacher and district principal Brooke Moore, Farm Roots bundles four courses in grades 10–12 and integrates it around the work of building, maintaining and growing a small market farm. Students on the farm are constantly engaged in real-world deci-sions with consequences for the wider group, and realise how intercon-nected not only they are, but the social, economic and environmental systems they rely on. Brooke describes the most important outcome of Farm Roots being the emergence of *co-agency*: 'we are all connected

---

[19] Fernandez, 'San Francisco High Schoolers Skip Senior Trip, Visit Afghan Boy in ICE Detention Center Instead'.
[20] Makovec, 'Students Rally in San Francisco for Afghan Teen Detained by ICE'.
[21] https://twitter.com/PSIIvictoria
[22] Graeme, 'Victoria to Participate in Global Student Strike for the Climate'.
[23] Times Colonist, 'Writers Challenged to Reflect Lives of Indigenous People on the Street'.

and can all move forward together – and the only way of enacting that is through dialogue'.

As the community at Farm Roots developed, Brooke and her colleagues realised that young people and their teachers needed an accessible and coherent way of making decisions collaboratively. This realisation led to the creation of *The Decision Maker Playbook*, a resource designed for teachers to help students in making 'thoughtful decisions that reflect their values'.[24] Written in a collaboration between educators and decision scientists, the Playbook walks young people and their teachers through the insights of decision theory (familiar to some adults through works such as Daniel Kahneman's *Thinking Fast and Slow*). This valuable resource serves also to demonstrate how agency is not the same thing as complete autonomy: fundamental to it is the assessment of the outcomes of decisions upon others.

This kind of decision making is a sophisticated set of skills, but ones that young children really can get to grips with. In her sixth-grade classroom, Delta teacher Joanne Calder has seen her students use the Playbook's 'Decision Maker Moves' in frequent and meaningful ways, moving through the year together in collaboration and co-agency. This orientation towards creating opportunities for students' decision making distributes responsibility for designing and maintaining the classroom learning community.

It is in these kinds of learning environments that young people engage in the very real work of collaboration and creating value. Whether one wants to call it twenty-first-century skills, transversal competencies or just a way of being and living, it looks like young people figuring out together how to grow, sustain and mutually benefit themselves and their environment.

We see some of the same values in the rise of schools that are leadership academies for 'ordinary' students, not just elites. One such is the Liger Leadership Academy of Cambodia,[25] which designs its programs explicitly to give learners a chance to make lasting beneficial change in their community, and adopt leadership roles. That could include practical projects (such as building an artificial reef off the coast of Cambodia); or working with experts and politicians to affect

---

[24] Failing et al., *The Decision Playbook: Making Thoughtful Choices in a Complex World (Teachers' Edition)*.
[25] www.ligeracademy.org/

policy change. Liger students work in partnership with the government to create STEM projects that are not too demanding of resources and money.

The concept and practice of learner agency is perhaps the most potent, the freshest and indeed the most challenging to established education systems. It can give rise to the mistaken notion that it is somehow at odds with teacher professionalism or expertise; or somehow curtails their exercise. Rather, the very reverse is true. In schools and systems where learner agency is nurtured, the skills of teachers are even more sophisticated and more highly valued. It offers a space for exciting extensions of innovation in teaching methods; and it not only liberates energy for the deep work of learning and teaching, but is central to the task of creating the empowered individuals we need to create the future we want and they deserve.

12.7 System Support for Promoting Agency: What Can Be Done?

If agency has entered the vocabulary and practice of pathfinding schools, what can systems do to promote and support this shift, and help ensure that it is done well?

Some system leaders are showing the way.

Victoria in Australia has undertaken a prototyping exercise with groups of volunteer schools, supported by Innovation Unit ANZ to develop models of practice that would be of value to schools across the state. This was an exercise in co-creation and design thinking: the state worked with schools to prototype and test approaches. The *Amplify Learning Labs* initiative brought together 100 school leaders from across 5 school networks to develop pedagogic and curricular models, case studies and support materials for schools across the system. Importantly, the state has asserted that:

Strengthening Student Voice Agency and Leadership (SVAL) in schools supports a paradigm shift from compliance and disengagement to commitment, motivation and deep intellectual engagement in learning. SVAL is critical to the achievement of contemporary goals of education, which aim for all students to develop as successful, lifelong learners.

The *Amplify* materials, which are now available to all schools is at time of writing, are the most popular resource that schools take up from the

State Department of Education.[26] From an analysis of the Learning Labs schools work, seven inter-related and mutually reinforcing approaches emerged as key areas of implementation:

- student voice/action teams
- student feedback
- curriculum co-design
- co-design of instructional approaches
- co-design of behaviour norms
- metacognition and self-regulation
- applied learning.

This endorsement and support from the state gives a powerful platform that can build a critical mass of practice and enable schools to push on to new territory, with a shared language. The state has begun to construct a new narrative.

The 'lab prototyping' method is a powerful way to enable grassroots co-creation and ownership, and through this means make the innovation more grounded, relevant and credible to practitioners across a system. In South Australia, a three-year initiative is underway to explore new models of learner agency. Under the auspices of AISSA (Association of Independent Schools of South Australia), schools are developing a robust theory and practice for student agency, creating practical, useful tools, methods and frameworks for schools, students, teachers and parents to develop learning that promotes agency. It is expected that the work will be shared widely through education systems in Australia and beyond. And these systems are giving the schools the gift of time: in times when other priorities crowd in, the time for schools to reflect, plan and innovate is invaluable.

12.8 Not Just the State: Other Players in the Ecosystem

Fortunately, schools can now look beyond state actors or even education-focused agencies for sources of support in fostering learner agency and competencies. In the last decade, multiple new organisations have sprung up to constitute a flourishing knowledge and innovation ecosystem to provide resources, models, frames and professional development to schools who seek to move in this direction. They may

---

[26] State Government of Victoria, 'Student Voice Practice Guide (Amplify)'.

be country-based; but all are now in effect global. To name but a few of the most vibrant: Education Re-Imagined (United States);[27] Next Gen Learning (USA);[28] HundrEd (Finland);[29] Innovation Unit (United Kingdom, Australia and New Zealand).[30] There are not-for-profit agencies doing superb work in supporting schools in specific issues and spaces. For example, *Agency by Design* (Harvard University) researches and supports schools to address the agency challenge by deploying the tools of design thinking. Dream a Dream (India) alluded to earlier in this chapter is dedicated to the task of helping educators to focus on thriving through fostering the agency of children in adversity. It is focused on the equity challenge: some learners face conditions of the utmost adversity. Empowering them to develop agency is one of the most significant contributions that can be made.

12.9 Making Agency a Part of the New Narrative ...

Students should emerge from education as purposeful, reflective responsible agents, investing themselves actively to achieve goals which they have understood and endorsed.[31]

We have argued that education needs a new narrative. Agency is an important part of the story's lexicon, and so its increased use is encouraging. The optimistic view is that a three-way pincer movement is possible:

- As learners identify the range of challenges (and opportunities) that the 'future pivots' described in earlier chapters have thrown up, and the tools they need to shape or adapt to them, they will likely grow more vocal about their own demands.
- As a critical mass of practice grows that is powerful, engaging and that demonstrates the value to learners, school leaders will be sharing and proliferating models that are both rigorous and creative.
- Systems leaders may start to perceive the valuable role they can play in shifting this paradigm for the good. Legitimised by international initiatives such as that by the OECD, they may become more relaxed about not assessing every aspect of education that moves.

---

[27] https://education-reimagined.org/   [28] www.nextgenlearning.org/
[29] https://hundred.org/en   [30] www.innovationunit.org/
[31] OECD, 'The Future We Want'.

State agencies have a particularly central role in supporting schools to incorporate learner agency into their teaching and learning. They can set the tone of the narrative; they can legitimate and endorse. They set the regulatory rules of what the state has a right to expect. They set regulations around assessment, which can have perhaps the greatest impact.

However, ecosystems of partners from every corner of society are offering help to bring agency, and the essential pillars of thriving, into learning for all. This is fortunate, because schools cannot really do this alone, or at least, not in a way that is adequate to the challenge. This new landscape of education ecosystems is the issue to which we now turn.

13 | From Schools to Learning Ecosystems

To reprise the argument so far: thriving in the transforming twenty-first-century world has to be seen holistically across four domains: the planetary, societal, interpersonal and intrapersonal. And recognising this leads to new goals for education. At the heart of achieving these goals is the effort to confer agency on learners; to cease to treat them as objects, but truly as subjects. What follows?

We have looked at pathfinder schools who are making huge strides towards designing curricula and pedagogies that effectively address these goals. The question in this chapter is: what supports do they need? How far can they take these new practices and philosophies as single institutions? Of course, changing the narrative and the discourse around education's purpose – the central objective of this book – will create a quite different climate in which schools can operate, innovate and explore. But in practical terms, our evidence suggests that schools that set out along this path are engaged in a journey that is not just an internal, organisational change programme. They also start to reach out more systematically to the resources for learning around them; and they become more permeable.

In every city, town and community there are multiple, almost infinite, resources for learning that are under- or unused. In general, schools do not exploit this potential. Of course 'community partnerships' are a familiar element of conventional schools' operating style: not many are total fortresses (though in some communities, the school can and needs to be a place of safety protecting learners from the dangers of its surroundings). But the pathfinder schools we have highlighted have pushed this notion much further: they have reached out to the wider communities – the businesses, creative and cultural organisations, entrepreneurs, not-for-profits, public services and multiple other categories – intentionally to create *local learning ecosystems*.

We first introduced the concept of learning ecosystems in Chapter 6, to describe the platforms and configurations of activities that support internships and learning pathways at the Met in Providence and Remake Learning in Pittsburgh. Below, we expand on how exactly those ecosystems developed. But we have also seen ecosystems at work through networks such as Making Caring Common, Naturally Smart Schools, and connected studies of mindfulness. Just as we saw in Chapter 4 how the planet's 'ecosystem services' provide (limited) 'carrying capacity' for human life, these wider support systems can be grown to increase the capacity available to schools.

13.1 Thinking in Ecosystems

Reflecting on the experience and practice of our pathfinders discussed above, we may start to ask questions about where these developments might lead. Could schools be more systematically focused on becoming a part of a social and digital network that is intentionally committed to optimising learning to thrive? Our own research and that of others finds that, across the world, there is interest, energy and funding going into the intentional creation of such ecosystems.[1] In a sense the COVID-19 shutdown of schools propelled them into a crash course of exploration about how to leverage the learning resources, whether digital or domestic, that are relatively under-exploited.

What is really meant by an 'ecosystem' here? Deriving from the field of evolutionary biology, an 'ecosystem' is a community of inter-dependent organisms acting in conjunction with the natural environment. Over the last decade, the term has proliferated as a metaphor for thinking differently about the future of education, moving beyond a top-down systems approach. The power of this metaphor has led both to a richness of debate and some confusion about what the term means. In earlier work, we have developed a simple typology of ecosystems to bring clarity to the work and support others navigating this territory:[2]

Knowledge Sharing Ecosystems

This type of ecosystem comprises complex, evolving networks of organisations including think tanks, foundations, governmental and

---

[1] Hannon et al., 'Local Learning Ecosystems: Emerging Models'; Luksha et al., 'Educational Ecosystems for Societal Transformation'.
[2] Hannon et al., 'Local Learning Ecosystems: Emerging Models'.

global agencies and others who are consciously connecting to *facilitate the sharing of new knowledge* about education and learning, innovation, funding opportunities and more. It is largely concerned with building the global shared knowledge base, scaling innovation and enabling better use of resources and opportunities to tackle shared global learning challenges, not only within but between networks.

Examples include the co-conveners of the Global Education Ecosystem advocacy effort, whose report *Investing in Knowledge Sharing to Advance SDG Four* calls for new means for how to improve knowledge sharing across borders in education (Center for Global Education at Asia Society, Results for Development, Teach For All, The Boston Consulting Group and World Innovation Summit for Education, 2018).[3] The aim here is to build an infrastructure that enables multiple stakeholders and initiatives to share knowledge in ways that are more organic, comprehensive and self-directed than in a traditional network.

Innovation Ecosystems

Some cities and regions are involved in designing deliberate conditions that drive and accelerate radical innovation – such as new designs for schooling – through the combination of multiple players, policies and platforms. These innovation ecosystems tend to contain traditional and new education providers, formal and informal learning opportunities, the involvement of business, edtech developers and providers and higher education, and are supported by digital technology.

By All Means (from Harvard's Education ReDesign Lab)[4] is an example of an innovation ecosystem. The New York iZone was another,[5] and there are strong networks of entrepreneurs and start-ups around education in Moscow and Tel Aviv, among others.

Learning Ecosystems

Learning ecosystems comprise diverse combinations of providers (schools, businesses, community organisations, government agencies,

[3] Center for Global Education at Asia Society et al., 'Investing in Knowledge Sharing to Advance SDG 4'.

[4] www.gse.harvard.edu/news-tags/all-means

[5] CPI, 'New York City Innovation Zone'.

not-for profits, entrepreneurs, edtech companies and so on) creating new learning opportunities and pathways to success. The diversity resides not just in the partners, but in the modes of learning: formal, informal, non-formal, digital. They are usually supported by an innovative credentialing system or technology platforms that replace or augment the traditional linear system of examinations and graduation. They need not, however, be confined to their geographic location in terms of resources overall. They may exploit the technologies now available to choreograph global learning resources. They are delivering new opportunities directly to learners.

13.2 Learning Ecosystems for Realising New Goals

With this clarification, we can hone in on the idea of *learning ecosystems* to examine in greater depth the contribution they are making towards the effort to realise new goals for education. Our own research has looked at the variety of local ecosystems springing up around the world, through a scanning exercise and some in-depth case studies.[6] Such ecosystems tend to be:

- *diversifying learning resources and pathways for learners*
- *activating and sharing resources for learning in new ways from diverse sources*
- *dynamic in composition and porous around the edges*
- *supported by helpful infrastructure*
- *comprised of formal and informal learning institutions, traditional and new entrants*
- *overseen by distributed governance*
- *learner driven or have learner agency at their heart*
- *attempting to meet twenty-first-century challenges through thriving, beyond academic attainment.*

These rather abstract qualities will be explored more fully in the practical examples we describe later in this chapter. But what they share is a simple conviction: education has to become everyone's concern. And the more connected, intertwined and inter-dependent societies become, the greater the opportunity to leverage our collective efforts. As new education innovations, organisations, resources and

---

[6] Hannon et al., 'Local Learning Ecosystems: Emerging Models'.

relationships develop, pathfinders profiled here see opportunities to transform the 'why', 'what' and 'how' of teaching and learning.

13.3 Learning Ecosystems in Practice: What Do They Look Like?

Diverse organisations are committed to the idea of ecosystems, but it is a different matter to bring one into being and sustain it. Many involved struggled to really envision what they are working towards. We offer some detailed case studies below therefore, to give a more tangible sense of the reality on the ground.[7]

It is rare for a school to be an initiator and sustainer of a learning ecosystem. One such, however, is The Met, in the United States, which we first introduced in Chapter 6.

The Metropolitan Regional Career and Technical Center, Rhode Island, United States ('The Met'): A School-Centric Ecosystem

The Met is a part of the network of schools known as the Big Picture Learning Company, and as the flagship of the movement.

Among its features is the development of a sophisticated learning ecosystem. The Met provides real-world, interest-led learning pathways by engaging mentors from the community, mobilising local businesses and building partnerships with further and higher education institutions. It operates a personalised learning design that allows each learner to pursue their passions and interests, in line with an individual learning plan negotiated between teacher, parent/carer and learner.

Students pursue real work, ventures and projects that have a consequence in the world, are assessed not on the basis of standardised tests, but on how they perform in the situations they are in at exhibitions and demonstrations of achievement, on motivation, and on the habits of mind, hand, and heart.[8] Over time, The Met has built an ecosystem of local organisations and community members deeply involved in

[7] The authors gratefully acknowledge the support of The World Innovation Summit on Education (WISE), which supported the original research on which the case studies are based.
[8] For a detailed discussion of the practice at the Met, see Hannon, Gillinson and Shanks, *Learning a Living*.

supporting the learning of students at the school through internships, projects and opportunities after leaving school.

For two days a week, learners connect with the community and gain real-world experience by working alongside mentors with whom they share a passion and interest. Placements – ranging from City Halls to the local skateboarding shop – involve extensive work in the situation they are in, projects and ventures that have authentic value in the real world, as well as for their studies. Internships are supported by an internship coordinator and the advisor who together help to source, administer and design internships. The students complete authentic work that benefits the student and the mentor with deep investigations. Through this work, students develop twenty-first century skills, real-world certifications, build adult relationships and begin establishing a professional network where people outside of school can validate who they are and what they know. They also learn to navigate the new landscape of work – one of the new goals associated with thriving.

The context and place of Rhode Island are leveraged to the full. The Met now has the advantage of many years of building relationships, most especially for the delivery of its internships, and the expertise required to sustain and develop these relationships, through new roles such as internship coordinators and advisors. This suggests that learning ecosystems will need to evolve such new roles and skillsets to realise their potential. The radical personalisation and real-world learning the Met provides would be impossible without its grounding in an extended ecosystem of providers and partners.

Big Picture Learning has now contributed hugely to the advancement of this work across other schools by the creation of Imblaze.[9] ImBlaze is a powerful platform that enables schools to curate a set of internships for students to request to pursue. Schools can monitor the search process, track internship attendance and ensure compliance, and ensure student success.

Swinburne University, Melbourne, Australia: A University-Centric Ecosystem

Although initiated and sustained by a university, this is a learning ecosystem that very much has schools at its heart. We have noted the

---

[9] www.imblaze.org/

importance of ecosystems for engaging young people in STEM learning, and also for ensuring that such learning is up-to-date and real-world. Swinburne University of Technology works with industry partners (such as Siemens and the Australian Synchrotron), local community expertise, primary and secondary schools, and the Australian government to provide enriching STEM learning programs as part of an ecosystem designed to raise awareness of STEM disciplines. Swinburne are investing heavily in building a dynamic, interactive, career management platform to connect groups across the ecosystem and allow users to meaningfully develop their own unique 'professional purpose', informed by real-time market data. Thus they aim at two (at least) of the learning goals we have proposed: to learn to navigate a disrupted landscape of work; and to find personal purpose and meaning.

At the time or writing, 400 schools across Victoria are engaged in STEM school engagement programs; 38,790 school students are engaged in STEM school engagement programs; and 116 Swinburne students are engaged in those STEM school engagement programs.

Swinburne's STEM ecosystem offers extensive enrichment programs that integrate with the curricula of schools. Programs connect schools, communities and industry, engaging students on multiple fronts. For connections between these groups to flourish, schools need to develop a trusting relationship with partners, like Swinburne, in providing the right support required for effectively running the programs. Swinburne supports teachers to practise facilitation skills that broker new relationships with universities, community organisations and industry that provide their students with the skills, such as creativity and problem solving, and behaviours needed to make a meaningful and positive contribution to society.

The engagement of Swinburne undergraduates and industry experts with schools has enabled a sense of passion and drive: this is what is needed to uplift the next generation of learners and engage them in authentic learning. Exposure to positive, enriching learning experiences equips students with a greater understanding of professional life. They become more self-, and socially, aware of personal interests and feel empowered to pursue pathways that are most meaningful to them. There is an equity dimension here: often these experiences are facilitated by parents in well-off families. Swinburne's ecosystem makes them available to all. Drawing on its success in the STEM area,

Swinburne is extending its ecosystem initiative to all other areas of the university, including the arts, law, business and innovation.

Remake Learning, Pittsburgh, United States: A City-Centric Ecosystem

In Chapter 6, we met Remake Learning and its work to define new pathways of learning in Pittsburgh. How did this develop into a learning ecosystem? The Remake Learning[10] ecosystem consists of more than 500 organisations in Western Pennsylvania, with 137 school districts, as well as museums, libraries, other out-of-school education non-profits, philanthropies, government bodies, industry partners and start-ups. It has trained over 5,300 educators (formal and non-formal) in innovative teaching methods, and has granted $70 million (USD) philanthropic support to local learning innovation. Their objective is their name: they seek to collectively 'remake learning' in order to best serve learners in a transforming world. Their vision is a future in which the creative members of Remake Learning support each other to ensure that learning is engaging, relevant and equitable across projects, organisations and programs.

The objectives of this ecosystem map directly onto the Thrive agenda. They seek to:

- Connect all the places learners live, work and play, including schools, libraries, museums, parks, clubs, community centres, centres of faith, at home and online.
- Encourage learners to explore and play; and support them to follow their curiosity using varied tools (including, but not limited to, technologies).
- Help develop deep and caring relationships between learners and their families, peers, educators and mentors.
- Connect learners to their communities and, in an interconnected world, help learners develop cross-cultural understandings that unlock opportunities to thrive both within and beyond their own communities.

The Remake Learning ecosystem also explicitly addresses the issue of growing learner agency. Learners are challenged to question,

---

[10] https://remakelearning.org/

examine and dissect social systems; to develop the confidence to address and deconstruct inequalities; and to construct a more just and equitable world.

13.4 Formidable, but Not Insuperable Obstacles

The encouraging appearance in the last few years of ecosystems that are focused on thriving should not mask the formidable problems the movement faces in becoming the norm and not the beautiful exceptions. Most learning ecosystems we have identified have been the outcome of the work of individual visionaries and institutions, forging alliances, and often supported by philanthropists who are prepared to take the risk of funding the initiating phase. The problems they face are substantial: institutional self-interest; funding and accountability regimes; lack of spare capacity in stretched schools to create discretionary effort.

Taking just the first of these, current trends in education exacerbate this problem of every-school-for-itself. School systems around the world are seeing an increase in quasi-markets, where schools compete for students and funding.[11] In these conditions, schools have very real incentives to compete and even altruistic school leaders face dilemmas engaging in time-consuming or risky collaborations.[12] Some funding and accountability regimes are also becoming less hospitable to ecosystem development. Decentralisation of budgets and decision-making to the school-level frees schools from some bureaucracy, but also leaves them without pooled resources to support external partnerships. Once disparate, it is hard to bring these resources back together. Recent efforts in New Zealand – one of the earliest countries to decentralise – to recreate 'communities of learning' across schools have illustrated the challenges of re-pooling budgets. Added to this is the difficulty – as with all disruptive innovations – of evidencing impact in complex social settings where a multitude of factors are at play, and where the metrics to indicate authentic success are not as developed as a simple set of standardised tests. Overall, it is evident that ecosystems are at odds with many education policy trends of the past two decades.

[11] Windle, *Making Sense of School Choice – Politics, Policies, and Practice under Conditions of Cultural Diversity*; Forsey, Davies, and Walford, *The Globalisation of School Choice?*
[12] Greany and Higham, 'Hierarchy, Markets and Networks'.

We call out these difficulties because they have collective solutions. School choice, decentralised funding and standardised testing create a logic of competition, but they can also create the foundations for an ecosystem. Schools that decide to take mutual responsibility for all the learners in their locality can find these policies supportive. They come with the freedom to specialise and develop distinctive school profiles. While the tendency is for schools to use this 'freedom' to ape traditional private schools to secure a second-best spot in a hierarchy,[13] an ecosystem perspective would encourage schools towards different niches, encouraged by the ability to draw on each others' resources to best serve their communities.

Moreover, for schools who are willing to take this perspective, there has been an explosion of potential new partners eager to work with schools to reinvent how we organise learning – the position is transformed from but a decade ago.

We do not underestimate how difficult it is for schools in the current climate to shift from a logic of competition to one of ecosystems. The study of institutional logics highlights how powerfully these ideas of what is right and necessary can grip organisations.[14] But the same body of research also illustrates how *individual leaders*, by using different language and modelling different values, can start to shift logics.[15] The next advance will be for *systems* to embrace and legitimate an ecosystemic approach.

13.5 Can *Systems* Go Ecosystemic?

Ironically the current 'systems' that organise public education do not generally think ecosystemically. They do little to encourage or enable schools to become a part of local learning ecosystems, and often include much that makes this difficult, such as encouraging schools to compete. Organisations tend to do what they get judged on.[16] In the case of schools, becoming part of learning ecosystems to enrich learners' opportunities is not usually seen as a priority.

Yet there are some exceptions.

---

[13] Lubienski, 'School Diversification in Second-Best Education Markets'.
[14] Thornton, Ocasio and Lounsbury, *The Institutional Logics Perspective*.
[15] Zietsma and Lawrence, 'Institutional Work in the Transformation of an Organizational Field'; Binder, 'For Love and Money'.
[16] Espeland and Sauder, *Engines of Anxiety*.

Finland's Ecosystemic Approach

The qualities and strengths of the Finnish system are now well known and analysed.[17] Excellence in teaching, intelligent assessment and accountability are all clearly identified as important features. What is less well known is how, in recent years, Finland has created the conditions for schools to flourish in rich local ecosystems.

The capital city of Helsinki is a good example. Despite its strengths, the goal is a shift to involving all of society. As Liisa Pohjolainen, Executive Director of the City of Helsinki, describes:

The goal in Helsinki is systemic change, with a focus on global future civic skills, the whole city as a learning environment, and the creation of a sustainable future.[18]

The whole city of Helsinki is regarded as a large learning environment in which learners work actively. Instead of learning taking place only at school and in the classroom during the school day, learning is now viewed as something tied neither to time or place.

Helsinki has a diverse natural environment and cultural history. Cooperation with various sectors offer a rich learning environment for learners of all ages. All of the city's parks, playgrounds, museums, theatres, cultural buildings and libraries are incorporated into schools' stocks of learning environments. In Helsinki, nature is nearby and available. Nature schools are very popular and there are forest pre-schools where, as a rule, everything is done out of doors.

For these educators, the city itself becomes the local learning ecosystem, as Pohjolainen describes again:

Helsinki is our learning environment. Even in kindergartens children go outside the classrooms and can learn in museums, theatres, libraries, streets, shopping centres and everywhere in the city. In this way, they learn about their home city of Helsinki.[19]

The cultural and creative sector is particularly closely tied in. Learners take part in film-making and joint productions have been created with the city orchestra and National Opera. One-off engagements such as these are of course not unfamiliar in other systems (though increasingly

---

[17] Sahlberg, *Finnish Lessons 2.0*.
[18] Noora, Lasse and Ilona, 'Forerunner: Improving Education in Helsinki', 4.
[19] Noora, Lasse and Ilona, 43.

under pressure). The point here is that they are embedded in every school's design for learning, and the connections are growing wider and deeper. This is not just for elites.

Helsinki is not alone. Kuopio is a small city in the centre of Finland sandwiched between two lakes. It has created a local learning ecosystem which has all the schools working in close relationship with the creative and cultural resources at the city's disposal. Kuopio Cultural Pathways has created a learning ecosystem to bring culture into the curriculum of individual subjects and larger subject areas in different grades of schooling, focusing on socialisation, cultural identity, media and responsibility for nature, environment and sustainable development.

The city has created a number of 'cultural paths' along which students 'trek'. There are nine 'paths' covering art, music and other cultural fields, with each path designed for the needs and curriculum objectives of a particular grade level, within and across different subjects. A path involves local institutions such as libraries, museums or galleries, and includes at least one cultural visit such as to the theatre or an exhibition, with options for many more. Each year, students in a year group 'trek' along a cultural path together. In the final year, students trek a personally chosen path. After eight years on the culture paths, ninth-graders can use the city's cultural services for free with a K9-card.

Every school has its own culture courier: a person that acts as a point of contact between schools and cultural facilities. In its original form, the culture path program coordinator would coordinate the program in interaction and cooperation with the teachers, cultural facilities and the educational services of the city of Kuopio. Like the example of The Met, this suggests that new roles need to evolve to construct and maintain the smooth working of the ecosystem.

The cultural pathways bring different styles of learning to environments outside the routines of school. Museums and theatres design activities around the curriculum from different perspectives and in different ways, while introducing real-world issues. For instance, the Kuopio Natural History Museum organises environmental education activities such as nature excursions or lectures in schools beyond the cultural pathways. Other examples include the 'Thank you for Friendship' project – a model to prevent school bullying through drama workshops. The approach involves participatory drama with

the student at the centre. The emphasis is on promoting communication and interaction skills as well as empathy, self-esteem, interaction
and recognition of emotions. The method is exploratory, humanistic
and hermeneutical.

STEM Learning Ecosystems in the United States

We have already noted the proliferation of ecosystemic approaches to
be found among US innovators. At the (national) level, an effort has
been made to draw together the wide and growing variety of STEM-
focused Learning Ecosystems right across the country, in a nationwide
Community of Practice.[20] STEM Local Learning Ecosystems are to be
found in more than 90 locations at the time of writing. They are
committed to designing new pathways to help all young people to
become engaged, knowledgeable and skilled in the STEM disciplines.
A rich array of learning opportunities is assembled to combine schools,
community settings such as after-school and summer programs, science centres and museums, and informal experiences at home and in a
variety of environments.

Ecosystems in the Fight for Equity

Finally, recalling the importance that equity has for the creation of
thriving societies, we should note the growing advocacy for the ecosystemic approach as a means to advance equity and overcome historic
and cyclical disadvantage. The STEM Ecosystems initiative in the
United States has been set up explicitly to focus on the under-served
and under-represented. Numerous other initiatives are predicated on
the same objective – *Educacio 360* in Catalonia[21] and Cities of
Learning in the UK[22] are good examples. It is clear that socio-economic
status in most societies determines young learners' access to the enriching learning experiences around them. Wealthier families will ensure it.

If we do not design intentionally for a vibrant learning ecosystem, we risk
creating a fractured landscape in which only learners whose families have the
time, money, and resources to customize or supplement their learning

---

[20] https://stemecosystems.org/   [21] www.fbofill.cat/educacio360
[22] www.thersa.org/cities-of-learning

journeys have access to learning that adapts to and meets their needs.
Katherine Prince, KnowledgeWorks[23]

We turn to this challenge of equity in the Chapter 14.

13.6 Conclusion

An active search is underway for new ways of learning and new organisational forms for education that will be consistent with the emergent conditions we face, and therefore new learning goals. In such a context, perhaps it is unsurprising that inspiration for change is sought from biological, as opposed to mechanical, analogues.

Thought leaders, system leaders and visionary practitioners have begun to explore whether the opportunity exists to create dynamic and evolving learning ecosystems that enable all young people to thrive and genuinely become lifelong learners. It will mean leveraging a broader and more powerful range of assets than ever before. Such a reconfiguration of education systems with broader resources is the only route to making the idea of 'real-world learning' a practical reality. Those involved in this work share an analysis that suggests the existing educational paradigm is exhausted, and there is an acute need to refocus on purpose. They see learning ecosystems as a fundamental element of the emergent paradigm.[24] Some writers consider that in aiming at empathy-based learning and an emphasis on human relationships and collective action, learning ecosystems can help shift human identity away from individualistic self-interest, towards one centred on humanistic changemaking.[25] Ashoka and others envision learning ecosystems to be suited to educating and empowering the 'whole human'.

We envisage new learning ecosystems in which whole communities work together to provide experiences that keep every young person on a journey to becoming a changemaker. [26]

---

[23] Prince, 'Innovating toward a Vibrant Learning Ecosystem: Ten Pathways for Transforming Learning', 6.
[24] Luksha et al., 'Educational Ecosystems for Societal Transformation'.
[25] Wagner, *Creating Innovators*.
[26] Hall and Ashoka Global Leadership Team, 'Empowering Young People to Create a Better World', 2.

It is worth noting that the application of the ecosystem metaphor to fields of human endeavour has a long history in disciplines other than education and learning. Ecosystem as both an analytical tool and a practical strategy has been explored in business and management theory for at least two decades and complexity economics has been gaining ground for around the same period.[27] In each case, the introduction of the ecosystem metaphor has been a response to the limitations of simple market equilibrium models or hierarchies for understanding and shaping systems, causing scholars to turn instead to an organic model that takes inspiration from biological work.

We note that it is the strengths of ecosystems that are foregrounded and not their fragility. In the natural world, they are threatened by, and sometimes succumb to, pollution, resource depletion and invasive species. They usually depend on 'keystone species' and 'ecosystem engineers' (like the beaver). So a question to be explored in the future, as local learning ecosystems develop and mature, will be: how resilient are they to the removal of initial catalytic funding, the entry of dysfunctional members or other unanticipated shifts in the environment? Furthermore, it will be observed that the case studies reported here are in the main from high-income countries. Yet natural ecosystems occur in relatively constrained environments (deserts and polar regions). It could be argued that it is even more imperative that learning ecosystems be encouraged in low-income countries, more optimally to utilise all the underused resources that might be available for learning. As philosopher Zak Stein has recently put it:

Education must no longer be something that is kept behind closed doors and that requires special privileges and capital to get. In a world pushed to the brink of crisis, education, like energy, must be made abundant, free, and healthy, if our species is to survive. Everyone everywhere must have access to educational resources that are good, true, and beautiful, even if only so that solutions can be found in time for the billions of community-level problems that are reverberating across our planet as it reels in crisis.[28]

The creation of stronger and richer educational ecosystems must be seen as part of the overall set of interactions that can sustain the planet, its species and its societies.

---

[27] Beinhocker, *The Origin of Wealth*; Moore, *Creating Public Value*.
[28] Stein, *Education in a Time between Worlds*.

14 | *Beyond Beautiful Exceptions*
The Challenge of Scale

How do we get from here to there? Expanding thriving at school will never be simple. There is no model that can be replicated, because there is more than one way to thrive. The schools in this book all have distinct purposes and approaches, based on their particular contexts. We have argued that part of what makes them work is their embeddedness *in* a context: their responsiveness to local narratives and their use of the resources available to them in that particular place. And yet, we have also argued that it is impossible to really thrive alone. The nature of ecosystems is that they are interdependent. Each level of thriving – the interpersonal, societal and planetary – relies on larger and larger groups respecting and promoting each others' needs. So we have to have some theory of change about how thriving at school grows.

14.1 The Nature of the Mission: Growth, Not Scale

Many of the schools in this book could be described as examples of educational innovation. In the world of business, when an innovation works, the next step is to *move to scale*. What would it look like to try to 'scale' thriving?

In education, most of what is scaled is products: electronic whiteboards, tablets, student information systems and behaviour apps. When it comes to scaling *practice*, there are two attempted paths to scale.[1]

The first is through state-led quality improvement. Over the past decades, education systems around the world have been engaged in an

---

[1] Robinson and Winthrop, 'Millions Learning: Scaling up Education in Development Countries' propose four pathways to scaling – horizontal, vertical, organisational and functional – but acknowledge that they take a broad perspective on the nature of scaling. We find their model very compelling but believe that the concept of growth better captures the key processes they describe.

almost continuous series of programmes and schemes aimed at 'transferring' and 'translating' – or, in the well-designed schemes 'adapting' – the practices of 'successful' schools to others.[2] These programmes often involve designating a lead school and expecting others to follow.

The second attempted path to scale is through markets. Increasing school choice was thought to be a way to stimulate schools to adopt the successful practices of others. In *theory*, in a market schools first diversify and generate new practices. Some of these practices are particularly successful in attracting students and then other schools, seeking to compete, adopt them. But in practice, markets do not produce diversification; increasing competition for students tends to increase homogeneity as schools stick with normal practice.[3] This phenomena is sometimes called 'isomorphism'.[4]

Neither of these routes has worked to reach scale. While there are individual contexts where state-led programmes or increase in school choice have produced moderate levels of improvement,[5] there are many more where the improvements have been sparse.[6]

What both routes have produced at scale is the proliferation of standardised measures of education outcomes and increased incentive for educators to focus time and energy on these measures. These metrics are fundamental to the operation of top-down improvement efforts and to markets and yet, as we have discussed before, they

---

[2] Canato, Ravasi and Phillips, 'Coerced Practice Implementation in Cases of Low Cultural Fit'; Redding, Cannata and Haynes, 'With Scale in Mind'.

[3] Windle, *Making Sense of School Choice – Politics, Policies, and Practice under Conditions of Cultural Diversity*; Lubienski, 'Innovation in Education Markets'.

[4] DiMaggio and Powell, 'The Iron Cage Revisited'.

[5] The London Challenge is an example of a state-led program that fostered sharing between schools. Some analyses suggest that the level of improvement observed was more to do with London's increased wealth over that period, but the schools involved say that they benefitted from the network. A – controversial – example of school markets that can be perceived as a success is New Orleans, where after being devastated by Hurricane Katrina the school system was converted to a system of charter schools. Here, it is difficult to disentangle the impacts of markets from the additional regeneration work occurring around schools.

[6] Payne, *So Much Reform, So Little Change*; Peurach and Glazer, 'Reconsidering Replication'; Lindgren, Oskarsson and Dawes, 'Can Political Inequalities Be Educated Away?'; Pritchett, 'The Risks to Education Systems from Design Mismatch and Global Isomorphism'.

cannot capture the range of valued goals of education. Instead, they tend to create unintended consequences.[7]

The problem with scaling as a goal is even more fundamental than its undesirable side-effects. We have argued in Chapters 12 and 13 that thriving is about the pursuit of meaningful purpose through agency and, consequently, we cannot *create* thriving but we can create the ecosystems to sustain it. Ecosystems do not scale; they grow. And while natural and social ecosystems are different, we can think about their growth in the same way: it is all about creating the right conditions. So where do we start?

14.2 Removing the Inhibitors of Growth

If a garden is choked by weeds, adding compost or watering will only spread the weeds as much as any flowers. Before creating a lot of new activity in the education system, it is important to identify what needs to be removed, so that this activity is not misdirected. There are currently three key inhibitors we see in education systems round the world.

Confusing Outputs and Outcomes

We have talked a number of times in this book about the limitations of educational measures. This is not because we are opposed to measurement – social science would be impossible without it – but because we want to emphasise that educational measurement is extremely *hard*. Recognising the real difficulty of educational measurement is the first step to resolving one of the key inhibitors in education systems: the confusion of outputs with outcomes.

In evaluation-speak, an output is what is produced by an activity, or its short-term result. An outcome is the ultimate value or utility of that result. Our ultimate goal is to know about outcomes, and so we would typically try to have some measure of outcomes so that we can check what is happening to them. Then, if we develop a clear theory as to how outputs and outcomes relate, we can rely on measures of outputs

---

[7] Espeland and Sauder, 'Rankings and Reactivity'; Lingard et al., *Globalizing Educational Accountabilities*.

going forward to tell us something about the outcomes we might expect.

In education, there are three major challenges to linking outputs and outcomes. First, there are many different outcomes we might care about. Already, the task is much more complex. Second, the gap between outputs and outcomes can often be many years, making it much more difficult to wait as long as necessary to be sure about outcomes, before we start to rely on our proxy outputs. Third, we do not actually have very clear theories about what links outputs and outcomes. The causal pathways of learning are multiple and complex and it is not clear what the good proxies are for the outcomes we care about.

As a result of these challenges, in education we often end up relying on measures of outputs, when we don't really have a warrant for doing so. A lot of activity is potentially misdirected in this way.

The above three problems apply, regardless what it is we are trying to teach or learn. But there is another, bigger, problem with relying on outputs when what we are trying to do is develop human expertise: for example, helping children on the way to becoming scientists, artists, mathematicians, inventors... With these sorts of aims, learning is made up of *convergent* and *divergent* phases. What this means is that sometimes the learning is aimed at learning the same things that everyone else knows – becoming fluent in the times-tables; mastering how to mix colours; learning the elements – and sometimes it is aimed at producing something *unique*. This second, divergent, type of learning might seem unusual but schools do it all the time: asking students to do a project, write a story, solve a problem, design a poster. All of these kind of activities anticipate that students will produce unique work. In fact, we would be concerned if two students submitted something identical, and they reflect the cultural valuation of individuals being able to produce individual work.

Ideally, these two kinds of learning work in tandem. We can be really focused on mastering something because we know that it will help us to produce something unique. More often than not, they do not work in tandem. But often that is because we rush them; we are trying to get everyone to master everything, and as a result not enough convergent learning is happening, and any time for divergent work is squeezed and the resultant work is of low quality.

We believe that thriving is closely related to divergent phases of learning. If thriving involves the exercising of agency, this is shown when we deviate from what has gone before by doing things that are unique? This does not mean that we do them alone. A unique creation might call on a whole class, a whole school, a network of schools – or, in the recent school strikes for the climate, school children from across the world. The important point is that it brings something new into being that would not have existed without us being there.

Recognising the distinction between divergent and convergent learning is important because it is only convergent learning that can be monitored using our current tools of measurement. Divergent learning calls for a different kind of valuation and in the penultimate section of this chapter, we describe what this might look like. But without the ability to measure the outputs of divergent learning, we will always be at risk of misdirection if we expect that we can rely on outputs as a proxy of educational outcomes. We have to keep our eyes on the real outcomes we care about, unique creations included.

Smothered by Scrutiny

There are many plants that die most easily from soaked roots. This happens through excessive watering. The plant does not have time to use the water it has and the excess water does not have space to drain through the soil. Likewise, smothering people and depriving them of the necessary time and space to do their thing can be one of the biggest inhibitors to learning.

In education, smothering comes in the form of excessive monitoring or 'hyper-accountability'. This can include districts or school leaders requiring termly or even weekly student learning data, regular inspections of classrooms or students' books, or lengthy reporting on students. This hyper-accountability is problematic because it misunderstands the complexity of teaching and learning. The learning of an individual student is already complex because it involves the interaction of attention, emotions, prior knowledge and the level of distraction in the environment. Coordinating the learning of multiple students – teaching – is vastly more complex.[8] It requires moment-by-moment judgement and discretion.

---

[8] Yurkofsky et al., 'Research on Continuous Improvement: Exploring the Complexities of Managing Educational Change'.

Trying to force this activity to look a certain way or produce certain products at particular times only distorts it. Instead of engaging with the complexity of it, the work becomes producing what is required at the particular time. Monitoring creates barriers to trying any new practice because of the uncertainty as to whether it will look the right way or hit the required targets. Professional conversations that could be about the specific purposes or activities of a particular community or discipline become supplanted by ones about techniques to ensuring that the accountability beast is fed.[9]

Excessive monitoring is by no means a universal problem. In many school systems, lack of oversight and accountability is just as much of a problem. We do not want to pretend that removing the structures of accountability would magically unleash a tide of energy and improved learning. Educators will always have lives to lead, wider interests and the normal human tendency towards rest or novelties that would likely take up more and more time without any oversight. But that oversight can come quite naturally from working in organisations full of other people doing the same work. There is no evidence that where there is a culture of valuing education, where expectations are realistic and people have the resources to do their jobs, teachers need external oversight to work hard for their students.

In the systems of high-income countries with strong teacher unions, such as those of Canada, New Zealand or Western Europe, there is considerably less oversight but measurable learning outcomes are no worse, and in some cases better, than in comparable countries such as the United Kingdom, United States or Australia.[10] Excessive monitoring seems to be related to the politics of education more than anything else: it is in countries where the control of education is more centralised, and consequently, further from the classroom, that the demands for improvement from the centre translate into layers of scrutiny that are divorced from the real activity of teaching and learning.

For accountability to work, educators have to be allowed to focus on coordinating learning, knowing that a by-product may be monitoring, instead of the focus being the monitoring, and learning possibly

[9] Ingram, Louis and Schroeder, 'Accountability Policies and Teacher Decision Making'; Coburn, 'Shaping Teacher Sensemaking'.

[10] OECD, *PISA 2018 Results Volume I: What Students Know and Can Do*; Moe and Wiborg, *The Comparative Politics of Education: Teacher Unions and Education Systems around the World*.

happening as a by-product. The key concern of all education system leaders should be whether they have this the right way round.

Resource Starvation: The Challenge of Educational Inequality

There is an additional reason why it is crucial to focus on how thriving schools are spreading. There is a tendency in education for new developments or innovations to most benefit the already privileged. This is sometimes called the 'Matthew effect', after a line in Matthew's book of the Bible: *For to everyone who has will more be given, and he will have abundance.* (Matthew 25–29).[11] It is unclear what exactly this line meant then, but today it describes the general phenomenon that those with more resources are often better placed to take advantage of new opportunities.

While we have seen in this book that some of the best examples of thriving come from the pressure of having too little, many also arise in areas of abundance. If we try to help schools to promote thriving, will this only exacerbate existing inequalities? Quite rightly, governments are criticised if they are seen to be focusing on only those schools that are 'doing okay'. If some kids have functioning buildings, qualified teachers and are passing their tests, but others do not, it would seem churlish to be worrying about the first group rather than focusing on the second.

This perspective makes two false assumptions. First, this should not be a zero-sum game. Promoting the possibility for schools to thrive need not and should not take the place of proper investment in school infrastructure and teachers. We have seen in this book that thriving is possible in a great range of situations; it does not rely on additional financial investment of any commensurate scale to what goes into infrastructure and teachers' salaries, which form the major component of education budgets all around the world. Most countries still have a way to go on ensuring the necessary size and equitable distribution of such budgets. This is a political problem that impacts on but is not integral to the goal of thriving. It should be possible to continue the argument for equitable investment while also promoting thriving.

Second, we have seen already the limitations of a vision of education's purpose based on test scores and achievement gaps. Tests are

[11] Kerckhoff and Glennie, *The Matthew Effect in American Education.*

designed to create differences, and socio-economic inequalities outside of schools will inevitably mean that tests show differences between groups. This is not an argument to get rid of the tests. It is important to keep monitoring these differences and, through reducing societal inequalities as well as through the work of schools, hope that they close. But making it the *purpose* of schools to close these gaps places a completely unfair role on teachers, results in dysfunctional practices, and, potentially, cements the notion of differences between groups in unhelpful ways.[12]

These two false assumptions arise from confusing thriving with a finite resource. Public spending on schools and good test scores are both, in the context of each school cohort, finite resources. Educational inequality arises when these finite resources are distributed unequally, or through processes that track prior socio-economic inequalities. Politicians would often have us believe that these things are not finite resources: that through maintaining an inequitable status quo we can grow the economy or all reach higher standards. But this does nothing for the generation in school now and nor does it prevent future inequalities; growing the pie does not change the way that it is divided. Consequently, we have a continuously misdirected debate about educational inequality.

But thriving is *not* a finite resource. Creating more thriving schools does not rely on arguments about who should get what or about growing a pie. It *is* possible for us all to thrive simultaneously. It is, perhaps, only really possible if we all do it simultaneously.

We are of course a long way from that point, and so this aspiration can start to sound utopian. But the key point is that we must not confuse thriving with the goal of equitably distributed resources. They are separate goals and we can work towards both.

When it comes to educational inequality, movements should focus first and foremost on inequalities in infrastructure and teachers, of the kind identified above, and direct public investment towards closing those gaps. This is the mission for reducing educational inequality, and it shapes our *political* commitments. But it should not shape *the practices of schools*. It should not be confused with a mission for promoting the thriving of all schools and children, *as schools and children*, not merely as representatives of their group as defined by

---

[12] Ladson-Billings, 'From the Achievement Gap to the Education Debt'.

political metrics. The rest of this chapter focuses on how we could achieve this latter mission.

14.3 Creating Healthy Growth

Removing the inhibitors above would make a big difference in creating the conditions for thriving. But nothing grows in a vacuum. Educational activity needs some things to shape it and energise it. What are these things?

Design Principles: Crafting a Frame

Across the cases in this book, we have seen that thriving schools have a clear sense of their *design principles*. Design principles are a little different from purposes. Where a purpose may be an abstract sense of what a school hopes to achieve with and for its pupils, a design principle says something about *how a school will be*.

The founding principles for the High Tech High schools we met in Chapter 4 were *personalisation*, *adult world connection*, *common intellectual mission* and *teacher-as-designer*.[13] Each of these principles had a special meaning to the staff at the schools and shaped all their work together, from how they hired to the design of projects. Each was linked to particular qualities of the school and detailed with questions.[14] But design principles can evolve over time as a school evolves. Today, the work of High Tech High schools is shaped by four slightly adjusted principles: *equity, personalisation, authentic work* and *collaborative design*. By keeping the number small and focused, they want no confusion about what they are about.

Most importantly, as one of High Tech High's founders Larry Rosenstock described to one of us back in 2012, the role of design principles is to make clear what you are *not* going to do. One of their early commitments was to allow no tracking – that is, offering of courses at different levels or with levelled groups. This is embodied in the principal of common intellectual mission and, now, of equity. They also committed to projects. By prioritising adult world connections,

---

[13] www.hightechhigh.org/about-us/
[14] An example of this is still available from *Unboxed*, High Tech High's journal: https://gse.hightechhigh.org/unboxed/issue1/cards/pdfs/High_Tech_High_ Design_Principles.pdf

and now, authentic work, they asserted what was going to be important to them and, simultaneously, acknowledged that some parts of subjects were not going to get taught (as is always the case with any curriculum choice). While Rosenstock and all at High Tech High have never tried to 'scale' the HTH model beyond their context of San Diego, they have always advocated for the value of the design principles.

Design principles come into their own when they are really a part of a school's daily decision-making. Alisa Berger, former founding Principal of the iSchool in New York City, describes how she knew she could move on when she heard staff talking through a decision and referring to the school's three design principles. They weren't doing it because she had asked them to or because they had just had a session on it; it had become how they made decisions in that school. Berger now works in other schools and always strongly advocates for limiting the number of design principles to three. Every decision needs to be able to pass all three design principles. This view is based on the ideas of one of her former teachers, the systems theorist Peter Senge. Senge talks about purpose as a three-legged stool: if one leg falls, it all falls.

We need more three-legged *schools*. Places that are clear about what they are committed to and seek to realise those commitments with all that they do. This is the first step to purpose becoming a living, breathing part of the lives of schools.

Networks: The Means to Grow

To thrive it is not enough to have aspirations or even purpose. Thriving takes activity and in the complex world of school, activities need to be coordinated through *practices* and *routines*. While we have stressed throughout this chapter that one cannot 'scale' thriving, practices and routines can scale. The practice of holding school exhibitions of projects, for example, is one that many schools in quite different contexts have now adopted. A routine of starting meetings by talking about an individual child or sharing some new interest from the week can create a more humane culture in schools, and continual reminders of what's important.

Some of these practices are routines that are simple enough that they can spread straightforwardly through books, conferences or online networks. Twitter is a haven of such ideas and examples. For these kinds of things, someone only has to see something once, or download a resource, and they can figure out how it works.

But some practices are more complex than this. The collections of practices we might call pedagogies tend to rely on extensive bodies ofexplicit and tacit knowledge, along with curricular resources and timetabling requirements. It is not possible to 'pick up' such pedagogies.

These more complex practices spread through social networks. These might be networks of friendships; teachers who work together for years or are friends across schools might gradually adopt or adapt each other's ways of doing things. They might be networks that are created through formal organisations or associations, such as Montessori or the International Baccalaureate. Or they can be somewhere in between: networks that start at an institute or conference but develop over time into ways to develop practice. Events then become distinguished by the social bonds that develop over time. There are many examples of such communities but two that we cherish are the Networks of Innovation and Inquiry in British Columbia and Whole Education in the United Kingdom, both places where social and professional regeneration are intertwined.

What typifies all these deeper networks is that they are often less about just sharing practice, and more about creating it together. Through work with Innovation Unit, we've been involved in a number of structured *communities of practice*: groups that are given time to work together on designing curriculum or practice. Again and again, we have seen teachers get inspired by creating something for *their* students. Many teachers are highly creative; they would not be a in a job that required them to continually be inventing new things for children to do if they were not. But often that inventing has to take place alone, in the evenings or at the weekends, trying to adapt materials or resources that were designed for other students and other purposes. This creativity can often be much more satisfying and productive when it is directed towards collaborative endeavours, where the scope is much greater to really make something that works. Networks can help teachers to do this, both within and across schools.

Nor are these deeper networks just for teachers. We have been fortunate to observe what happens when education system leaders are given the time and space to work together on shared complex problems. They, too, thrive on this. Not only is it rare for them to have the opportunity to engage with people who are in a similar position to their own, but just as for teachers they relish the opportunity to really work on what they think is most important, rather than going through the motions of the daily demands of their job.

No matter what the position, the work of educators is often isolating and lonely. Other than in the rare (but from our observations hugely beneficial) cases of team-teaching, no one teaches quite the same subject to the same group of students. It is difficult to find opportunity to externalise thoughts and bounce ideas around. Moreover, even when educators do get to talk, talk is often focused on the proximate demands, not on the big questions. It is amazing how often when educators are posed with a question about purpose or the challenges of the future they say, as they eagerly get stuck in, 'we never get to think about this'. For many, it requires a structured opportunity to look up and think about what they are doing and why. When these opportunities translate into social networks, individuals then have a circle of people they can have that conversation with in an ongoing way.

It feels, however, as if more and more educators want to focus on the big questions. Whether because they share with their students the sense of the climate emergency or are simply sick of unreasonable or misdirected demands from their governments, educators are pushing back and demanding more say in what happens in schools and why. We hope that communities like *Flip the System* or *ResearchED*, who are admirably focused on working out what is best for the children in our schools, will continue to push the boundaries of what teachers can lead on.

Social Movements: Sending Up a Flare

Networks of teachers and system leaders can create new practices and try to create new system conditions, but their work remains shaped by the desires and demands of parents and students. System leaders remain very sensitive to the public, and for many, their position relies on public support. For teachers, even apparently simple acts such as changing a report card can bring a barrage of parental questioning that can undercut momentum for change.

Parents have to *demand* schools where young people thrive, not be a barrier to them. This means working to shift the narrative and norms around schooling. Parents and students, quite understandably, are concerned often first and foremost with the 'results' they will get from schools: the grades, the qualifications, the next steps. This is inevitably part of what schools have to provide and, particularly in the upper years of schooling, it can place considerable constraints on what is possible.

But, often the sense of restriction that comes from the emphasis on results is due to a misunderstanding of what good results look like. There is a great tendency in education to mistake anything that is traditional or longstanding with what is prestigious and therefore successful. This is a simple error of misattribution. Mimicking prestige does nothing to change the power relations in our societies, which keep opportunity very restricted. Driving young people to focus on nothing other than a rigged game is setting them up for a fall. This does not mean that examinations should not be a major focus – of course young people need preparation for whatever major hurdles their system offers – but they *must* have something else besides. Long-term mental health, a sense of purpose or vocation, the capability to contribute: these are surely the things parents really want for their children.

But these more long-term desires can so easily be misdirected if social norms prioritise something else. It is so much easier to trade in the social currency of grades, hobbies and recognised achievements, than it is to talk about a child's more unique hopes or contributions to the world.

In the social sciences, there is a problem known as the Nash equilibrium.[15] In any given situation, it is possible for things to be better if we all act simultaneously. But if we do not, the optimal action for each of us is to do nothing. This is a mass version of what is known as 'the prisoner's dilemma'. To overcome this problem, we *coordinate*. We use the communication tools we have to signal to each other that we would be willing to act, we would be willing to do a particular thing for the good of the whole, and then we all have to trust each other that we will follow through on these actions.[16]

Coordination happens on a daily basis. Most of us pick up our litter, stop at stop signs, pay our taxes, even if it might be easier or better for

---

[15] *The Economist*, 'What Is the Nash Equilibrium and Why Does It Matter?'
[16] For a more detailed theoretical account of this see Gray, Purdy and Ansari, 'From Interactions to Institutions'; For an account grounded in history, see Thelen, *How Institutions Evolve*; or Culpepper, *Creating Cooperation*.

us in that instance if we did not. We call these actions that have become so regularised as to be assumed habits, or, more formally, *social institutions*. Almost everything we do, including most of what we do in schools, relies on these bundles of norms, laws and practices that result from coordination. But it is very hard to create new moments of coordination at scale.

This is the magic of social movements. At some point, there is a tipping point, where enough people realise that others also want something different, and are willing to act for it, and everyone acts differently. Social movements might be associated with marches in the street or public disruption, but these are just the visible signals that allow coordination to happen. The integral part of social movements is that change in perception, that alignment of new values; 'Are you thinking what I'm thinking?'; 'Can I trust you to act on it?'.

We're not proposing a march in the street for thriving – though if anyone would like to do this we'll be there with the banners. But with everything else going on in the world, the goal of changing the narrative around schooling is not sufficiently simple or acute for traditional acts of protest to communicate strongly. The signal for coordination will need to be different. It will come in the questions that we ask: of our colleagues, of children's teachers or school leaders, of our friends. What does it mean for our children to thrive? How might our schools contribute to a thriving society, and planet? What do we hope for?

If we work in education, it will come in what we do and worry about on a daily basis. How are our children caring for each other? What are they using their time for? What message are we sending about what matters? And for all of us, it will come in what we talk about as 'a good school'.

Some people may have ways to amplify these signals. Through tweets or blogs, or podcasts, or the old school ways: books, documentaries and films. However we communicate, the signal will come in the stories we tell and share: what we signal are valuable stories of things that happen in schools. The signal will come when we raise our expectations of what young people and schools can do, towards thriving.

15 | *Getting Purposeful*

Education has long been cast as a key solution to the many ills that humanity faces, and the route for its progress. But to contribute to the solution – as opposed to being part of the problem – education must change. In this context, transformative education is what philosopher of education Zak Stein calls a planetary frontier, a place to turn to where renewal becomes possible. The evidence now available to us is overwhelmingly clear that today's children face acute dangers, as well as astounding opportunities. We cannot look only to the past to determine how education can be leveraged to do the job we need it to do. In any case, in the past, education systems were never designed to have *everybody* thrive: on the contrary, they were designed to filter and select for the needs of the economic and social conditions of the time.

Across the world, some level of consensus is starting to emerge about the kinds of competencies people – young and old – will need. The distinctive argument of this book is that this is necessary, but insufficient. The acquisition of those competencies (even assuming that we get better at teaching people to acquire them) will not guarantee that they are deployed to promote a thriving humanity and natural world in transformed circumstances. Consequently, we need to begin a debate about our new purposes for education. It is overdue.

Purpose is about why we do things. For too long in education, we have neglected to address that issue. Ironically, research from the business world indicates a growing interest in the issue of purpose: a commissioned report from the Harvard Business Review analyses the strength of the 'business case' for addressing purpose. It concludes:

Today more than ever, companies are searching for a new genetic code that will help them continuously evolve—to survive and to thrive .... We found a very high level of consensus among (the executives interviewed) that purpose matters, and a widespread belief that it has positive effects on key performance drivers. The survey also demonstrates that companies who clearly articulate their purpose enjoy higher growth rates and higher levels of success in transformation and innovation initiatives. Given the strong sentiment that purpose is important and the clear benefits it seems to accrue, it is curious that purpose is utilized by only a minority of companies as a driver of strategy and decision-making.[1]

It is even more curious in the case of education, and how ironic that we might – again – be looking to the business world for a different perspective. Nevertheless, debates about skills, pedagogy, structures, assessment and curriculum cannot be resolved if there is no clarity about the job we look to education to do: its core purposes.

The schools reviewed in this book have thought hard about their purpose, sometimes against the tide. They have thought beyond their test scores and assumptions about college and work, to a more profoundly important set of goals – which in all instances do in fact tick off the accountability requirements that systems lay down, because students became powerfully engaged and motivated learners. The accumulation of data and evidence about the future now gives a stronger foundation upon which to refocus the purpose of education in a more holistic and less partial way. The educators of High Tech High reflect on the bigger picture of purpose:

While the content of any learning experience is important … what really matters is how students react to it, shape it, or apply it. The purpose of learning in this century is not simply to recite inert knowledge, but, rather, to transform it. It is time to change the subject.[2]

15.1 Reinvent and Save 'the School'

Critics of current schooling systems (and the numbers are growing) increasingly point to the disintermediation in other spheres of social life, through which institutions previously thought essential to a process – booking a holiday, getting a divorce, investing in stocks – are being circumvented by platforms which allow direct producer-to-consumer contact.

---

[1] Harvard Business Review, 'The Business Case for Purpose'.
[2] Riordan, 'Change the Subject'.

Techno-solutionists in education point to a similar trajectory. As the channels for learning and skill acquisition become ever more open and accessible, the need for the institution of school diminishes and perhaps will disappear. Indeed, data about the rise of home schooling would appear to support this analysis. Although overall the proportion is low (3.4 per cent in the United States), the numbers are rising with the advent of a flourishing market in online packages and resources, businesses dedicated to home-schooling support, and an increase in social-media supported group networks. In some areas in the United States, the numbers are growing by 10 per cent per year.[3] Across the United Kingdom, there has been a consistent rises in home schooling over the past decade[4] and there is similar growth in Australia.[5] It remains to be seen whether the enforced experience of home schooling, as a result of the COVID-19 shutdown, will accelerate this growth or not.

Of course, there will be many reasons for this growth. But it is to be hoped that reports of the 'death of school' are premature. Schools provide one of the last places in increasingly stratified societies where people can come together face-to-face to create community. In schools, young learners can encounter some of the variety of the world, and in safe spaces where they can develop strong identities. It was clear throughout the 2020 shutdown how many of them yearned for this. Moreover, it is only schools that can foster the sense of collective purpose set out in Chapters 3 and 5. However, it is vital – *literally* for the future of humanity – that schools are reinvented for the new conditions and the new challenges our children face. The 'Great Pause' brought about by COVID-19 afforded the possibility for educators to think freshly about what reinvention might look like and how to bring it about.

Part of that reinvention will need to involve a period of experimentation and diversification. This is why school leaders, and not just system leaders, should have more responsibility for expanding the purposes of their institutions. The work of the pathfinder schools offers some potential models; as they grow stronger and increasingly

---

[3] Russell, 'Why Homeschooling Is Growing'.

[4] Jeffreys, 'Rising Numbers of Pupils Home Educated'; Camden, 'Children's Commissioner to Publish Home Education Figures for Every School'.

[5] Tovey, 'Home Schooling up 65% in Four Years'; English, 'Homeschooling Is on the Rise in Australia. Who Is Doing It and Why?'

attractive to parents and learners, there will be more, not less, diversity in approaches. This is of not of course to underestimate the importance of systems: the whole point of this book is to speed up the process of broader adoption and adaptation, and particularly to contribute towards a shift in the prevalent discourse about education. It is necessary to go beyond the beautiful exceptions. But this cannot be done at the behest of systems. Rather, the complexity and speed of change in the contemporary world makes it increasingly problematic to set highly specified agendas successfully from a system level. This creates a more important role for schools as key decision makers, not just 'deliverers', when it comes to education. As various kinds of 'school autonomy' increase, schools are asked to be the integrators of diverse educational purposes within their settings, and we want to highlight the potential of that role.

From the evidence so far, some characteristics of schools working to achieve goals related to the real challenges we face have started to emerge.

15.2 Ecosystems as Part of the Solution

The first is that schools cannot achieve these purposes alone. As we argue in Chapter 13, they need to become part of learning ecosystems; this is exemplified by many of the cases reviewed in this book. Increasingly we see the emergence in a few schools – in the right project or with visionary leaders – of *inter-dependent systems of providers dedicated to supporting human learning across the full life cycle.* These ecosystems of learning will incorporate diverse partners in the learning business, bringing a multiplicity of resources, skills, methods and opportunities to the piece. It entails exploiting the full the range of digital connections and resources now available that sprung into greater visibility during the COVID-19 shutdown.

15.3 Systems, System Conditions and a New 'Public Narrative'

Some schools are achieving these shifts *in spite of* rather than because of the conditions that governments create. This is true even in low-income countries, where, sadly, incipient schooling systems are still being created to ape the out-dated factory model of the global north's recent past. For the shift to take place, governments need to assume a different role: vision-setting, enabling, regulating and attending to equity.[6] And as above, acting as the midwife to local learning ecosystems. Some public systems are stepping up to the plate: developments in Finland, in British Columbia and New Zealand will be worth watching in the years to come.

It is surely timely for a fresh debate about the job we want and need education to do. This book is but a beginning, a foundation, which we hope many will contribute to, contest and take forward. What is unacceptable is the assumption that no debate is required. A huge amount of work is necessary, some of it already underway. Among the many dimensions of this – including curricular and pedagogic questions – is that of measures or indicators. We have become so accustomed to the narrow range of indicators deemed by most systems to 'count', that broadening the focus seems unthinkable. The race to attain better qualifications to win an elite job (better paid and more immune to automation) will become harder. Moreover, the areas of employment that are expanding do not regard the existing systems of credentials with much confidence. And, by definition, that 'race' can only be won by a very few. Tunnel vision on this narrow set of goals will not be conducive to thriving societies.

But what if schools were encouraged to think about outputs such as:

- the global competence of their learners when they graduate
- the school's collective contribution to local sustainability and students' involvement in such an endeavour
- academic achievement evidenced both by appropriate testing but also by application of knowledge and skills in real situations
- learner performance in internships or work-based learning
- entrepreneurial skill and achievement evidenced by real-world products, and participation in business or social enterprise competitions
- effective engagement in community programs, campaigns and civic involvement, documented in terms of time, products and achievements
- experience of a learning relationship, built up over time, with individuals from an older generation

---

[6] For an expanded discussion of such new roles, see Hallgarten, Hannon and Beresford, 'Creative Public Leadership: How School System Leaders Can Create the Conditions for System-Wide Innovation'.

- contributions to the school as a thriving micro-community with positive, caring relationships as the norm
- good mental health indicated by clinical outcomes and surveys
- strong learner agency – evidenced by learners' initiation and leadership of aspects of learning
- physical fitness habits and evidenced application of knowledge and understanding to personal health.

Many schools featured in this book, and others like them around the world, are already attending to some of these outcomes. Too often, however, it is a struggle when there is little support for, or incentive to, observe and systematically record the relevant evidence. The above is not necessarily the ideal list; but when a school can connect its broader goals to indicators and measures it has a much stronger ability to protect those outcomes against other encroaching pressures. A serious debate is required about how to support schools to evidence and communicate these outcomes – one that needs to involve learners and their families, employers and civil society, as well as the professions directly involved in education. This debate also needs politicians with the bravery to go beyond the usual clichés about what schools are for, and give schools the support and accountability structures to achieve a better balance across the goals of education. Ahead of that, political leaders need to tell a different story, create a new narrative, one that builds the public will for change,

This book is written for anyone with an interest in schools – which, we hope we have shown, should include all of us. But more than anyone else, it is written for school leaders, who we think hold incredible positions of power in shaping what happens in education. We want to close by focusing on two school leaders we have come to learn about since writing the first edition of this book, because they particularly illustrate the catalytic potential of a clear sense of purpose.

Rae Snape has been a head teacher for 13 years, most recently at Milton Road Primary in Cambridge, England, and previously at another primary in the city, The Spinney. As a leader, she believes strongly that it is only possible for a school to become the place it needs to be if everyone can be part of that work: 'How do you coach people to come on the same journey with you, so they are receptive to change and are part of change?' She quotes the German poet Rainer Maria Rilke: 'the only journey is the journey within'. What she is highlighting is the deeply personal work that is at the heart of changing the purpose of a school. It is one thing to have a new mission statement, but to really manifest a different sense of purpose in actions, daily routines and practices is another matter.

In the past, Rae has started with rules. She wants her schools to be guided by rules that are not arbitrary but essential, rules that could apply to every sort of context. She started framing these as a series of expanding circles: take care of yourself, take care of each other, take care of your learning, take care of school, take care of community, take care of the world, take care of the future. In essence, this is the message of this book. When Rae read the first edition of *Thrive*, she says, it immediately resonated because of this framing of thriving rippling outwards from the intrapersonal to the global. She highlighted for us that while *Thrive* focuses on a very broad agenda, 'it starts with the self at the centre'. In this edition, we have placed more emphasis on agency as this is really the key shift. As Rae would put it, it's about recognising that 'we are crew, not passengers'.

Across the other size of the country, down the river from Merseyside, Andy Moor is head of a multi-academy trust that includes two secondary schools and two primaries. For the past 10 years, he has been head teacher of one of these primaries, St. Bernard's. Now, Andy's sense of purpose for his school – and the wider group of schools – is focused on 'global thriving'. This stems from the realisation of all that is happening in the world that schools could be working on, and, more importantly, the transformative effect it can have on both teachers and students when they are allowed to do so. His journey in this was furthered through a partnership with local Chester Zoo, which started with a single project to equip young people as educators about palm oil, and has developed into a curriculum designed by a teaching schools alliance and multiple partners, focused on conservation, social justice, relationships and personal development. For clarifying the school's vision, he describes *Thrive* as "the most important book I've ever read". But it is evident that his work has been inspired and furthered by a wide range of people, and is a testament to the power of networks. Just as a single relationship with a zoo's education specialist resulted in Chester becoming the world's first city to source is palm oil from sustainable sources, an individual engagement with Action Transport Theatre resulted in his school co-commissioning an hour-long production on refugees, rehearsed in school and associated with a whole term's curriculum of history, geography and literature built around it. Across the teaching alliance and wider networks, the curriculum development has involved 83 schools and 22,500 children.

For Andy, the question that educators have to ask themselves currently is not just 'why this, why now?' (the new questions of the United Kingdom's curriculum inspection) but 'why this at all?' His sights are firmly set on how their work as a school can have wider impact in the world. As he describes, reflecting on his first conversation with the Director of Learning at Chester Zoo, 'We said, let's launch the next army of conservationists! That was fanciful talk, but by god, it's not a fanciful idea.' Indeed, it's never been more important. And with 20,000 children and counting, it's looking less fanciful by the minute.

Andy describes himself as 'just a small cog in an education wheel', but sees huge potential as schools 'connect together'. Rae has planned a 'Big Education Conversation', a community conversation about education and its purpose. She is hoping for a time when education policy will no longer be decided only in central government and instead people can sit down and ask, 'what is the point of what we're doing?'

For both Rae and Andy, part of the challenge they face is balancing their sense of a school's real purpose with that of external demands. But they are adamant that developing children's academic skills – something they take very seriously – can be combined and indeed furthered by helping children connect with their deeper and wider purposes. Both ultimately talk about their work as regenerating communities. For Andy, this is about how the work of schools can directly transform the lives of their wider community, not just their students. For Rae, it is about seeing how a school can become a learning community, with each teacher taking up their opportunity to have impact far into the future. The notion of regeneration comes from biology and ecology. It is a reminder that living things have enormous resilience, but a living thing cannot be restored from the outside. Each must do its own regeneration.

For these two leaders, the book *Thrive* has proved a useful tool in holding conversations about purpose, making the case for a broader perspective and developing simple frameworks that their schools can live by. All the real work must take place outside its pages, but we hope that it can serve others in this same way. Paolo Freire is famous for articulating the special balance of individual and shared purpose that is

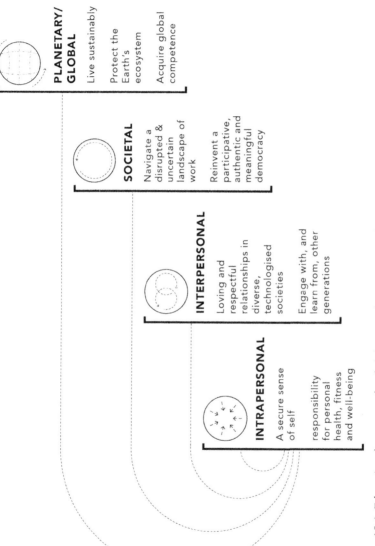

PLANETARY/ GLOBAL

Live sustainably

Protect the Earth's ecosystem

Acquire global competence

SOCIETAL

Navigate a disrupted & uncertain landscape of work

Reinvent a participative, authentic and meaningful democracy

INTERPERSONAL

Loving and respectful relationships in diverse, technologised societies

Engage with, and learn from, other generations

INTRAPERSONAL

A secure sense of self

responsibility for personal health, fitness and well-being

Figure 15.1 Educational purposes for thriving people, societies and planet

tied up in education. It is one of Rae's favourites, and we would not try to put it better. As Freire puts it, 'if you have come to help me then you are wasting your time, but if you have come because your liberation is bound up with mine, then let us work together.' We hope that we have shown in this book how we are, indeed, all bound together.

We have to find ways to harness education to the project of our collective, and individual, thriving. Reinvented schools are critical to this process, but let's create the conditions where it can happen at scale – rather than as rare exceptions. (See Figure 15.1.)

Bibliography

ABC News. 'SJ Hardware Store Uses Robot to Help Customers'. ABC7 San Francisco, 3 December 2014. https://abc7news.com/419533/.

Abraham, John. 'An Inconvenient Sequel – The Science, History, and Politics of Climate Change'. *The Guardian*, 15 November 2017, sec. Environment. www.theguardian.com/environment/climate-consensus-97-per-cent/2017/nov/15/an-inconvenient-sequel-the-science-history-and-politics-of-climate-change.

Abraham, Maurie. 'Principal Possum: Die in the Ditch – Non-Negotiable Principles for Learning Design'. *Principal Possum* (blog), 16 January 2017. http://principalpossum.blogspot.com/2017/01/die-in-ditch-non-negotiable-principles.html.

'Principal Possum: It's Not Only The Kids Who Learn Here!' *Principal Possum* (blog), 18 May 2015. http://principalpossum.blogspot.com/2015/05/danger-super-heroes-at-work-i-have.html.

Achen, Christopher H. and Larry M. Bartels. *Democracy for Realists: Why Elections Do Not Produce Responsive Government*. Princeton, NJ: Princeton University Press, 2016.

AgeUK. 'Loneliness and Isolation Evidence Review'. London: AgeUK, 2012. www.ageuk.org.uk/documents/en-gb/for-professionals/evidence_review_loneliness_and_isolation.pdf?dtrk=true.

Ahmed, Kamal. 'Bank Warns on AI Jobs Threat'. *BBC News*, 20 August 2018, sec. Business. www.bbc.com/news/business-45240758.

Albrecht, Glenn. '"Solastalgia". A New Concept in Health and Identity'. *PAN: Philosophy Activism Nature*, no. 3 (2005): 41.

American Psychological Association. 'Mental Health Issues Increased Significantly in Young Adults over Last Decade: Shift May Be Due in Part to Rise of Digital Media, Study Suggests'. *ScienceDaily* (blog), 15 March 2019. www.sciencedaily.com/releases/2019/03/190315110908.htm.

Anderson, Kevin. 'Climate Change Going beyond Dangerous: Brutal Numbers and Tenuous Hope'. In *Development Dialogue: What Next Volume III: Climate, Development and Equity*. London, 2012.

anthropocene.info. 'The Anthropocene'. Accessed 8 February 2020. www
.anthropocene.info/.

Arts Action Fund. 'ESSA (Every Student Succeeds Act)'. Alexandria, VA:
National Arts Education Association, 19 November 2015. www
.arteducators.org/advocacy/essa-every-student-succeeds-act.

Asada, Takashi. 'Epidemiology of Dementia in Japan'. In *Neuroimaging
Diagnosis for Alzheimer's Disease and Other Dementias*, edited by
Hiroshi Matsuda, Takashi Asada, and Aya Midori Tokumaru, 1–10.
Tokyo: Springer Japan, 2017. https://doi.org/10.1007/978-4-431-
55133-1_1.

Asia Society and OECD. *Teaching for Global Competence in a Rapidly
Changing World*. OECD, 2018. https://doi.org/10.1787/
9789264289024-en.

Atkinson, Anthony B. *Inequality: What Can Be Done?* 1st edition.
Cambridge, MA: Harvard University Press, 2015.

Attoun, Marti. 'Students and Elders Share Camaraderie'. *American Profile*,
29 July 2010. https://americanprofile.com/articles/students-elders-share-
camaraderie/.

Autor, David H. 'Why Are There Still So Many Jobs? The History and
Future of Workplace Automation'. *The Journal of Economic
Perspectives* 29, no. 3 (2015): 3–30.

Aviezer, Ora, Marinus H. Van IJzendoorn, Abraham Sagi and Carlo
Schuengel. '"Children of the Dream" Revisited: 70 Years of Collective
Early Child Care in Israeli Kibbutzim'. *Psychological Bulletin* 116, no. 1
(1994): 99–116. https://doi.org/10.1037/0033-2909.116.1.99.

Awartani, Marwan and Janet Looney. 'Learning and Well-Being: An Agenda
for Change'. Research Report. WISE (World Innovation Summit on
Education), 7 October 2015.

Anthropocene Working Group (AWG). 'Results of Binding Vote by AWG'.
Anthropocene Working Group, Subcommission on Quaternary
Stratigraphy, International Union of Geological Sciences, 21 May
2019. http://quaternary.stratigraphy.org/working-groups/anthropo
cene/.

Bakhshi, Hasan, Jonathan M. Downing, Michael A. Osborne and Philippe
Schneider. *The Future of Skills: Employment in 2030*. Harlow: Pearson,
2017.

Bakhshi, Hasan, Carl Benedikt Frey and Michael Osborne. 'Creativity vs
Robots: The Creative Economy and the Future of Employment'.
London: Nesta, April 2015.

Ball, Philip. *How to Grow a Human: Adventures in Who We Are and How
We Are Made*. London: HarperCollins, 2019.

Ballotpedia: Local Ballot Measures. 'Toledo, Ohio, Question 2, "Lake Erie Bill of Rights" Initiative (February 2019)', 26 February 2019. https:// ballotpedia.org/Toledo,_Ohio,_Question_2,_%22Lake_Erie_Bill_of_ Rights%22_Initiative_(February_2019).

Banulescu-Bogdan, Natalia. 'When Facts Don't Matter: How to Communicate More Effectively about Immigration's Costs and Benefits'. Washington, DC: Migration Policy Institute, November 2018.

Barber, Michael and Mona Mourshed. 'How the World's Best-Performing School Systems Come out on Top | McKinsey & Company'. McKinsey & Co., 2007. www.mckinsey.com/industries/social-sector/our-insights/ how-the-worlds-best-performing-school-systems-come-out-on-top.

Barlińska, Julia, Anna Szuster and Mikołaj Winiewski. 'Cyberbullying among Adolescent Bystanders: Role of the Communication Medium, Form of Violence, and Empathy'. *Journal of Community & Applied Social Psychology* 23, no. 1 (2013): 37–51. https://doi.org/10.1002/casp .2137.

Bates Ramirez, Vanessa. 'Inching towards Abundant Water: New Progress in Desalination Tech'. *Singularity Hub* (blog), 18 June 2019. https:// singularityhub.com/2019/06/18/inching-towards-abundant-water-new- progress-in-desalination-tech/

BBC News. 'Depression Looms as Global Crisis', 2 September 2009. http:// news.bbc.co.uk/1/hi/health/8230549.stm.

Becker, Gary Stanley. *Human Capital; a Theoretical and Empirical Analysis, with Special Reference to Education*, General Series (National Bureau of Economic Research); No. 80. New York: National Bureau of Economic Research; distributed by Columbia University Press, 1964.

Beinhocker, Eric D. *The Origin of Wealth: Evolution, Complexity, and the Radical Remaking of Economics*. London: Random House Business, 2007.

Bellanca, James A. and Ron Brandt. *21st Century Skills: Rethinking How Students Learn*. 1st ed. Bloomington, IN: Non Basic Stock Line, 2011.

Bentley, Tom. 'OECD Transformative Competencies 2030: Coping with Tensions, Dilemmas.' EDU/EDPC. Future of Education and Skills 2030: Reflections on Transformative Competencies. Unpublished: OECD, 2017.

Berger, Ron. *An Ethic of Excellence: Building a Culture of Craftsmanship with Students*. Portsmouth, NH: Heinemann Educational Books, 2003.

Bertrand, Philippe, Jérôme Guegan, Léonore Robieux, Cade Andrew McCall and Franck Zenasni. 'Learning Empathy through Virtual Reality: Multiple Strategies for Training Empathy-Related Abilities Using Body

Ownership Illusions in Embodied Virtual Reality'. *Frontiers in Robotics and AI* 5 (2018). https://doi.org/10.3389/frobt.2018.00026.

Biesta, Gert J. J. *Beautiful Risk of Education: Interventions Education, Philosophy, and Culture.* Abingdon: Routledge, 2016. www.amazon.co.uk/Beautiful-Risk-Education-Interventions-Philosophy/dp/1612050271.

Beyond Learning: Democratic Education for a Human Future. Boulder, CO: Paradigm Publishers, 2006.

Bigler, Rebecca, Amy Roberson Hayes and Veronica Hamilton. 'The Role of Schools in the Early Socialization of Gender Differences'. In *Encyclopedia on Early Childhood Development* (online resource). Montreal: Centre of Excellence for Early Childhood Development (CEECD), 2013. http://www.child-encyclopedia.com/sites/default/files/textes-experts/en/2492/the-role-of-schools-in-the-early-socialization-of-gender-differences.pdf

Binder, Amy. 'For Love and Money: Organizations' Creative Responses to Multiple Environmental Logics'. *Theory and Society* 36, no. 6 (20 September 2007): 547–571. https://doi.org/10.1007/s11186-007-9045-x.

Blair, Tony. 'Leader's Speech'. Presented at the British Political Speech Archive, Brighton, 1995. www.britishpoliticalspeech.org/speech-archive.htm?speech=201.

Blaug, Mark. *The Economics of Education and the Education of an Economist.* Cheltenham: Edward Elgar Publishing, 1987. https://ideas.repec.org/b/elg/eebook/48.html.

Boffey, Daniel. 'Amsterdam to Embrace "doughnut" Model to Mend Post-Coronavirus Economy'. *The Guardian*, 8 April 2020, sec. World news. www.theguardian.com/world/2020/apr/08/amsterdam-doughnut-model-mend-post-coronavirus-economy.

Boix Mansilla, Veronica and Anthony Jackson. 'Educating for Global Competence: Preparing Our Youth to Engage the World'. Washington, D.C. & New York: Council of Chief State School Officers' EdSteps Initiative & Asia Society Partnership for Global Learning, 2011.

Boone Grove High School (BGHS). 'Course Descriptions: Multidiciplinary Course Offerings'. Boone Grove High School, 2019. https://bghs.ptsc.k12.in.us/guidance/course-descriptions/

Bostrom, Nick. *Superintelligence: Paths, Dangers, Strategies.* Oxford: Oxford University Press , 2014.

Bragg, Rachel and Gavin Atkins. *A Review of Nature-Based Interventions for Mental Health Care.* Commissioned Report 204. Natural England, 2016.

Braunschweiger, Amy and Matthieu Rytz. 'Interview: Climate Change and the Disappearing Islands of Kiribati'. *Human Rights Watch*, 15 June 2018. www.hrw.org/news/2018/06/15/interview-climate-change-and-disappearing-islands-kiribati.

Brey, Philip. 'Human Enhancement and Personal Identity'. In *New Waves in Philosophy of Technology*, edited by Jan Kyrre Berg Olsen Friis, Evan Selinger and Søren Riis, 169–185. Basingstoke, Hampshire; New York, NY: Palgrave-Macmillan, 2009.

Brown, Philip, Hugh Lauder and David Ashton. *The Global Auction: The Broken Promises of Education, Jobs and Incomes*. New York, NY: Oxford University Press, 2011. www.oxfordscholarship.com.ezp-prod1.hul.harvard.edu/view/10.1093/acprof:oso/9780199731688.001 .0001/acprof-9780199731688.

Brynjolfsson, Erik and Andrew McAfee. *The Second Machine Age: Work, Progress, and Prosperity in a Time of Brilliant Technologies*. 1st ed. New York; London: W. W. Norton & Company, 2016.

Bunten, Alexis. 'What Do the Rights of Nature Have to Do with Indigeneity?' *Bioneers* (blog). Accessed 8 February 2020. https:// bioneers.org/rights-nature-indigeneity/.

Cambridge Assessment. 'The International Popularity of STEM Subjects'. *Cambridge Assessment* (blog), February 2017. www .cambridgeassessment.org.uk/our-research/data-bytes/the-international-popularity-of-stem-subjects/.

Camden, Billy. 'Children's Commissioner to Publish Home Education Figures for Every School'. *Schools Week*, 4 February 2019. https:// schoolsweek.co.uk/childrens-commissioner-to-publish-home-educa tion-figures-for-every-school/.

Campbell, David E., Meira Levinson and Frederick M. Hess, eds. *Making Civics Count: Citizenship Education for a New Generation*. Cambridge, MA: Harvard Education Press, 2012.

Campbell, Peter. 'Trucks Headed for a Driverless Future'. *Financial Times*, 31 January 2018, sec. Special Report Driverless vehicles. www.ft.com/ content/7686ea3e-e0dd-11e7-a0d4-0944c5f49e46.

Canato, Anna, Davide Ravasi and Nelson Phillips. 'Coerced Practice Implementation in Cases of Low Cultural Fit: Cultural Change and Practice Adaptation during the Implementation of Six Sigma at 3M'. *Academy of Management Journal* 56, no. 6 (December 2013): 1724–1753. https://doi.org/10.5465/amj.2011.0093.

Cappon, Paul and Jarrett Laughlin. 'Canada's Composite Learning Index: A Path towards Learning Communities'. *International Review of Education* 59, no. 4 (September 2013): 505–519. https://doi.org/10 .1007/s11159-013-9374-0.

Carbon Brief. 'Mapped: How Climate Change Affects Extreme Weather around the World'. Carbon Brief, 11 March 2019. www.carbonbrief .org/mapped-how-climate-change-affects-extreme-weather-around-the-world.

Cardinale, Bradley J., J. Emmett Duffy, Andrew Gonzalez, David U. Hooper, Charles Perrings, Patrick Venail, Anita Narwani et al. 'Biodiversity Loss and Its Impact on Humanity'. *Nature* 486, no. 7401 (June 2012): 59–67. https://doi.org/10.1038/nature11148.

Carrington, Damian. 'Three-Quarters of UK Children Spend Less Time Outdoors than Prison Inmates – Survey'. *The Guardian*, 25 March 2016, sec. Environment. www.theguardian.com/environment/2016/ mar/25/three-quarters-of-uk-children-spend-less-time-outdoors-than-prison-inmates-survey.

Carver, Courtney. *Project 333: The Minimalist Fashion Challenge That Proves Less Really Is So Much More.* New York, NY: Tarcherperigree – Penguin Publishing Group, 2020.

Ceballos, Gerardo, and Paul R. Ehrlich. 'The Misunderstood Sixth Mass Extinction'. *Science* 360, no. 6393 (8 June 2018): 1080–1081. https:// doi.org/10.1126/science.aau0191.

Center for Global Education at Asia Society, Results for Development, Teach For All, The Boston Consulting Group, and World Innovation Summit for Education. 'Investing in Knowledge Sharing to Advance SDG 4'. A report prepared in support of a recommendation of the International Commission on Financing Global Education Opportunity (Education Commission). Education Commission, 2018. https://educationcommission .org/wp-content/uploads/2018/09/Investing-in-Knowledge-Sharing-to-Adv ance-SDG-4.pdf.

Chamie, Joseph. 'Student Debt Rising Worldwide'. YaleGlobal Online, 18 May 2017. https://yaleglobal.yale.edu/content/student-debt-rising-worldwide.

Champion, Marc. 'The Rise of Populism'. *Bloomberg.Com.* 5 December 2018. www.bloomberg.com/quicktake/populism.

Chapron, Guillaume, Yaffa Epstein and José Vicente López-Bao. 'A Rights Revolution for Nature'. *Science* 363, no. 6434 (29 March 2019): 1392–1393. https://doi.org/10.1126/science.aav5601.

Children & Nature Network, and IUCN. '*Children & Nature Worldwide: An Exploration of Children's Experiences of the Outdoors and Nature with Associated Risks and Benefits'.* Minneapolis, MN: Children & Nature Network, 2012.

Chow, Denise. '5 Places Already Feeling the Effects of Climate Change'. *Livescience.Com*, November 21. www.livescience.com/41380-climate-change-places-at-risk.html.

Christensen, Clayton, Curtis Johnson and Michael Horn. *Disrupting Class: How Disruptive Innovation Will Change the Way the World Learns.* New York, NY: McGraw-Hill Education, 2008.

CIC. 'UK Creative Employment'. Creative Industries Council, June 2019. www.thecreativeindustries.co.uk/uk-creative-overview/facts-and-fig ures/employment-figures.

Circle Economy. 'The Amsterdam City Doughnut: How to Create a Thriving City for a Thriving Planet'. *Medium* (blog), 12 June 2019. https:// medium.com/circleeconomy/the-amsterdam-city-doughnut-how-to-create-a-thriving-city-for-a-thriving-planet-423afd6b2892.

'The Grave Disconnect: Aligning School Reform with Ecological Change'. Glasgow, 2016.

Clarke, Paul. 'Naturally Smart'. Naturally Smart toolkit. Accessed 9 February 2020. https://naturallysmart.world.

Claxton, Guy. *What's the Point of School?: Rediscovering The Heart of Education.* Reprint ed. Oxford: Oneworld Publications, 2008.

Climate & Migration Coalition. 'The Climate & Migration Coalition'. Accessed 9 February 2020. http://climatemigration.org.uk/.

Coburn, Cynthia E. 'Shaping Teacher Sensemaking: School Leaders and the Enactment of Reading Policy'. *Educational Policy* 19, no. 3 (7 January 2005): 476–509. https://doi.org/10.1177/0895904805276143.

Collins. 'The Collins Word of the Year 2019 Is...' Collinsdictionary.com, 2019. www.collinsdictionary.com/woty.

Collins, Rebecca L., Victor C. Strasburger, Jane D. Brown, Edward Donnerstein, Amanda Lenhart and L. Monique Ward. 'Sexual Media and Childhood Well-Being and Health'. *Pediatrics* 140, Supplement 2 (1 November 2017): S162–166. https://doi.org/10.1542/peds.2016-1758X.

Colvin, Geoff. *Humans Are Underrated: What High Achievers Know That Brilliant Machines Never Will.* London: Nicholas Brealey Publishing, 2015.

Connor, Linda, Glenn Albrecht, Nick Higginbotham, Sonia Freeman and Wayne Smith. 'Environmental Change and Human Health in Upper Hunter Communities of New South Wales, Australia'. *EcoHealth* 1, no. 2 (1 November 2004): SU47–58. https://doi.org/10.1007/s10393-004-0053-2.

Conway, Maree. *An Overview of Foresight Methodologies.* Melbourne, Victoria, Australia: Thinking Futures, 2006.

Cookson, Clive. 'Robot Trained to Be Useful Teaching Assistant in Three Hours'. *Financial Times,* 23 October 2019. www.ft.com/content/ 5458d814-f4bd-11e9-b018-3ef8794b17c6.

Coote, Anna, and Edanur Yazici. 'Universal Basic Income – A Union Perspective'. London: Public Services International (PSI), April 2019.

Council, National Academy of Engineering and National Research (NAENR). *STEM Integration in K-12 Education: Status, Prospects, and an Agenda for Research*, 2014. https://doi.org/10.17226/18612.

Cowen, Tyler. *Average Is Over: Powering America beyond the Age of the Great Stagnation*. New York, NY: E P Dutton & Co Inc, 2013.

CPI. 'New York City Innovation Zone'. Case Study. Arlington, VA: Centre for Public Impact (CPI), 8 April 2016. www.centreforpublicimpact.org/case-study/new-york-city-innovation-zone/.

Croft, Jane. 'More than 100,000 Legal Roles to Become Automated'. *Financial Times*, 15 March 2016. www.ft.com/content/c8ef3f62-ea9c-11e5-888e-2eadd5fbc4a4.

Culpepper, Pepper D. *Creating Cooperation: How States Develop Human Capital in Europe*. Ithaca, NY: Cornell University Press, 2002.

CYP Now. 'NSPCC Reports Rise in Children Seeking Mental Health Support'. *Children & Young People Now* (blog), 15 November 2019. www.cypnow.co.uk/news/article/nspcc-reports-rise-in-children-seeking-mental-health-support.

Damian Carrington Environment. ed., 'Public Concern over Environment Reaches Record High in UK'. *The Guardian*, 5 June 2019, sec. Environment. www.theguardian.com/environment/2019/jun/05/greta-thunberg-effect-public-concern-over-environment-reaches-record-high

Damon, William. *The Path to Purpose: How Young People Find Their Calling in Life*. New York: Free Press, 2008.

Davis, Lauren Cassani. 'What Happens When Mindfulness Enters Schools'. *The Atlantic*, 31 August 2015. www.theatlantic.com/education/archive/2015/08/mindfulness-education-schools-meditation/402469/.

DCSF. *Social and Emotional Aspects of Learning for Secondary Schools*. Nottingham: Department for Children, Schools and Families, 2007.

DeAngelis, Tori. 'Children and the Internet – Web Pornography's Effect on Children'. *APA Monitor*, November 2007.

Deloitte. 'Plateauing at the Peak The State of the Smartphone'. Global Mobile Consumer Survey: UK cut. Deloitte, 2019.

Delors, Jacques. *Learning: The Treasure within; Report to UNESCO of the International Commission on Education for the Twenty-First Century*. Paris: UNESCO Publishing, 1996. https://unesdoc.unesco.org/ark:/48223/pf0000109590.

Diamandis, Peter H. 'Merging Mind with Machine'. *Techblog* (blog). Accessed 10 February 2020. www.diamandis.com/blog/brain-computer-interfaces-neuralink.

Diamandis, Peter H. and Steven Kotler. *The Future Is Faster Than You Think: How Converging Technologies Are Transforming Business, Industries, and Our Lives.* New York, NY: Simon & Schuster, 2020.

Dice, Mark. *The True Story of Fake News: How Mainstream Media Manipulates Millions.* San Diego, CA: The Resistance Manifesto, 2017.

DiMaggio, Paul J. and Walter W. Powell. 'The Iron Cage Revisited: Institutional Isomorphism and Collective Rationality in Organizational Fields'. *American Sociological Review* 48, no. 2 (April 1983): 147–160.

Dirzo, Rodolfo, Hillary S. Young, Mauro Galetti, Gerardo Ceballos, Nick J. B. Isaac and Ben Collen. 'Defaunation in the Anthropocene'. *Science* 345, no. 6195 (25 July 2014): 401–406. https://doi.org/10.1126/science.1251817.

Division of Economic Research. 'National Income, 1929–1932: Letter from the Acting Secretary of Commerce Transmitting in Response to Senate Resolution No. 220 (72nd Congress) a Report on National Income, 1929-32'. Document. 73d Congress, 2d Session. Washington, DC: United States Government Printing Office, 4 January 1934.

Dobbs, Richard, James Manyika and Jonathan Woetzel. *No Ordinary Disruption: The Four Global Forces Breaking All the Trends.* PublicAffairs, 2015.

Doughnut Economics Action Lab, Biomimicry 3.8, Circle Economy, and C40 Cities. 'The Amsterdam City Doughnut: A Tool for Transformative Action'. Amsterdam, March 2020. www.circle-economy.com/insights/the-amsterdam-city-doughnut-a-tool-for-transformative-action.

Dream a Dream. 'Project Thrive : A Research Study by Quantum Consumer Solutions for Dream a Dream to Explore the Nuances of Thriving Amongst People from Adverse Backgrounds'. Bangalore: Dream a Dream, 25 June 2019. http://dreamadream.org/reports/quantumreport.pdf.

Duncan-Andrade, Jeffrey M., and Ernest Morrell. *The Art of Critical Pedagogy: Possibilities for Moving from Theory to Practice in Urban Schools.* 1st ed. New York, NY: Peter Lang Publishing, 2008.

Duncan, Greg J. and Richard J. Murnane, eds. *Whither Opportunity?: Rising Inequality, Schools, and Children's Life Chances.* New York, NY: Russell Sage Foundation, 2011.

The Economist, 'The New Local'. Accessed 9 February 2020. www.economist.com/international/2014/12/17/the-new-local.

'What Is the Nash Equilibrium and Why Does It Matter?'. Accessed 10 February 2020. www.economist.com/the-economist-explains/2016/09/06/what-is-the-nash-equilibrium-and-why-does-it-matter.

Education Revolution – Alternative Education Resource Organization. 'Democratic Schools – Find a School'. Accessed 9 February 2020. www.educationrevolution.org/storc/findaschool/democraticschools/

Egan, Kieran. *Learning in Depth: A Simple Innovation That Can Transform Schooling*. Chicago, IL: University of Chicago Press, 2011.

Elfert, Maren. 'Learning to Live Together: Revisiting the Humanism of the Delors Report – UNESCO Digital Library'. ERF Working Papers Series. Paris: UNESCO Publishing, 2015. https://unesdoc.unesco.org/ark:/48223/pf0000233814.

Ellen MacArthur Foundation. 'What Is a Circular Economy? Accessed 8 February 2020. www.ellenmacarthurfoundation.org/circular-economy/concept.

English, Rebecca. 'Homeschooling Is on the Rise in Australia. Who Is Doing It and Why?' *The Conversation*, 14 April 2019. http://theconversation.com/homeschooling-is-on-the-rise-in-australia-who-is-doing-it-and-why-110268.

Erikson Institute. 'Amanda Moreno, Director, Child Development Program'. Erikson Institute. Accessed 10 February 2020. www.erikson.edu/about/directory/amanda-moreno/.

Espeland, Wendy Nelson and Michael Sauder. *Engines of Anxiety: Academic Rankings, Reputation, and Accountability*. Russell Sage Foundation, 2016. www.jstor.org/stable/10.7758/9781610448567.

'Rankings and Reactivity : How Public Measures Recreate Social Worlds'. *American Journal of Sociology* 113, no. 1 (2007): 1–40.

European Commission. 'Beyond GDP: Measuring Progress, True Wealth, and Well-Being'. European Commission: Environment, 29 January 2020. https://ec.europa.eu/environment/beyond_gdp/index_en.html.

EY. 'Cultural Times: The First Global Map of Cultural and Creative Industries'. EY and CISAC – The International Confederation of Societies of Authors and Composers, December 2015.

Facer, Keri. *Learning Futures: Education, Technology and Social Change*. Abingdon: Routledge, 2011. www.amazon.co.uk/Learning-Futures-Keri-Facer/dp/0415581435.

'Learning to Live with a Lively Planet: The Renewal of the University's Mission in the Era of Climate Change'. Uppsala University, 2019. https://media.medfarm.uu.se/play/video/9204.

'The Problem of the Future and the Possibilities of the Present in Education Research'. *International Journal of Educational Research*, 61 (2013): 135–143. https://doi.org/10.1016/j.ijer.2013.03.001.

Fadel, Charles, Bernie Trilling and Maya Bialik. *Four-Dimensional Education: The Competencies Learners Need to Succeed*. 1st ed., Scotts Valley, CA: CreateSpace Independent Publishing Platform, 2015.

Fahle, Erin M., Sean F. Reardon, Demetra Kalogrides, Ericka S. Weathers and Heewon Jang. 'Racial Segregation and School Poverty in the United States, 1999–2016'. *Race and Social Problems* 12, no. 1 (1 March 2020): 42–56. https://doi.org/10.1007/s12552-019-09277-w.

Failing, Lee, Robin Gregory, Graham Long and Brooke Moore. *The Decision Playbook: Making Thoughtful Choices in a Complex World (Teachers' Ed)*. Vancouver: GutsNHeads Project, 2019. https://deltalearns.ca/decisions/the-decision-playbook/.

Fernandez, Lisa. 'San Francisco High Schoolers Skip Senior Trip, Visit Afghan Boy in ICE Detention Center Instead'. *KTVU FOX 2*, 18 December 2018. www.ktvu.com/news/san-francisco-high-schoolers-skip-senior-trip-visit-afghan-boy-in-ice-detention-center-instead.

FinAid.org. 'Student Loan Debt Clock'. Accessed 7 February 2020. www.finaid.org/loans/studentloandebtclock.phtml.

Fioramonti, Lorenzo. *The World After GDP: Politics, Business and Society in the Post Growth Era*. Malden, MA: Polity Press, 2017.

First Nations Education Steering Committee (FNESC). 'First People's Principles of Learning'. British Columbia, Canada, 2008. http://www.fnesc.ca/wp/wp-content/uploads/2015/09/PUB-LFP-POSTER-Principles-of-Learning-First-Peoples-poster-11x17.pdf

Foer, Jonathan Safran. *We Are the Weather: Saving the Planet Begins at Breakfast*. London: Hamish Hamilton – Penguin Books, 2019.

Forsey, Martin, Scott Davies and Geoffrey Walford. *The Globalisation of School Choice?* Didcot, Oxford: Symposium Books Ltd, 2008.

Frey, Carl Benedikt and Michael Osborne. 'The Future of Employment: How Susceptible Are Jobs to Computerisation?' *Technological Forecasting and Social Change* 114 (January 2017): 254–280. https://doi.org/10.1016/j.techfore.2016.08.019.

Gawande, Atul. *Being Mortal: Medicine and What Matters in the End*. 1 ed. New York, NY: Metropolitan Books, 2014.

George, Daniel, Catherine Whitehouse and Peter Whitehouse. 'A Model of Intergenerativity: How the Intergenerational School Is Bringing the Generations Together to Foster Collective Wisdom and Community Health'. *Journal of Intergenerational Relationships* 9, no. 4 (1 October 2011): 389–404. https://doi.org/10.1080/15350770.2011.619922.

Gerdin, Jonas and Hans Englund. 'Contesting Commensuration'. *Accounting, Auditing & Accountability Journal*, 24 May 2019. https://doi.org/10.1108/AAAJ-09-2016-2717.

Ghosh, Amitav. *The Great Derangement: Climate Change and the Unthinkable*. Chicago, IL: University of Chicago Press, 2016.

Giaoutzi, Maria and Bartolomeo Sapio, eds. *Recent Developments in Foresight Methodologies. Complex Networks and Dynamic Systems.*

New York, NY: Springer US, 2013. https://doi.org/10.1007/978-1-4614-5215-7.

Gilens, Martin and Benjamin I. Page. 'Testing Theories of American Politics: Elites, Interest Groups, and Average Citizens'. *Perspectives on Politics* 12, no. 03 (September 2014): 564–581. https://doi.org/10.1017/S1537592714001595.

Global Commission on Adaptation. 'Adapt Now: A Global Call for Resilience on Climate Resilience'. Global Center on Adaptation and World Resources Institute, 13 September 2019.

Global Water Forum. 'Water Outlook to 2050: The OECD Calls for Early and Strategic Action', 21 May 2012. https://globalwaterforum.org/2012/05/21/water-outlook-to-2050-the-oecd-calls-for-early-and-strategic-action/

Goodhart, David. *The Road to Somewhere: The Populist Revolt and the Future of Politics*. London: C. Hurst & Co. Publishers, 2017.

Gore, Al. *The Future: Six Drivers of Global Change*. New York, NY: Random House Trade, 2013.

Goyal, Madhav, Sonal Singh, Erica M. S. Sibinga, Neda F. Gould, Anastasia Rowland-Seymour, Ritu Sharma, Zackary Berger, et al. 'Meditation Programs for Psychological Stress and Well-Being: A Systematic Review and Meta-Analysis'. *JAMA Internal Medicine* 174, no. 3 (1 March 2014): 357–368. https://doi.org/10.1001/jamainternmed.2013.13018.

Graeme, Mike. 'Victoria to Participate in Global Student Strike for the Climate', 11 March 2019. www.martlet.ca/victoria-to-participate-in-global-student-strike-for-the-climate/.

Graham, Carol. 'American Optimism, Longevity, and the Role of Lost Hope in Deaths of Despair'. *Brookings* (blog), 7 November 2019. www.brookings.edu/blog/up-front/2019/11/07/american-optimism-longevity-and-the-role-of-lost-hope-in-deaths-of-despair/.

Gratton, Lynda and Andrew Scott. *The 100-Year Life: Living and Working in an Age of Longevity*. London; New York, NY: Bloomsbury Information Ltd, 2016.

Gray, Barbara, Jill M. Purdy and Shahzad (Shaz) Ansari. 'From Interactions to Institutions: Microprocesses of Framing and Mechanisms for the Structuring of Institutional Fields'. *Academy of Management Review* 40, no. 1 (1 January 2015): 115–143. https://doi.org/10.5465/amr.2013.0299.

Greany, Toby and Rob Higham. Hierarchy, Markets and Networks. The Institute of Education University of London, London, 2018, 116.

Gregory, Mark. 'UK Economy Headed for Record Contraction as Coronavirus Has Heavy Near-Term Impact', 27 April 2020. www.ey.com/en_uk/growth/ey-item-club/uk-economy-headed-for-record-contraction.

Griffin, Patrick and Esther Care. *Assessment and Teaching of 21st Century Skills: Methods and Approach*. Vol. 142. Educational Assessment in an Information Age. Dordrecht: Springer Netherlands, 2015.

Haldane, Andrew G. 'Ideas and Institutions – A Growth Story'. Speech given by Andrew G. Haldane Chief Economist Bank of England presented at the The Guild Society, University of Oxford, 23 May 2018.

'Labour's Share'. Speech given by Andrew G. Haldane, Chief Economist, Bank of England presented at the Trades Union Congress, London, 12 November 2015.

Hall, Ross and Ashoka Global Leadership Team. 'Empowering Young People to Create a Better World'. Ashoka, August 2016. https://issuu.com/asho kachangemakers/docs/empowering_young_people_to_create_a.

Hallgarten, Joe, Valerie Hannon and Tom Beresford. 'Creative Public Leadership: How School System Leaders Can Create the Conditions for System-Wide Innovation'. Research Report. WISE (World Innovation Summit on Education), 2015.

Hammer, Kate. 'Kindergarten in a Retirement Home Proves a Hit with Young and Old'. *The Globe and Mail*, 30 December 2011, Update May 8, 2018 ed. www.theglobeandmail.com/news/national/kindergarten-in-a-retire ment-home-proves-a-hit-with-young-and-old/article4103165/.

Hannon, Valerie, Louise Thomas, Sarah Ward and Tom Beresford. 'Local Learning Ecosystems: Emerging Models'. Research Report. WISE (World Innovation Summit on Education), 30 April 2019. www.wise-qatar.org/app/uploads/2019/05/wise_report-rr.1.2019-web.pdf.

Hannon, Valerie, Sarah Gillinson and Leonie Shanks. *Learning a Living: Radical Innovation in Education for Work*. 1st ed. London: Bloomsbury Academic, 2013.

Harari, Yuval Noah. *Homo Deus: A Brief History of Tomorrow*. 1st ed. London: Harvill Secker, 2016.

Sapiens: A Brief History of Humankind. London: Harvill Secker, 2014.

Harvard Business Review. 'The Business Case for Purpose'. Sponsored by EY. Cambridge, MA: Harvard Business School Publishing, 2015.

harvardstudy. 'Harvard Second Generation Study'. Accessed 9 February 2020. www.adultdevelopmentstudy.org.

Haste, Helen. 'Ambiguity, Autonomy and Agency: Psychological Challenges to New Competence'. *Defining and Selecting Key Competencies*, 2001, 93–120.

Hawkes, Denise, Mehmet Ugur and EPPI-Centre. *Evidence on the Relationship between Education, Skills and Economic Growth in Low-Income Countries: Systematic Review*. London: EPPI-Centre, Social Science Research Unit, Institute of Education, University of London, 2012.

Hawksworth, John, Richard Berriman and Saloni Goel. 'Will Robots Really Steal Our Jobs? An International Analysis of the Potential Long Term Impact of Automation', PwC, February 2018, 47.

Hendrickson, Clara and William A. Galston. 'The Educational Rift in the 2016 Election'. *Brookings* (blog), 18 November 2016. www.brookings .edu/blog/fixgov/2016/11/18/educational-rift-in-2016-election/.

Henson, Audrey. 'Dementia Crisis in Japan'. Project. Pulitzer Center, 31 October 2019. https://pulitzercenter.org/projects/dementia-crisis-japan.

High Tech High. 'High Tech High – About Us'. Accessed 9 February 2020. www.hightechhigh.org/about-us/.

Hodgson, Camilla. 'Hottest Decade Ever Recorded "Driven by Man-Made Climate Change"'. Financial Times, 15 January 2020. www.ft.com/ content/5f4b30ee-36e6-11ea-a6d3-9a26f8c3cba4.

Holley, Peter. 'Domino's Will Start Delivering Pizzas via an Autonomous Robot This Fall'. Washington Post, 17 June 2019, sec. Innovations. www.washingtonpost.com/technology/2019/06/17/dominos-will-start-delivering-pizzas-via-an-autonomous-robot-this-fall/.

Horgan, John. 'Flashback: My Report on First Consciousness Powwow in Tucson. How Far Has Science Come Since Then?' *Scientific American Blog Network* (blog), 26 April 2016. https://blogs.scientificamerican .com/cross-check/flashback-my-report-on-first-consciousness-powwow-in-tucson-how-far-has-science-come-since-then/.

Hough, Lory. 'Get under the Hood'. *Ed. Harvard Ed. Magazine*, 2015. www .gse.harvard.edu/news/ed/15/08/get-under-hood.

House of Commons Library. 'General Election 2019: Turnout'. *House of Commons Library* (blog), 7 January 2020. https://commonslibrary .parliament.uk/insights/general-election-2019-turnout/.

Huijnen, Claire A. G. J., Monique A. S. Lexis, Rianne Jansens and Luc P. de Witte. 'Roles, Strengths and Challenges of Using Robots in Interventions for Children with Autism Spectrum Disorder (ASD)'. *Journal of Autism and Developmental Disorders* 49, no. 1 (1 January 2019): 11–21. https://doi.org/10.1007/s10803-018-3683-x.

IET. 'Studying Stem: What Are the Barriers?' Fact File. The Institution of Technology and Engineering, 2008.

IFS, 'Inequalities in the Twenty-First Century: Introducing the IFS Deaton Review'. Accessed 9 February 2020. www.ifs.org.uk/inequality/chapter/ briefing-note/.

Ingram, Debra, Karen Seashore Louis and Roger G. Schroeder. 'Accountability Policies and Teacher Decision Making: Barriers to the Use of Data to Improve Practice'. *Teachers College Record* 106, no. 6 (June 2004): 1258–1287. https://doi.org/10.1111/j.1467-9620.2004 .00379.x.

International Child Development Centre, ed. *Child Well-Being in Rich Countries: A Comparative Overview*. Innocenti Report Card 11. Florence: UNICEF Nations Children's Fund, 2013.

IOM. 'Global Migration Trends'. International Organization for Migration (IOM) United Nations, 30 October 2018. www.iom.int/global-migration-trends.

IPBES. 'Global Assessment Report on Biodiversity and Ecosystem Services'. Intergovernmental Science-Policy Platform on Biodiversity and Ecosystem Services (IPBES), 2019. https://ipbes.net/global-assessment-report-biodiversity-ecosystem-services.

Jeffreys, Branwen. 'Rising Numbers of Pupils Home Educated'. *BBC News*, 21 December 2015, sec. Education & Family. www.bbc.com/news/education-35133119.

Jiang, Jingjing. 'How Teens and Parents Navigate Screen Time and Device Distractions'. *Pew Research Center: Internet, Science & Tech* (blog), 22 August 2018. www.pewresearch.org/internet/2018/08/22/how-teens-and-parents-navigate-screen-time-and-device-distractions/.

Jordan, Kyle, and Yascha Mounk. 'What Populists Do to Democracies'. *The Atlantic*, 26 December 2018. www.theatlantic.com/ideas/archive/2018/12/hard-data-populism-bolsonaro-trump/578878/.

Kahneman, Daniel, and Angus Deaton. 'High Income Improves Evaluation of Life But Not Emotional Well-Being'. *Proceedings of the National Academy of Sciences* 107, no. 38 (21 September 2010): 16489–16493. https://doi.org/10.1073/pnas.1011492107.

Kamarck, Elaine. 'The Challenging Politics of Climate Change'. *Brookings (blog), 23 September 2019*. www.brookings.edu/research/the-challenging-politics-of-climate-change/.

Karabarbounis, Loukas, and Brent Neiman. 'The Global Decline of the Labor Share'. Working Paper. National Bureau of Economic Research, June 2013. www.nber.org/papers/w19136.

Kegan, Robert. *In Over Our Heads: The Mental Demands of Modern Life*. 4th printing ed. Cambridge, MA: Harvard University Press, 1998.

Kelly, Yvonne, Afshin Zilanawala, Cara Booker and Amanda Sacker. 'Social Media Use and Adolescent Mental Health: Findings From the UK Millennium Cohort Study'. *EClinicalMedicine* 6 (1 December 2018): 59–68. https://doi.org/10.1016/j.eclinm.2018.12.005.

Kent, David. 'The Countries Where People Are Most Dissatisfied with How Democracy Is Working'. *Pew Research Center* (blog), 31 May 2019. www.pewresearch.org/fact-tank/2019/05/31/the-countries-where-people-are-most-dissatisfied-with-how-democracy-is-working/.

Kerckhoff, Alan C., and Elizabeth Glennie. *The Matthew Effect in American Education*. Vol. 12, 1999. www.researchgate.net/publication/257936416_The_Matthew_Effect_in_American_Education.

Khan, Salman. *The One World Schoolhouse: Education Reimagined*. Reprint ed. New York, NY: Twelve, 2013.

Klees, Steven J. 'A Quarter Century of Neoliberal Thinking in Education: Misleading Analyses and Failed Policies'. *Globalisation, Societies and Education* 6, no. 4 (1 November 2008): 311–348. https://doi.org/10.1080/14767720802506672.

Klein, Alice. 'Eight Low-Lying Pacific Islands Swallowed Whole by Rising Seas'. *New Scientist*, 7 September 2017. www.newscientist.com/article/2146594-eight-low-lying-pacific-islands-swallowed-whole-by-rising-seas/.

This Changes Everything: Capitalism vs. the Climate. 1st ed. London: Penguin, 2015.

Klein, Naomi. *On Fire: The Burning Case for a Green New Deal*. London: Penguin , 2019.

Kolbert, Elizabeth. *The Sixth Extinction: An Unnatural History*. London: Bloomsbury Publishing, 2014.

Konrath, Sara H., Edward H. O'Brien and Courtney Hsing. 'Changes in Dispositional Empathy in American College Students Over Time: A Meta-Analysis'. *Personality and Social Psychology Review* 15, no. 2 (1 May 2011): 180–198. https://doi.org/10.1177/1088868310377395.

Koretz, Daniel. *The Testing Charade: Pretending to Make Schools Better*. Chicago, IL; London: University of Chicago Press, 2017.

Kowalski, Robin M., Susan P. Limber and Patricia W. Agatston. *Cyber Bullying: Bullying in the Digital Age*. 2nd ed. Malden, MA: Wiley-Blackwell, 2012.

Kulp, Scott A. and Benjamin H. Strauss. 'New Elevation Data Triple Estimates of Global Vulnerability to Sea-Level Rise and Coastal Flooding'. *Nature Communications* 10, no. 1 (29 October 2019): 1–12. https://doi.org/10.1038/s41467-019-12808-z.

Kuo, Frances E. and Andrea Faber Taylor. 'A Potential Natural Treatment for Attention-Deficit/Hyperactivity Disorder: Evidence from a National Study'. *American Journal of Public Health* 94, no. 9 (September 2004): 1580–1586.

Kwak, James. *Economism: Bad Economics and the Rise of Inequality*. New York, NY: Pantheon Books, 2017.

Kyllonen, Patrick C. 'Inequality, Education, Workforce Preparedness, and Complex Problem Solving'. *Journal of Intelligence* 6, no. 3 (16 July 2018): 33. https://doi.org/10.3390/jintelligence6030033.

Ladson-Billings, Gloria. 'From the Achievement Gap to the Education Debt: Understanding Achievement in U.S. Schools'. *Educational Researcher* 35, no. 7 (2006): 3–12.

Larry Elliott Economics. ed., 'Robots Threaten 15m UK Jobs, Says Bank of England's Chief Economist'. *The Guardian*, 12 November 2015, sec. Business. www.theguardian.com/business/2015/nov/12/robots-threaten-low-paid-jobs-says-bank-of-england-chief-economist

Laville, Sandra and Jonathan Watts. 'Across the Globe, Millions Join Biggest Climate Protest Ever'. *The Guardian*, 23 September 2019. www.theguardian.com/environment/2019/sep/21/across-the-globe-millions-join-biggest-climate-protest-ever.

Leadbeater, Charles. '*Education 2030 – Conceptual Learning Framework: Background Papers*'. Paris: OECD, 2017. www.oecd.org/education/2030-project/contact/Conceptual_learning_framework_Conceptual_papers.pdf.

Leakey, Richard E. and Roger Lewin. *The Sixth Extinction: Patterns of Life and the Future of Humankind*. New York: Doubleday, 1995.

Lee, Shirley and Avis Mysyk. 'The Medicalization of Compulsive Buying'. *Social Science & Medicine* 58, no. 9 (1 May 2004): 1709–1718. https://doi.org/10.1016/S0277-9536(03)00340-X.

LeGrain, Philippe. 'The Future of Globalisation Is in Doubt'. *CapX*, 17 April 2015. https://capx.co/the-future-of-globalisation-is-in-doubt/.

Lindgren, Karl-Oskar, Sven Oskarsson and Christopher T. Dawes. 'Can Political Inequalities Be Educated Away? Evidence from a Large-Scale Reform'. *American Journal of Political Science* 61, no. 1 (1 January 2017): 222–236. https://doi.org/10.1111/ajps.12261.

Lingard, Bob, Wayne Martino, Goli Rezai-Rashti and Sam Sellar. *Globalizing Educational Accountabilities*. Reprint ed. New York, NY; London: Routledge, 2016.

Lister, Josephine. 'How Can We Meaningfully Include Students' Voices in Schools?' *HundrED* (blog), 1 August 2019. https://hundred.org/en/articles/how-can-we-meaningfully-include-students-voices-in-schools.

Louv, Richard. *Last Child in the Woods: Saving Our Children from Nature-Deficit Disorder*. Main ed. London: Atlantic Books, 2010.

Lubienski, Christopher. 'Innovation in Education Markets: Theory and Evidence on the Impact of Competition and Choice in Charter Schools'. *American Educational Research Journal* 40, no. 2 (1 July 2003): 395–443.

'School Diversification in Second-Best Education Markets: International Evidence and Conflicting Theories of Change'. *Educational Policy* 20, no. 2 (1 May 2006): 323–344. https://doi.org/10.1177/0895904805284049.

Luksha, Pavel, Joshua Cubista, Alexander Laszlo, Mila Popovich and Ivan Ninenko. 'Educational Ecosystems for Societal Transformation'. Global Education Futures Report. Moscow: Global Education Futures, 2018.

www.academyforchange.org/educational-ecosystems-societal-trans
formation/.

Lund, Susan, James Manyika, Jonathan Woetzel, Jacques Bughin, Mekala
Krishnan, Jeongmin Seong and Mac Muir. 'Globalization in Transition:
The Future of Trade and Global Value Chains'. McKinsey Global
Institute: McKinsey & Company, January 2019. www.mckinsey.com/
featured-insights/innovation-and-growth/globalization-in-transition-the
-future-of-trade-and-value-chains.

Makovec, Anne. 'Students Rally in San Francisco for Afghan Teen Detained
by ICE'. *CBS SF BayArea*, 8 June 2018. https://sanfrancisco.cbslocal
.com/2018/06/08/students-rally-in-san-francisco-for-afghan-teen-detained-
by-ice/.

Manney, P. J. 'Is Technology Destroying Empathy? (Op-Ed)'. *LiveScience*,
30 June 2015. www.livescience.com/51392-will-tech-bring-humanity-
together-or-tear-it-apart.html.

Manocha, Ramesh, Deborah Black and Leigh Wilson. 'Quality of Life and
Functional Health Status of Long-Term Meditators'. *Evidence-Based
Complementary and Alternative Medicine* 2012 (7 May 2012):
e350674. https://doi.org/10.1155/2012/350674.

Manyika, James, Susam Lund, Byron Auguste and Sreenivas Ramaswamy.
'Help Wanted: The Future of Work in Advanced Economies'. McKinsey
Global Institute, 2012. file:///C:/Users/IU50/Downloads/Help_wanted_
future_of_work_full_report.pdf.

Maraz, Aniko, Mark D. Griffiths and Zsolt Demetrovics. 'The Prevalence of
Compulsive Buying: A Meta-Analysis'. *Addiction (Abingdon, England)*
111, no. 3 (March 2016): 408–419. https://doi.org/10.1111/add.13223.

Margil, Mari and Ryan Dickinson. 'Toledo Passed a "Lake Erie Bill of
Rights" to Protect Its Water. The State Is Trying to Stop It.' *In These
Times*, 15 August 2019. http://inthesetimes.com/article/22018/rights-of-
nature-toledo-ohio-state-industry-repression-lake-erie.

Marginson, Simon. 'The Worldwide Trend to High Participation Higher
Education: Dynamics of Social Stratification in Inclusive Systems'.
Higher Education 72, no. 4 (1 October 2016): 413–434. https://doi
.org/10.1007/s10734-016-0016-x.

Markovits, Daniel. *The Meritocracy Trap: How America's Foundational
Myth Feeds Inequality, Dismantles the Middle Class, and Devours the
Elite*. New York: Penguin Press, 2019.

Martin. 'UN Report: Nature's Dangerous Decline "Unprecedented"; Species
Extinction Rates "Accelerating"'. *United Nations Sustainable
Development* (blog), 6 May 2019. www.un.org/sustainabledevelop
ment/blog/2019/05/nature-decline-unprecedented-report.

Martin, Alan. 'Driverless Truck Convoys Cross Europe'. *Alphr*, 7 April 2016. www.alphr.com/cars/1003136/driverless-truck-convoys-cross-europe.

Mason, Paul. *PostCapitalism: A Guide to Our Future*. London: Allen Lane, 2015.

Mcafee, Andrew and Erik Brynjolfsson. *Machine, Platform, Crowd: Harnessing the Digital Revolution*. 1st ed. Hardback. Dust Jacket. ed. New York: W. W. Norton & Company, 2017.

McDougall, Dan. '"Ecological Grief": Greenland Residents Traumatised by Climate Emergency'. *The Guardian*, 12 August 2019, sec. World news. www.theguardian.com/world/2019/aug/12/greenland-residents-trauma tised-by-climate-emergency.

McGivney, Eileen and Rebecca Winthrop. 'Why Wait 100 Years? Bridging the Gap in Global Education'. Washington, DC: Brookings Institution, June 2015. www.brookings.edu/research/why-wait-100-years-bridging-the-gap-in-global-education/.

McGrath, Matt. 'Coronavirus: Five Charts about the Biggest Carbon Crash'. *BBC News*, 6 May 2020, sec. Science & Environment. www.bbc.com/news/science-environment-52485712.

McRae, Mike. 'Latest Report on Finland's Universal Basic Income Trial Says It Makes People Happier'. ScienceAlert, 8 May 2020. www.sciencealert .com/latest-report-on-finland-s-universal-basic-income-trial-suggests-we-d-be-happier-with-it.

Mehta, Jal and Sarah Fine. *In Search of Deeper Learning: The Quest to Remake the American High School*. Cambridge, MA: Harvard University Press, 2019.

Michaels, F. S. *Monoculture: How One Story Is Changing Everything*. Kamloops, BC: Red Clover, 2011.

Milanovic, Branko. *Global Inequality: A New Approach for the Age of Globalization*. Cambridge, MA: Harvard University Press, 2016.

Milk, Chris. *How Virtual Reality Can Create the Ultimate Empathy Machine*. TED2015, 2015. www.ted.com/talks/chris_milk_how_vir tual_reality_can_create_the_ultimate_empathy_machine.

Miller, Riel. 'Futures Literacy – Embracing Complexity and Using the Future'. *Ethos*, no. 10 (October 2011). www.academia.edu/8268282/Futures_Literacy_Embracing_Complexity_and_Using_the_Future.

Moe, Terry M. and Susanne Wiborg. *The Comparative Politics of Education: Teacher Unions and Education Systems around the World*. Cambridge; New York: Cambridge University Press, 2016. www .cambridge.org/us/academic/subjects/politics-international-relations/comparative-politics/comparative-politics-education-teachers-unions-and-education-systems-around-world?format=PB.

Moore, Mark H. *Creating Public Value: Strategic Management in Government*. Revised ed. Cambridge, MA: Harvard University Press, 1995.

Morris, Marla. 'The Eighth One: Naturalistic Intelligence'. In *Multiple Intelligences Reconsidered*, edited by Joe L. Kincheloe, 159–173. New York: Peter Lang, 2004.

Moss, Stephen. *Our Natural Childhood*. National Trust, 2012. https://nt .global.ssl.fastly.net/documents/read-our-natural-childhood-report.pdf.

Mourshed, Mona, Diana Farrell and Dominic Barton. *Education to Employment: Designing a System That Works*. Washington, DC: McKinsey & Company, January 2013. http://mckinseyonsociety.com/ downloads/reports/Education/Education-to-Employment_FINAL.pdf.

Naam, Ramez. *More Than Human*. New York, NY: Broadway Books – Penguin Random House, 2005.

Narayan, Ambar, Roy Van der Weide, Alexandru Cojocaru, Christoph Lakner, Silvia Redaelli, Daniel Gerszon Mahler, Rakesh Gupta N. Ramasubbaiah and Stefan Thewissen. *Fair Progress?: Economic Mobility across Generations around the World*. The World Bank, 2018. https://doi.org/10.1596/978-1-4648-1210-1.

Nathan, Max, Tom Kemeny, Andy Pratt and Greg Spencer. *Creative Economy Employment in the US, Canada and the UK: A Comparative Analysis*. London: Nesta, March 2016. www.nesta .org.uk/report/creative-economy-employment-in-the-us-canada-and-the-uk/.

The Nature Conservancy. 'Connecting America's Youth to Nature'. Survey Results. Arlington, VA: The Nature Conservancy; Toyota USA Foundation & Foundation for Youth Investment; Fairbank, Maslin, Maullin, Metz & Associates and Public Opinion Strategies, 2011.

NCES. *Arts Education in Public Elementary and Secondary Schools: 1999-2000 and 2009-10*. Statistical Analysis Report. Washington, DC: National Center for Education Statistics, 2 April 2012. https://nces.ed .gov/pubs2012/2012014rev.pdf.

NCSL. *The Journey of Sustainable Schools: Developing and Embedding Sustainability*. London: National College for School Leadership, March 2011.

nesta. 'Democratic Innovations'. Accessed 9 February 2020. www.nesta.org .uk/project/democratic-innovations/.

Newland, Kathleen and Randy Capps. 'Why Hide the Facts about Refugee Costs and Benefits?' Commentaries. Washington, DC: Migration Policy Institute, 20 September 2017. www.migrationpolicy.org/news/why-hide-facts-about-refugee-costs-and-benefits.

NHS. 'Children Treated for Computer Gaming Addiction under NHS Long Term Plan'. News. NHS England, 8 October 2019. www.england.nhs .uk/2019/10/children-treated-for-computer-gaming-addiction-under-nhs-long-term-plan/.

Nies, Yunji de. 'President Obama Outlines Goal to Improve College Graduation Rate in U.S.' *ABC News*, 9 August 2010. https://abcnews .go.com/WN/president-barack-obama-outlines-college-education-goal-university/story?id=11359759.

Noora, Ruoho, Leponiemi Lasse and Taimela Ilona. 'Forerunner: Improving Education in Helsinki'. Research Report. Helsinki: HundrED, November 2019.

Nosowitz, Dan. 'How Alarming Is It That Islands Are Just Disappearing?' Atlas Obscura, 28:00 400AD. www.atlasobscura.com/articles/are-islands-disappearing.

Nourbakhsh, Illah. 'Fears and Joys of a Life with Social Robots'. *Financial Times*, 6 May 2016, sec. Opinion. www.ft.com/content/6cb943f4-12ac-11e6-91da-096d89bd2173?ftcamp=crm/email//nbe/techFT/product.

NPR. *Keynes Predicted We Would Be Working 15-Hour Weeks. Why Was He So Wrong?* Planet Money, August 13, 2015. www.npr.org/2015/08/13/432122637/keynes-predicted-we-would-be-working-15-hour-weeks-why-was-he-so-wrong.

NSPCC. '40% of Teenage Girls Pressured into Having Sex'. NSPCC, 11 February 2015. www.nspcc.org.uk/what-we-do/news-opinion/40-percent-teenage-girls-pressured-into-sex/.

Nussbaum, Martha C. 'Education and Democratic Citizenship: Capabilities and Quality Education'. *Journal of Human Development* 7, no. 3 (1 November 2006): 385–395. https://doi.org/10.1080/14649880600815974.

O'Brien, Dave, Daniel Laurison, Andrew Miles and Sam Friedman. 'Are the Creative Industries Meritocratic? An Analysis of the 2014 British Labour Force Survey'. *Cultural Trends* 25, no. 2 (2 April 2016): 116–131. https://doi.org/10.1080/09548963.2016.1170943.

OECD. 'Comparative Child Well-Being across the OECD'. In *Doing Better for Children*, 21–63. Paris: OECD Publishing, 2009.

Education Policy Outlook 2015 – Making Reforms Happen. Paris: OECD Publishing, 2015. https://doi.org/10.1787/9789264225442-en.

'The Future We Want'. The Future of Education and Skills: Education 2030. OECD, 2018.

Getting Skills Right: Assessing and Anticipating Changing Skill Needs. OECD Publishing, 2016. https://doi.org/10.1787/9789264252073-en.

'Health at a Glance 2019: OECD Indicators'. Paris: OECD Publishing, 2019. www.oecd.org/health/health-systems/health-at-a-glance-19991312.htm.

'Inclusive Growth – Economic Growth That Is Distributed Fairly across Society'. Accessed 7 February 2020. www.oecd.org/inclusive-growth/.

'Making Physical Education Dynamic and Inclusive for 2030'. International Curriculum Analysis. OECD Future of Education 2030. Paris: OECD, 2019. www.oecd.org/education/2030-project/contact/ OECD_FUTURE_OF_EDUCATION_2030_MAKING_PHYSICAL_ DYNAMIC_AND_INCLUSIVE_FOR_2030.pdf.

'OECD Better Life Index'. Accessed 8 February 2020. www .oecdbetterlifeindex.org/.

'PISA 2015 Results (Volume III) Students Wellbeing'. Paris: OECD Publishing, 2017.

'PISA 2018 Global Competence', n.d. www.oecd.org/pisa/pisa-2018-global-competence.htm.

PISA 2018 Results Volume I: What Students Know and Can Do. Paris: OECD Publishing, 2019. www.oecd-ilibrary.org/docserver/5f07c754-en .pdf?expires=1576159668&id=id&accname=guest&checksum=4A15E7 AD16E1E19B353CA8665AE93C97.

PISA 2018 Results Volume II: Where All Students Can Succeed. Paris: OECD Publishing, 2019. www.oecd-ilibrary.org/docserver/b5fd1b8f-en .pdf?expires=1576158959&id=id&accname=guest&checksum=F0237 23B8808EB9D4D68F3D4B4C4BB66.

PISA 2018 Results Volume III: What School Life Means for Students' Lives. Paris: OECD Publishing, 2019. www.oecd-ilibrary.org/docser ver/acd78851-en.pdf?expires=1576159673&id=id&accname=guest& checksum=A1DA538ED0D8D5F03CDFAD090DC8D00F.

'Preparing Our Youth for an Inclusive and Sustainable World: The OECD PISA Global Competence Framework'. Paris: OECD Publishing, 2018.

TALIS 2013 Results: An International Perspective on Teaching and Learning. TALIS. OECD, 2014. https://doi.org/10.1787/ 9789264196261-en.

TALIS 2018 Results (Volume I) – Teachers and School Leaders as Lifelong Learners. Paris: OECD Publishing, 2019. www.oecd.org/edu cation/talis-2018-results-volume-i-1d0bc92a-en.htm.

Ofcom. *Online Nation: 2019 Report.* London: Ofcom, 30 May 2019.

Ofsted. *XP School'. School Report.* Manchester: Ofsted, 12 July 2017.

Okamura, Hitoshi, Shinya Ishii, Tomoyuki Ishii and Akira Eboshida. 'Prevalence of Dementia in Japan: A Systematic Review'. *Dementia and Geriatric Cognitive Disorders* 36, no. 1–2 (2013): 111–118. https://doi.org/10.1159/000353444.

ONS. *Changes in the Value and Division of Unpaid Care Work in the UK.* London: Office for National Statistics, 10 November 2016.

Orenstein, Peggy. *Girls & Sex: Navigating the Complicated New Landscape*. New York, NY: Harper, 2016.

Osborne, Michael, Carl Benedikt Frey and Hasan Bakhshi. 'Creativity vs Robots'. *Nesta* (blog), 17 April 2015. www.nesta.org.uk/report/creativity-vs-robots/.

Oxfam. 'Just 8 Men Own Same Wealth as Half the World'. Oxfam International, 1 March 2018. www.oxfam.org/en/press-releases/just-8-men-own-same-wealth-half-world.

Panova, Tayana and Xavier Carbonell. 'Is Smartphone Addiction Really an Addiction?' *Journal of Behavioral Addictions* 7, no. 2 (1 June 2018): 252–259. https://doi.org/10.1556/2006.7.2018.49.

Parijs, Phillipe Van and Yannick Vanderborght. *Basic Income: A Radical Proposal for a Free Society and a Sane Economy*. Cambridge, MA: Harvard University Press, 2017.

Partington, Richard. 'Is It Time to End Our Fixation with GDP and Growth?' The Guardian, 17 June 2019, sec. News. www.theguardian.com/news/2019/jun/17/is-time-to-end-our-fixation-with-gdp-and-growth.

Payne, Charles M. *So Much Reform, So Little Change: The Persistence of Failure in Urban Schools*. Third ed., Cambridge, MA: Harvard Education Press, 2010.

Pearson, Natalie, Lauren B. Sherar and Mark Hamer. 'Prevalence and Correlates of Meeting Sleep, Screen-Time, and Physical Activity Guidelines among Adolescents in the United Kingdom'. *JAMA Pediatrics* 173, no. 10 (1 October 2019): 993–994. https://doi.org/10.1001/jamapediatrics.2019.2822.

Perez, Rafael E. and Steven D. Schwaitzberg. 'Robotic Surgery: Finding Value in 2019 and Beyond'. *Annals of Laparoscopic and Endoscopic Surgery* 4, no. 51 (30 May 2019). https://doi.org/10.21037/ales.2019.05.02.

Peters, Adele. 'This Cute Robot Is Designed to Help Children with Autism'. *Fast Company*, 15 June 2016. www.fastcompany.com/3059604/this-cute-robot-is-designed-to-help-children-with-autism.

Peurach, Donald J. and Joshua L. Glazer. 'Reconsidering Replication: New Perspectives on Large-Scale School Improvement'. *Journal of Educational Change* 13, no. 2 (May 2012): 155–190. https://doi.org/10.1007/s10833-011-9177-7.

Pew Research Center, 'Millennials in Adulthood'. *Pew Research Center's Social & Demographic Trends Project* (blog), 7 March 2014. www.pewsocialtrends.org/2014/03/07/millennials-in-adulthood/.

Pickett, Kate and Richard Wilkinson. *The Spirit Level: Why Equality Is Better for Everyone*. 2nd ed. London: Penguin, 2010.

Pietari, Kyle. 'Ecuador's Constitutional Rights of Nature: Implementation, Impacts, and Lessons Learned', 2016, 58.

Piketty, Thomas and Arthur Goldhammer. *Capital in the Twenty-First Century*. Cambridge MA: Harvard University Press, 2014.

Pimm, Stuart L., Gareth J. Russell, John L. Gittleman and Thomas M. Brooks. 'The Future of Biodiversity'. *Science* 269, no. 5222 (21 July 1995): 347–350. https://doi.org/10.1126/science.269.5222.347.

Podesta, John. 'The Climate Crisis, Migration, and Refugees'. *Brookings* (blog), 25 July 2019. www.brookings.edu/research/the-climate-crisis-migration-and-refugees/.

Pomerantsev, Peter. *This Is Not Propaganda: Adventures in the War against Reality*. Main ed. London: Faber & Faber, 2019.

Pooley, Cat Rutter. 'Lawyers' next Challenge: Too Much Technology'. *Financial Times*, 23 October 2019. www.ft.com/content/d9d475c2-d544-11e9-8d46-8def889b4137.

Pope Francis. 'Encyclical Letter Laudato Si' of the Holy Father Francis on Care for Our Common Home', 24 May 2015. http://w2.vatican.va/content/francesco/en/encyclicals/documents/papa-francesco_20150524_enciclica-laudato-si.html.

Postman, Neil. *The End of Education: Redefining the Value of School*. 1st Vintage Books ed. New York, NY: Vintage Books, 1996.

Power, Michael. *The Audit Society: Rituals of Verification*. Oxford; New York, NY: Oxford University Press, 1997.

Pratt, Russ. 'The "Porn Genie" Is out of the Bottle: Understanding and Responding to the Impact of Pornograph'. *InPsych (Australian Psychological Society)*, April 2015. www.psychology.org.au/inpsych/2015/april/pratt.

Price, David. *Open: How We'll Work, Live and Learn in the Future*. Horley, Surrey: Crux Publishing Ltd, 2013.

Prince, Katherine. *Innovating toward a Vibrant Learning Ecosystem: Ten Pathways for Transforming Learning. Forecast*. Cincinnati, OH: KnowledgeWorks, 2014.

Pritchett, Lant. 'The Risks to Education Systems from Design Mismatch and Global Isomorphism: Concepts, with Examples from India'. Working Paper Series. World Institute for Development Economic Research (UNU-WIDER), 2014. http://econpapers.repec.org/paper/unuwpaper/wp2014-039.htm.

Purohit, Tanmaya. 'Social Innovators of Udaipur: Interview with Vidhi Jain'. *Shikshantar: The People's Institute for Re-Thinking Education and Development* (blog), 28 January 2016. http://shikshantar.org/innovations-shiksha/families-learning-together-unschooling/social-innovators-udaipur-interview-vidhi.

Rallings, Jonathan. *Youth and the Internet: A Guide for Policy Makers.* Ilford Essex: Barnados, April 2015.

Ratey, John J. and Eric Hagerman. *Spark: The Revolutionary New Science of Exercise and the Brain.* 1st ed. New York, NY: Little, Brown and Company, 2008.

Raworth, Kate. *Doughnut Economics: Seven Ways to Think Like a 21st-Century Economist.* London: Random House Business, 2017.

Reardon, Sean F., Demetra Kalogrides and Kenneth Shores. 'The Geography of Racial/Ethnic Test Score Gaps'. *American Journal of Sociology* 124, no. 4 (1 January 2019): 1164–1221. https://doi.org/10.1086/700678.

Redding, Christopher, Marisa Cannata and Katherine Taylor Haynes. 'With Scale in Mind: A Continuous Improvement Model for Implementation'. *Peabody Journal of Education* 92, no. 5 (20 October 2017): 589–608. https://doi.org/10.1080/0161956X.2017.1368635.

Reeves, Richard V. *Dream Hoarders: How the American Upper Middle Class Is Leaving Everyone Else in the Dust, Why That Is a Problem, and What to Do about It.* Washington DC: Brookings Institution Press, 2017. https://muse-jhu-edu.ezp-prod1.hul.harvard.edu/book/51694.

Reimers, Fernando M. and Connie K. Chung, eds. *Teaching and Learning for the Twenty-First Century: Educational Goals, Policies, and Curricula from Six Nations.* Cambridge, MA: Harvard Education Press, 2016.

Richardson, Will. *Why School?: How Education Must Change When Learning and Information Are Everywhere.* EBook. TED, 2012. www .amazon.co.uk/Why-School-Education-Information-Everywhere-ebook/dp/B00998J5YQ.

Richter, Felix. 'Always On: Media Usage Amounts to 10+ Hours a Day (Based on Nielsen Total Audience Report Q2 2018)'. *Statista Infographics*, 16 January 2019. www.statista.com/chart/1971/elec tronic-media-use/.

Riordan, Rob. 'Change the Subject: Making the Case for Project-Based Learning'. *Edutopia* (blog), 17 January 2013. www.edutopia.org/blog/ 21st-century-skills-changing-subjects-larry-rosenstock-rob-riordan.

Ripple, William J., Christopher Wolf, Thomas M. Newsome, Phoebe Barnard and William R. Moomaw. 'World Scientists' Warning of a Climate Emergency'. *BioScience* 70, no. 1 (1 January 2020): 8–12. https://doi.org/10.1093/biosci/biz088.

Robinson, Jenny Perlman and Rebecca Winthrop. 'Millions Learning: Scaling up Education in Development Countries'. Washington, DC: Brookings Institution, 2016.

Rosborough, Trish, Judy Halbert and Linda Kaser. 'Aboriginal Enhancement Schools Network: Walking Together in a Spirit of

Respect and Inquiry'. In *Learning, Knowing, Sharing: Celebrating Successes in K-12 Aboriginal Education in British Columbia | Faculty of Education*, edited by Jo-Ann Archibald, Q'um Q'um Xiiem and Jan Hare, 28–43. Vancouver, BC, Canada: BC Principals' & Vice-Principals' Association (BCPVPA), 2017. https://educ.ubc.ca/learning-knowing-sharing-celebrating-successes-in-k-12-aboriginal-education-in-british-columbia/.

Rosenstock, Larry. 'I Used to Think... That Traditional Public Education Was the Institution with the Most Promise...' *The Daily Riff* (blog), 3 May 2012. www.thedailyriff.com/articles/i-used-to-think-that-traditional-public-education-was-the-institution-with-the-most-promise-526.php.

Ross, Alec. *The Industries of the Future*. London; New York, NY; Sydney; Toronto; New Delhi: Simon & Schuster UK, 2016.

Rowson, Jonathan. 'Bildung in the 21st Century – Why Sustainable Prosperity Depends upon Reimagining Education'. Centre for the Understanding of Sustainable Prosperity (CUSP), June 2019. cusp.ac.uk/essay/m1-9.

Roy, Eleanor Ainge. 'New Zealand's World-First "Wellbeing" Budget to Focus on Poverty and Mental Health'. *The Guardian*, 14 May 2019, sec. World news. www.theguardian.com/world/2019/may/14/new-zealands-world-first-wellbeing-budget-to-focus-on-poverty-and-mental-health.

RSA, 'Circular Economy – RSA'. Accessed 8 February 2020. www.thersa.org/discover/topics/circular-economy.

RSPB. *Connecting with Nature: Finding out How Connected to Nature the UK's Children Are*. Bedfordshire: Royal Society for the Protection of Birds, 2013.

Rudgard, Olivia. '"Alexa Generation" May Be Learning Bad Manners from Talking to Digital Assistants, Report Warns'. *The Telegraph*, 31 January 2018. www.telegraph.co.uk/news/2018/01/31/alexa-generation-could-learning-bad-manners-talking-digital/.

Rushkoff, Douglas. *Throwing Rocks at the Google Bus: How Growth Became the Enemy of Prosperity*. New York, NY: Portfolio, 2016.

Russell, Nicole. 'Why Homeschooling Is Growing'. *The Federalist*, 1 September 2015. https://thefederalist.com/2015/09/01/why-homeschooling-is-growing/.

Sadofsky, Mimsy. 'What Is "Agency"?' *Sudbury Valley School* (blog), 18 November 2019. https://sudburyvalley.org/blog/what-agency-0.

Sahlberg, Pasi. *Finnish Lessons 2.0: What Can the World Learn from Educational Change in Finland?* 2nd ed. New York, NY: Teachers College Press, 2014.

Saldana, Justin. 'Power and Conformity in Today's Schools'. *International Journal of Humanities and Social Science* 3, no. 1 (2013): 5.

Schonert-Reichl, Kimberly A., Eva Oberle, Molly Stewart Lawlor, David Abbott, Kimberly Thomson, Tim F. Oberlander and Adele Diamond. 'Enhancing Cognitive and Social–Emotional Development through a Simple-to-Administer Mindfulness-Based School Program for Elementary School Children: A Randomized Controlled Trial'. *Developmental Psychology* 51, no. 1 (2015): 52–66. https://doi.org/10 .1037/a0038454.

Schwab, Klaus. *The Fourth Industrial Revolution*. New York, NY: The Fourth Industrial Revolution, 2016.

Schwitzer, Gary. 'New Questions about the $3B/Year Robotic Surgery Business'. HealthNewsReview.org, 28 August 2018. www .healthnewsreview.org/2018/08/new-questions-about-the-3b-year-robotic-surgery-business/.

Scott, Bill. 'Another Ministerial Stonewalling'. *Bill Scott's Blog, University of Bath* (blog), 2 January 2015. http://blogs.bath.ac.uk/edswahs/2015/01/ 02/another-ministerial-stonewalling/.

Sedlacek, Tomas. *Economics of Good and Evil: The Quest for Economic Meaning from Gilgamesh to Wall Street*. Oxford: Oxford University Press, 2011.

Shademan, Azad, Ryan S. Decker, Justin D. Opfermann, Simon Leonard, Axel Krieger and Peter C. W. Kim. 'Supervised Autonomous Robotic Soft Tissue Surgery'. *Science Translational Medicine* 8, no. 337 (4 May 2016): 337ra64-337ra64. https://doi.org/10.1126/scitranslmed.aad9398.

Shorthouse, Ryan, ed. *Disconnected: Social Mobility and the Creative Industries*. London: Social Market Foundation, 2010.

Siddique, Haroon. 'British Researchers Get Green Light to Genetically Modify Human Embryos'. *The Guardian*, 1 February 2016, sec. Science. www.theguardian.com/science/2016/feb/01/human-embryo-genetic-modify-regulator-green-light-research.

'Mental Health Disorders on Rise among Children'. *The Guardian*, 22 November 2018, sec. Society. www.theguardian.com/society/2018/ nov/22/mental-health-disorders-on-rise-among-children-nhs-figures.

Skidelsky, Robert. 'How to Work Less: Lord Skidelsky on Reducing the Working Week'. *PoliticsHome* (blog), 20 September 2019. www .politicshome.com/news/uk/technology/house/house-magazine/106680/ how-work-less-lord-skidelsky-reducing-working-week.

'Rise of the Robots: What Will the Future of Work Look like? *The Guardian*, 19 February 2013, sec. Business. www.theguardian.com/ business/2013/feb/19/rise-of-robots-future-of-work.

Slayback, Zachary. *The End of School: Reclaiming Education from the Classroom*. Scotts Valley, CA: CreateSpace Independent Publishing, 2016.

Smedley, Tim. 'Is the World Running out of Fresh Water?' Accessed 8 February 2020. www.bbc.com/future/article/20170412-is-the-world-running-out-of-fresh-water.

Smil, Vaclav. *Growth: From Microorganisms to Megacities*. Cambridge, MA: The MIT Press, 2019.

Spang, Rebecca. 'Thing Theory: Contemplating the Culture of Consumption'. *Financial Times*, 29 January 2016. www.ft.com/content/9c57c12c-c517-11e5-808f-8231cd71622e.

St Cuthbert's School, Auckland, New Zealand, 'Kahunui Times: Intake 6', 2008. www.stcuthberts.school.nz/wp-content/uploads/2013/07/Intake-6-2008.pdf

Standing, Guy. *The Precariat: The New Dangerous Class*. Revised ed. London; New York, NY: Bloomsbury Academic, 2014.

State Government of Victoria. 'Student Voice Practice Guide (Amplify)'. Department of Education and Training, 11 December 2019. www.education.vic.gov.au/school/teachers/teachingresources/practice/improve/Pages/amplify.aspx.

Stein, Zachary. *Education in a Time between Worlds: Essays on the Future of Schools, Technology, and Society*. San Francisco CA: Bright Alliance, 2019.

Steinberg, Lawrence. 'OECD Transformative Competencies 2030: Taking Responsibility.' Paris: OECD, 2017. www.oecd.org/education/2030-project/contact/Conceptual_learning_framework_Conceptual_papers.pdf.

Steinemann, Namji. *Student Agency in Asia: Educators' Perceptions on Its Promises and Barriers*. Paris: OECD, 2017. www.oecd.org/education/2030-project/contact/Conceptual_learning_framework_Conceptual_papers.pdf.

STEM Women. 'Percentages of Women in STEM Statistics'. *STEM Women* (blog), 26 September 2019. www.stemwomen.co.uk/blog/2019/09/women-in-stem-percentages-of-women-in-stem-statistics.

Stiglitz, J. E., A. Sen and J. P. Fitoussi, Report by the Commission on the Measurement of Economic Performance and Social Progress, Paris, 2009

Stone, Jon. 'Over-Focus on Exams Causing Mental Health Problems and Self-Harm among Pupils Study Find'. *The Independent*, 6 July 2015. www.independent.co.uk/news/uk/politics/over-focus-on-exams-causing-mental-health-problems-and-self-harm-among-pupils-study-finds-10368815.html.

Streeck, Wolfgang. *Buying Time: The Delayed Crisis of Democratic Capitalism*. Brooklyn, NY: Verso Books, 2014.

The Students of High Tech High. *Perspectives of San Diego Bay: A Field Guide*. Providence, R.I.: Next Generation Press, 2006.

Surridge, Paula. 'What Lies behind the UK's New Political Map? Education, Education, Education'. *Prospect*, 18 December 2019. www .prospectmagazine.co.uk/politics/what-lies-behind-the-uks-new-polit ical-map-education-education-education.

Susskind, Daniel. 'Robot Doctors and Lawyers? It's a Change We Should Embrace'. *The Guardian*, 2 November 2015, sec. Opinion. www .theguardian.com/commentisfree/2015/nov/02/robot-doctors-lawyers-profes sions-embrace-change-machines.

  A World without Work: Technology, Automation and How We Should Respond. London: Allen Lane, 2020.

Susskind, Richard, and Daniel Susskind. *The Future of the Professions: How Technology Will Transform the Work of Human Experts*. 1st ed. Oxford: Oxford University Press, 2015.

The Sutton Trust. 'Social Mobility and Education: Academic Papers Presented at a High Level Summit Sponsored by the Carnegie Corporation of New York and the Sutton Trust', 1 June 2008. www.suttontrust.com/wp-content/uploads/2020/01/academic_papers_report.pdf.

Tait, Peter. 'Causes of Growing Mental Health Problems Sit Largely within Schools', *Telegraph*, 2 December 2015, sec. Education. www.telegraph .co.uk/education/educationopinion/12025711/Schools-largely-to-blame-for-rising-mental-health-issues.html.

Talreja, Vishal. 'Student Agency: The Impact of Adversity'. EDU/EDPC. Education 2030 – Conceptual Learning Framework: Background Papers. OECD, 2017.

Taylor, Matthew. 'Democratic Renewal, or Else…' *RSA* (blog), 5 April 2016. www.thersa.org/discover/publications-and-articles/matthew-tay lor-blog/2016/04/democratic-renewal-or-else.

Thelen, Kathleen. *How Institutions Evolve: The Political Economy of Skills in Germany, Britain, the United States, and Japan*. Cambridge; New York, NY: Cambridge University Press, 2004.

Thompson, Clive. 'May A.I. Help You?' *The New York Times*, 14 November 2018, sec. Magazine. www.nytimes.com/interactive/2018/11/14/maga zine/tech-design-ai-chatbot.htmlwww.nytimes.com/interactive/2018/ 11/14/magazine/tech-design-ai-chatbot.html, www.nytimes.com/inter active/2018/11/14/magazine/tech-design-ai-chatbot.html.

Thornton, Patricia H., William Ocasio and Michael Lounsbury. *The Institutional Logics Perspective: A New Approach to Culture, Structure, and Process*. Oxford: Oxford University Press, 2012.

Times Colonist. 'Writers Challenged to Reflect Lives of Indigenous People on the Street'. *Times Colonist*, 17 March 2019. www .timescolonist.com/islander/writers-challenged-to-reflect-lives-of-indigen ous-people-on-the-street-1.23666081?fbclid=IwAR26Fn_3HqH_D4-aHbS3h0qM3YKDiVQBf6c1i3-gAkcg0VSuOpjoIxSj6S0.

TNN. 'Why Populist Leaders Are Shunning the Pundits'. *The Economic Times*. 24 May 2019.

Torres, Julia and Elizabeth Macpherson. 'The Tour to Save the World: Colombia Wins the Yellow Jersey for the Rights of Nature'. *International Journal of Constitutional Law Blog* (blog), 23 August 2019. www.iconnectblog.com/2019/08/the-tour-to-save-the-world-colombia-wins-the-yellow-jersey-for-the-rights-of-nature/.

Tovey, Josephine. 'Home Schooling up 65% in Four Years'. *The Sydney Morning Herald*, 7 September 2013. www.smh.com.au/education/ home-schooling-up-65-percent-in-four-years-20130907-2tcj8.html.

Trilling, Bernie and Charles Fadel. *21st Century Skills: Learning for Life in Our Times*. 1st ed. San Francisco, CA: Jossey-Bass, 2012.

Tucker, Marc. *Leading High-Performance School Systems: Lessons from the World's Best*. Alexandria, VA: ASCD, 2019.

Turkle, Sherry. *Alone Together*. First Trade Paper Ed ed. New York, NY: Basic Books, 2013.

Turner, Karen. 'Meet "Ross," the Newly Hired Legal Robot'. *Washington Post*, 16 May 2016. www.washingtonpost.com/news/innovations/wp/ 2016/05/16/meet-ross-the-newly-hired-legal-robot/.

Twenge, Jean M., and W. Keith Campbell. *The Narcissism Epidemic: Living in the Age of Entitlement*. New York, NY: Free Press, 2010.

UCL. 'British Teenagers Don't Hit 24-Hour Movement Guidelines'. UCL Institute of Epidemiology & Health Care, 9 September 2019. www.ucl .ac.uk/epidemiology-health-care/news/2019/sep/british-teenagers-dont-hit-24-hour-movement-guidelines.

UN DESA. '2018 Revision of World Urbanization Prospects'. United Nations Department of Economic and Social Affairs, 16 May 2018. www.un.org/development/desa/publications/2018-revision-of-world-urban ization-prospects.html.

'The World Population Prospects: 2015 Revision'. Report. New York, NY: United Nations Department of Economic and Social Affairs, 29 July 2015. world-population-prospects-2015-revision.html.

UN News. 'Migration and the Climate Crisis: The UN's Search for Solutions'. UN News, 31 July 2019. https://news.un.org/en/story/2019/ 07/1043551.

UNCTAD. 'Creative Economy Bucks the Trend, Grows Despite Slowdown in Global Trade'. Geneva, Switzerland: United Nations Conference on Trade and Development, 14 January 2019. https://unctad.org/en/pages/PressRelease.aspx?OriginalVersionID=499.

UNESCO. *Cracking the Code: Girls' and Women's Education in Science, Technology, Engineering and Mathematics (STEM)*. Paris: UNESCO Publishing, 2017. https://unesdoc.unesco.org/ark:/48223/pf0000253479.

  Rethinking Education: Towards a Global Common Good? Paris: UNESCO Publishing, 2015.

  'UNESCO 'Moving Forward the 2030 Agenda for Sustainable Development; 2017'. Paris: UNESCO Publishing, 2017.

UNICEF. *A Child Is a Child: Protecting Children on the Move from Violence, Abuse and Exploitation*. New York, NY: UNICEF, 2017. www.unicef.org/publications/index_95956.html.

  ed. *Children in a Digital World*. The State of the World's Children 2017. New York, NY: UNICEF, 2017.

University of Bath. 'Rise of "Eco-Anxiety" Affecting More and More Children Says Bath Climate Psychologist'. Press Release. University of Bath communications, 19 September 2019. www.bath.ac.uk/announcements/rise-of-eco-anxiety-affecting-more-and-more-children-says-bath-climate-psychologist/.

Valenti, Jessica. *He's a Stud, She's a Slut and 49 Other Double Standards Every Woman Should Know*. Berkeley, CA: Seal Press, 2008.

Volante, Louis and John Jerrim. 'Why a Good Education Isn't Always the Key to Social Mobility'. *World Economic Forum* (blog), 19 November 2018. www.weforum.org/agenda/2018/11/education-does-not-always-equal-social-mobility/.

Wagner, Tony. *Creating Innovators: The Making of Young People Who Will Change the World*. New York, NY: ATRIA BOOKS, 2012.

Waldinger, Robert. 'Transcript of "What Makes a Good Life? Lessons from the Longest Study on Happiness"'. TED Talk, TEDxBeaconStreet, November 2015. www.ted.com/talks/robert_waldinger_what_makes_a_good_life_lessons_from_the_longest_study_on_happiness/transcript.

Warrier, Varun, Roberto Toro, Bhismadev Chakrabarti, Anders D. Børglum, Jakob Grove, David A. Hinds, Thomas Bourgeron and Simon Baron-Cohen. 'Genome-Wide Analyses of Self-Reported Empathy: Correlations with Autism, Schizophrenia, and Anorexia Nervosa'. *Translational Psychiatry* 8, no. 1 (12 March 2018): 1–10. https://doi.org/10.1038/s41398-017-0082-6.

theWeather Club (Royal Meterological Society). 'Wildfires across the Globe', 30 August 2019. www.theweatherclub.org.uk/node/590.

Wellcome Trust. 'Large-Scale Trial Will Assess Effectiveness of Teaching Mindfulness in UK Schools'. Press release. Wellcome Trust, 16 July 2015. https://wellcome.ac.uk/press-release/large-scale-trial-will-assess-effectiveness-teaching-mindfulness-uk-schools.

White, Mathew P., Ian Alcock, James Grellier, Benedict W. Wheeler, Terry Hartig, Sara L. Warber, Angie Bone, Michael H. Depledge and Lora E. Fleming. 'Spending at Least 120 Minutes a Week in Nature Is Associated with Good Health and Wellbeing'. *Scientific Reports* 9, no. 1 (13 June 2019): 1–11. https://doi.org/10.1038/s41598-019-44097-3.

Whiteford, Harvey A., Louisa Degenhardt, Jürgen Rehm, Amanda J. Baxter, Alize J. Ferrari, Holly E. Erskine, Fiona J. Charlson et al. 'Global Burden of Disease Attributable to Mental and Substance Use Disorders: Findings from the Global Burden of Disease Study 2010'. *Lancet (London, England)* 382, no. 9904 (9 November 2013): 1575–1586. https://doi.org/10.1016/S0140-6736(13)61611-6.

WHO. 'Child and Adolescent Mental Health'. World Health Organization, 2020. www.who.int/mental_health/maternal-child/child_adolescent/en/.

——— ed. *Global Report on Diabetes*. Geneva, Switzerland: World Health Organization, 2016.

Wilkinson, Alissa. 'Al Gore's New Inconvenient Truth Sequel Is a Strange Artifact of a Post-Truth Year'. Vox, 28 July 2017. www.vox.com/culture/2017/7/28/16035852/an-inconvenient-sequel-review-post-truth.

Willingham, Daniel T. *Why Don't Students Like School?: A Cognitive Scientist Answers Questions about How the Mind Works and What It Means for the Classroom*. 1st ed. San Francisco, CA: Jossey Bass, 2010.

Windle, Joel A. *Making Sense of School Choice – Politics, Policies, and Practice under Conditions of Cultural Diversity*. New York, NY: Palgrave Macmillan, 2015. //www.palgrave.com/br/book/9781137483522.

Wolf, Alison. *Does Education Matter?: Myths about Education and Economic Growth*. London: Penguin Global, 2003.

Wolfram, Conrad, 'Making Maths Beautiful'. Accessed 9 February 2020. www.youtube.com/watch?v=gsWKyFg9IdM.

Wong, Joon Ian. 'Workers in These Countries Are Most Scared Robots Will Replace Them'. *World Economic Forum* (blog), 21 March 2016. www.weforum.org/agenda/2016/03/workers-in-these-countries-are-most-scared-robots-will-replace-them/.

World Bank. *Turn Down the Heat: Confronting the New Climate Normal'*. Washington, DC: World Bank, November 2014. www.worldbank.org/en/topic/climatechange/publication/turn-down-the-heat.

Turn down the Heat: Why a 4°C Warmer World Must Be Avoided. A Report for the World Bank by the Potsdam Institute for Climate Impact Research and Climate Analytics. Washington, D.C.: The World Bank, 1 November 2012. http://documents.worldbank.org/ curated/en/865571468149107611/Turn-down-the-heat-why-a-4-C-warmer- world-must-be-avoided.

World Economic Forum. *The Future of Jobs: Employment, Skills and Workforce Strategy for the Fourth Industrial Revolution*' Global Challenge Insight Report. Geneva, Switzerland: World Economic Forum, January 2016. https://reports.weforum.org/future-of-jobs- 2016/.

Yamanaka, Shinya. 'Creating New Value'. OECD Learning Compass 2030: Transformative Competencies. Paris: OECD, 2019.

Yang, Yanbing, Xiangdong Yang, Ling Liang, Yuyan Gao, Huanyu Cheng, Xinming Li, Mingchu Zou, Renzhi Ma, Quan Yuan and Xiangfeng Duan. 'Large-Area Graphene-Nanomesh/Carbon-Nanotube Hybrid Membranes for Ionic and Molecular Nanofiltration'. *Science* 364, no. 6445 (14 June 2019): 1057–1062. https://doi.org/10.1126/science .aau5321.

Young, Sarah. 'Social Media Being Used by Growing Number of Children under 11 despite Age Limits'. *The Independent*, 31 January 2019. www .independent.co.uk/life-style/children-social-media-use-age-limit-facebook- instagram-profiles-a8756096.html.

Young Minds. 'Young People's Mental Health Statistics'. YoungMinds. Accessed 10 February 2020. https://youngminds.org.uk/about-us/ media-centre/mental-health-stats/.

Yule, Jeffrey V., Robert J. Fournier and Patrick L. Hindmarsh. 'Biodiversity, Extinction, and Humanity's Future: The Ecological and Evolutionary Consequences of Human Population and Resource Use'. *Humanities* 2, no. 2 (2 April 2013): 147–159. https://doi.org/10.3390/ h2020147.

Yurkofsky, Maxwell M, Amelia Peterson, Jal D. Mehta, Rebecca Horwitz- Willis and Kim Frumin. 'Research on Continuous Improvement: Exploring the Complexities of Managing Educational Change'. *Review of Research in Education* 44, no. 1 (2020): 403–433. https:// doi-org.ezp-prod1.hul.harvard.edu/10.3102/0091732X20907363.

Zero Tolerance. *"He's the Stud and She's the Slut" Young People's Attitudes to Pornography, Sex and Relationships.*' Edinburgh: Zero Tolerance, 2014. www.zerotolerance.org.uk/resources/Hes-the-stud- and-shes-the-slut.pdf.

Zhao, Yong. *World Class Learners: Educating Creative and Entrepreneurial Students*. Thousand Oaks, CA: Corwin Press, 2012.

Zietsma, Charlene and Thomas B. Lawrence. 'Institutional Work in the Transformation of an Organizational Field: The Interplay of Boundary Work and Practice Work'. *Administrative Science Quarterly* 55, no. 2 (1 June 2010): 189–221. https://doi.org/10.2189/asqu.2010.55.2.189.

Zuboff, Shoshana. *The Age of Surveillance Capitalism: The Fight for a Human Future at the New Frontier of Power*. London: Profile Books, 2019.

Index

Printed in Great Britain
by Amazon